D1807144

Writings By The Way

You are holding a reproduction of an original work that is in the public domain in the United States of America, and possibly other countries.You may freely copy and distribute this work as no entity (individual or corporate) has a copyright on the body of the work.This book may contain prior copyright references, and library stamps (as most of these works were scanned from library copies).These have been scanned and retained as part of the historical artifact.

This book may have occasional imperfections such as missing or blurred pages, poor pictures, errant marks, etc. that were either part of the original artifact, or were introduced by the scanning process. We believe this work is culturally important, and despite the imperfections, have elected to bring it back into print as part of our continuing commitment to the preservation of printed works worldwide. We appreciate your understanding of the imperfections in the preservation process, and hope you enjoy this valuable book.

COLLEGE LIBRARY
Apr. 21 1892
PRINCETON, N.J.

WRITINGS BY THE WAY

WRITINGS BY THE WAY

BY

JOHN CAMPBELL SMITH, M.A.
ADVOCATE

WILLIAM BLACKWOOD AND SONS
EDINBURGH AND LONDON
MDCCCLXXXV

PREFACE.

For want of some expression more appropriate, I have adopted that which appears on the title-page, to designate this volume. In form the first three papers are lectures. They have not been printed hitherto, except a few phrases, sentences, or paragraphs, in newspaper reports.

Nearly all the rest of the volume has been previously printed and published. Most of the articles appeared in the 'Scotsman' during the days of the editorship of Alexander Russel, to whose memory I desire to pay the tribute of grateful respect. He was a king of good fellows, and almost all that a newspaper editor ought to be, mainly intent on educating the public mind in what is true, just, and moderate, though joyfully using the means of a satirist oftener than the propositions of a theorist; not at all an unscrupulous special pleader, a blind political partisan, or manufacturer of extempore printed twaddle that will sell and

(RECAP) 85226

seem victorious for a day, but a man of wide living information touching men and affairs, who could maturely reflect, and promptly act for himself, preferring as a public teacher, when occasion required, the dictates of conviction to the discipline of party ; a man of the swiftest natural shrewdness, of a lively, sudden, saltatory, not unkindly humour allied with the readiest and sharpest of mother-wit, and a pious antipathy to all falsehood and humbug, whether appearing in Church or in State, or among the pretentious conventionalities of Edinburgh. In supplement to his skilful rapid touches, they had the benefit of the revision of Mr John Ritchie Findlay, then assistant editor, now proprietor; and to his delicate taste they owe the removal of blemishes, some of which would have escaped the notice of a less careful and fastidious critic.

All the 'Scotsman' articles are indicated, and the date of publication given, except that on Sir William Hamilton. The first part of that article was the 'Scotsman' review of Professor Veitch's Memoir; the latter part of it appeared in the St Andrews University Magazine. Perhaps it may be not improper to remark that the article on Positivism appeared early in 1868, because, since its publication, there has been a good deal either of appropriation of its views, or of concurrence in them, occasionally even among persons slightly deficient in the spirit of toleration, and inclined rather to persecute a new religion than to laugh at it. In denouncing Positivism, I may be ashamed of some of my allies, but of the denunciation itself I never shall be ashamed. I cannot help looking upon Positivism, be it a pretended scientific system or a religious faith, as next to nothing short of sheer insanity. Still it would appear to be not unworthy of toleration, and to have in it some odd little element of the *quasi* miraculous, otherwise it could not keep its hold on its votaries, some, indeed ·I daresay most, of whom live lives worthy of a noble and rational creed. The English Positivists are, I believe, really sincere, benevolent persons, doing and trying to do good as they have opportunity, and having among them one eloquent and more than one excellent writer. But this is too surely "a mad world," of which the Positivists are not unworthy inmates, being in their creed not madder than many, and in their conduct not so mischievous as most who suffer from a religious craze.

The articles on Lord Murray, Lord Colonsay, and Henry Glassford Bell, are reprinted without material change from the 'Journal of Jurisprudence;' that on Lord Colonsay having in part appeared also in the 'Scotsman.' The article on Sir Isaac Newton appeared as the review of Sir David Brewster's

life of that celebrated philosopher in a short-lived
periodical entitled the 'Edinburgh Weekly Review.'
I hesitated about resuscitating it, for I cannot help
feeling that it contains rather more than enough of
irreverent criticism, both of Newton and of Brewster.
But I know that it contains truths about both of
them that cannot be readily found elsewhere; and I
think that they are both great enough to bear to
have the whole truth known about them, whatever
the skilful suppression of circumspect persons may
suggest to the contrary.

The knowledge that Brewster sometimes lost his temper, and was not much of a mathematician or logician,
does not prevent me from looking back in memory to
my St Andrews College years (1848-53), and remembering, with sincere regard, Brewster as Principal of the
United College lecturing to us students, sometimes
angry at such provocation as peas, or, as he called
them, " pieces of solid matter, being thrown all about
the room," but always looking like a philosopher,
even when the flush of indignation was on his pale
face,—a beautiful old man, with sloping roundish forehead, and silvery silken hair, who manifestly had
devoted his life unreservedly to the pursuit of knowledge, and who could talk of physical science with
a contagious enthusiasm not matched in any other
man I have ever seen. He did verily in his aspect,

and in his whole walk and conversation, approach to the ideal philosopher. The students doubted much, but never his thorough genuineness. We could see that he was able as well as modest—painfully modest, until the demon in him was fairly roused,—but we never saw in him anything that did not proclaim the true nobility of ministering at the altars of science.

The lecture on Carlyle was delivered to the Edinburgh Literary Institute on the 31st January 1883. The five volumes published by Mr Froude since then have not materially altered any opinion expressed in it. Certainly they have not diminished my admiration for Carlyle, though they tend to show that his eye for character was not quite infallible, or he could not have placed such unlimited confidence in Mr Froude. Still I must give him the benefit of the doubt, seeing that I cannot conjecture where he would have found a biographer more likely to prove in every way suitable. He suppresses nothing; he may not have been duly called upon to suppress anything, except his spontaneous suspicions. These, however, sown a little too profusely in his first two volumes, are pretty well dissipated in the last two. The idea of the unfeeling domestic tyrant, who could see into and sympathise with all humanity, and yet did not understand or sympathise with his own wife, can hardly survive these last two volumes. That Mr Froude should have originated or cherished such an idea proves that in writing the first instalment of the biography he did not know the materials available for the second, as also, that he must have very little real human insight; for no man or woman of insight could have seen the Carlyles in their own home and remained so blind to their mutual affection and to their real devotion to each other as he appears to have done.

One statement of doubtful accuracy in regard to Carlyle's theological studies I have made, which I had not the means of qualifying until too late to alter the text. I have represented him as studying divinity to become a minister in the Burgher Church of which his father and mother were members. But the fact (not before published, I think) is, that the Church for which he did study was the Established Church. Professor Flint has kindly ascertained for me, from the Edinburgh Divinity Hall Register, that "on November 16, 1813, Thomas Carlyle, of the parish of Hoddam and Presbytery of Annan, was enrolled as a *regular* student of theology; on December 29, 1814, as a *partial* student; and on December 22, 1815, as a *partial* student. He was recommended on all three occasions by Mr Yorstoun — the Rev. James Yorstoun—who was parish minister of Hoddam

from 1784 to 1834." [1] For Carlyle to have become
a licentiate of the Established Church like Irving,
would have been the regular end of the course of
theological study upon which he had entered. His
entrance upon this course may have been his first
open step aside from the old narrow Burgher paths,
vexatious enough in all likelihood to the old folks at
home: or it may have been merely his plan to procure
the best education then procurable in Scotland for a
minister, whatever his Church might be. But in all its
aspects this proceeding must have had a dangerously
latitudinarian look to the eye of Burgher bigotry; and
it seems to me that the most probable explanation of
it is, that even at the early age of eighteen, Carlyle had
come to conclude that, if he must enter some Church,
he would be likely to find more scope for honest
freedom in the Established Church than in any other.

---

[1] Edward Irving's name appears also as a student from 1809-10 to
1814-15, both inclusive. For the last two sessions he is described as
belonging to Kirkcaldy, and is recommended by the Rev. Mr Martin
of Kirkcaldy.

CONTENTS.

BIOGRAPHICAL NOTICES—*continued.*

CARLYLE

THOMAS CARLYLE.

———◆———

NOTHING is more interesting to the living than life. To man, the more human it is, the more interesting. In the struggles of existence, all men are brethren who sympathise with the wounded, condemn the coward, and applaud the brave. Distance may lend enchantment, but it does not induce indifference. It only engenders doubt and the conviction that the more remote in years, in space, in race, in culture, in general environment, the less intelligibility will there be, the less genuine, practical human enlightenment. The man that lies nearest us is the man of our own time and country. We can better understand him than any other. He speaks our own dialect, wrestles with our own difficulties, fights battles like unto our own. His life has been illuminated by the same books, the same arts, the same sciences, the same philosophies, the same gospels. He has listened to the same temptations, especially to the temptation of getting rich, "honestly if you can, but get rich," and has heard occasional sermons, most of them short and suggestive rather than eloquent, upon various texts in the Gospel according to Mammon, the "gospel of getting on," and other modern non-miraculous gospels which are expected to supplement, if not to supersede, the antiquated copies of the law and the prophets. He has known poverty, perhaps hunger, though willing to work. He may have penetrated secrets of natural law, of human history, of social development, and arrived at no marketable result. He may have peeped through the high fences of the learned professions, have seen how the tares are greener than the wheat, and have felt that entry was neither possible nor desirable. He may have asked in desperation—

"What is that that I should turn to, lighting upon days like
    these ?
Every door is barred with gold, and opens but to golden keys.
Every gate is thronged with suitors, all the markets overflow :
I have but an angry fancy : what is that which I should do ?"

Yes; he may have asked—must have asked—many questions which the Sphinx of existence did not put before Jew or Greek or Roman, and which they can give little or no help to answer. Out of the pre-historic man there is still less help to be got. He, poor fellow, even if we were sure of him, which we are not soon likely to be, and could get our fingers and eyes on his fossil, petrified bones, is of no more practical consequence to us than the water-kelpie. The man who is of practical consequence to us is the man who has worked at, if not solved, the problems lying before us, which rise up before us importunate for solution every day—the man whose experience may give us instruction, may save us trouble, may protect us from disaster, may guide us in safety, if not with ease, along thorny, dangerous paths, and impart to us, to some extent, the benefits of his dear-bought wisdom. Such a man I think Thomas Carlyle. I know of no other modern man whose life and labours are so pregnant with wholesome instruction to the present generation as his, in every department that is worthily human, worthy of man as a Son of the Highest, with a heaven above him and a moral sense within, and not a mere beast, who has settled with himself, "Let me eat and drink, for to-morrow I die."

The materials for discoursing on Carlyle are all but overwhelming. His collected writings form a small library of themselves—the octavo edition, published during his life, numbering thirty volumes. Since his death, Mr Froude has published two volumes of 'Reminiscences,' of which all the world has heard—probably more than enough—as also two volumes dealing with the first forty years of his life, and embracing a great many of his letters. I know of many interesting letters of his, some of them already printed, which do not appear in Froude's book, there being plainly in the background a set of influences that has prevented the publication of letters, the chief among them being the not unnatural hostility of Carlyle's nearest living relatives. Many other biographies, great and small,

have issued to the light since his death ; and the list,
I should fancy, is far from complete. Certainly I am
very far from thinking that his final biography is yet
written, Mr Froude's work being little other than a
hasty conglomeration of materials, regulated not at all
by any views of hero-worship, or biographic discretion,
or art hitherto expounded, but regulated apparently
rather by the notion that the infirmities of a great
man, actual or conjectural, give a zest to the world's
curiosity about him, and gratify the ant-hill of
small Pharisees who piously thank heaven that they
are not as he was. Besides, there are plenty of
unpublished — perhaps as yet unwritten — reminiscences. Carlyle was the greatest talker of this century
—talked as he wrote, only more fiercely outspoken ;
and plenty that he said is perfectly well remembered.
He printed thirty volumes, and he probably talked
3000. What the Boswellism of the day may do for
his talk I don't know—that must remain an unsettled
factor in future estimates of the man ; but I know
enough to satisfy me that in power of eloquent,
earnest, penetrating talk, he was unequalled by any
man of his time—unequalled by any man since Burns
and Dr Johnson. And then others have talked and
shrieked abundantly about him. No merely literary
man was ever the theme of so much and so frequent
newspaper comment, generally condemnatory. Out of
acres of printed criticism, what fruit is forthcoming ?
He did not gather much of it, and we shall be content
with recognising that it is there, ready for the reaper or

the fire, like the corn of the Philistines, that stood waiting for Samson's foxes.

So much for the complex and multiplex outward
manifestation of materials; next as to its inward
essence, which is, if possible, still more varied and
many-sided, but all converging, as if a circle of concave
mirrors, to throw light upon man in the present era
and his duties. Carlyle was a philosopher in the
broadest and best sense of the word,—not a mere
dabbler in bread-and-butter science, but a searcher
after truth for its own sake in its highest spheres and
relations, if haply he might find it,—an interrogator of
books and of living men, though for the most part a
solitary student, devouring libraries, yet also a citizen
of the world, ready and eager to elicit information
from every creature of intellect who had any information to give. I conclude, from a host of considerations,
that hardly any man ever more completely gathered to
himself the whole wisdom of his age. Of his Scottish
predecessors, George Buchanan and David Hume most
nearly attained a like success. They, too, knew whatsoever their respective centuries could teach them; as
did also the French Voltaire, the superior of them all
in versatility of productive intellect, though not in
integrity of conscience. Goethe, too, was another of
the wisest of the wise. I believe Carlyle would have
accorded him that title over all the family of man.
He had swept the whole horizon of the knowable, had
enlarged the limits of physical science, was a courtier,
a politician, a philosopher, a poet, perhaps even a pro-

phet. But this German Solomon, like Solomon of old, who also aspired to know wisdom and folly, was a good deal encumbered with feminine and other the like baggage, which are bound to be fatal impediments in the search after the highest, most sacred truth; for it is "the pure in heart," and they alone, that can "see God,"—the self-denying Dante, or Milton, or Spinoza, and not Solomon or Epicurus. I think, to the inquiring spirit of to-day, no modern writings have so much instruction to give as Carlyle's writings. I think he is a safer teacher than Voltaire, or Solomon, or Goethe; that he has deeper views of human duty and nobler views of human destiny; and that even on the low ground of utility, his tidings from the vast Unknown are fresher than those of the earlier sages, and bear more directly upon the toils and troubles, the certain temptations and possible triumphs, of to-day— our poor little to-day, so trivial and commonplace to appearance, but the heir of myriad yesterdays, and the sovereign of to-morrow.

Thomas Carlyle was born on 4th December 1795, and died at Chelsea on 5th February 1881, his life having thus lasted eighty-five years and two months. His birth took place at, and his childhood was spent in, the village of Ecclefechan, in Dumfriesshire—a village far enough from aristocratic, with a stream running through it all unsung but by the boy who had played by it, celebrated in 'Sartor Resartus' as the Kuhbach, and lifted out of the realm of prose and cow accommodation into the "grand world-circulation of waters," murmuring on across the wilderness all unseen "when Cæsar swam the Nile and Joshua forded Jordan." His father's house was one of the best in the village at its date, built by himself, then and for years after a stone-mason, contracting in a small way for farmers and lairds thereabouts, and doing, chiefly with his own hands, the rough mason-work of an agricultural district. Fortunate he was in both father and mother, they being both excellent specimens of the best of the Scottish peasantry, such as produced Burns, and hundreds that have no name—uncommonly fortunate, even if large qualifications be attached to the eulogy he wrote upon his father between his death and funeral, when he, far away in London, was brooding upon all his father had been to him, and soothing his grief by praise of the dead, which no sober neutral judgment can think other than extravagant, the love and gratitude of the son having temporarily quite darkened the insight of the critic. Some of the father's letters are published in Froude's Life, and they show no sign of "natural faculty" to warrant his son's suggestion of comparison with that of Burns for a single moment. Still the father had a stern honest eye that could see into the truth of things; a singular talent for sarcastic speech and inventing nicknames that would stick, as Dumfriesshire tradition still records; as also a very ready pair of fists, well known and greatly dreaded on market - days in the Ecclefechan district. A much rougher, wilder man he was than his son seems to have been aware of, though it was to be expected from a youth spent in masoning and poaching. No doubt he was a religious man all the while, but a poacher may be a religious man. I have known a religious poacher—many a good honest fellow among poachers: as to certain game-selling game-preservers, I am not quite so sure, even though they do not feed their flocks on farmers' victual, and have them killed without consideration by other gentlemen's powder and shot. An exemplary elder of the Kirk, latterly of the Free Kirk, well known to me, and dearly and gratefully remembered, had poached at times in his youth, and, like James Carlyle, had no objection to give a troublesome fellow a solid knock-down blow, or what he used to call "a nievefu' o' Dalkeith meal." Among the descendants of the Covenanters, lineal and spiritual, I think there lingered an inclination to observe the precepts of natural justice, and to settle personal disputes by processes more summary than those of courts of law.

There can be no doubt of the perfect sincerity of James Carlyle and his wife, and that it stamped itself upon their gifted son, and coloured his whole life from the beginning to the end. He drifted far from the narrow creed of the little Burgher meeting-house in which he sat among decent bigots and fanatics who had travelled five, ten, and fifteen miles to listen to dull sermons, perhaps to fall asleep—as I, too, have often seen in a similar tabernacle; but the spirit remained to the end, vivifying the dry bones of the age of Cromwell, and spitting curses upon the cant, the dishonesty, and the hypocrisy of this. The religion of Carlyle has been half jocularly described as that of an old Covenanter with the Confession of Faith and the Solemn League and Covenant left out. There is, however, part of the backbone of all possible religions in the Confession of Faith; but the fact underlying the jest is, that Carlyle's creed declined to be put upon paper and tied to positive dogmas, it being largely made up of negations.

His early education was achieved amid the rustic scenes and horny-handed people of Dumfriesshire— not an education in which books played the chief part, but an education gathered out of talk in the fields and by the fireside, out of the workshops of village artisans, and out of the voices of the woods and the hills and the streams. Tinkers and pedlars, jolly beggars, joiners, shoemakers, blacksmiths, were among his tutors. His education was far from genteel, but it had in it that rough, stern genuineness which is not without its value for those who are born to use the horn spobn and the wooden ladle. Reading he learned from his mother earlier than he remembered, and he went on still learning to read at Ecclefechan school, at Annan Academy, at Edinburgh University — a little teaching to read in a few languages and sciences being all that he admits to have got from teachers and professors. For that somewhat pompous order of gentry he did not cherish much gratitude, but has a kindly word for the Ecclefechan schoolmaster, "a down-bent, broken-hearted, underfoot martyr," who pronounced

him " a genius fit for the learned professions "; a little
praise for Adam Hope of Annan, rigid Seceder, walking
every Sunday several miles to Ecclefechan kirk, "inexorable logician," as also an enemy of sham knowledge,
with his thorough ways of drilling, his cat, not of nine
tails, but of one only, and his two jet-black teeth in
front, made out of cork by the frugal penknife, and
dyed with tobacco-juice; a fund of sincere but only
half-expressed gratitude for Sir John Leslie, who really
gave him the bulk of the good he got out of Edinburgh College; and a pretty hearty contempt for
all the rest of them, and their College, and its
impostures and pomposities. In mathematics alone
Carlyle attained distinction, and that was chiefly due
to the impulse given by Sir John Leslie, himself a
kind of genius, not for mathematics and physical
science alone, but also for literature, who, having
himself begun life as a cow-herd on Largo Law, was
not without sympathy for a youth in hodden grey
gifted with intellectual parts which poverty and shy-
ness might darken a little, but could not quench eventually. Sir John was really the first effectual discoverer of Carlyle, Edward Irving was the second, and
his wife the third; and without these, or some adequate
substitutes, he might have gone to an early grave and
made no sign.

His father, too, deserves some credit, though I doubt
if he had any proper conception of his son's abilities.
I rather think, if some magician could have unveiled
the future to him and showed him his son's course in

life, and the manner that he was to deviate not merely
from Burgher orthodoxy but from all orthodox creeds
of which he had ever heard, that he would not have sent
him from home to be educated as he did. Like many
Scotch fathers, and still more Scotch mothers, he hoped
his son would "wag his pow in a poopit"; and his
highest hopes for him, when he sent him to Annan and
to Edinburgh, was that he should turn out a shining
light in his paltry, but, I admit, simple and sincere
Burgher Church. Sir John Leslie, over whose indication
that he had agreed with Hume as to cause and effect
all the bigots of Edinburgh and of Scotland had, four
or five years before (1804-5), grown frantic, to the
convulsion of Church courts and the vast effusion of
General Assembly oratory, was not a good guide for
a youth on his way to the Burgher priesthood old or
new; for though a great authority on the dew-point,
geometrical analysis, and the radiation of heat, the
dews which fall upon Burgher graces, and the analysis
of their molehills, and the thermometrical apparatus
suitable to determine and estimate the heat generated
in Burgher controversies, was beyond the sphere of his
scientific capacities. Edinburgh in his day, like St
Andrews in the great Dr John Hunter's, was not a safe
college for an intellectual lad on his way to a Burgher
or Cameronian pulpit. The intellectual lad was not
unlikely to learn a little too much—and this was what
happened with Carlyle; and dutiful, affectionate son
as he was, especially to his mother, even her pious ex-
hortations, now touchingly pathetic, though a sort of

comic too, to read at least a chapter every day, by-and-by failed of their effect. Doubt began to arise in him darker and darker. The cloud, at first no bigger than a man's hand, enveloped his horizon, blotting out sun and stars, and blocking up his path to all pulpits finally and for ever. He was not to preach what he could not believe: he would, he resolved, die of starvation rather. The beautiful way in which his father and mother bore their bitter disappointment, does them an amount of honour which only those who have understood how the pulpit is reverenced among the peasantry of Scotland, can adequately gauge. To be a minister was, in their estimation, far better and grander than to be a marquis; and perhaps they were right, — much would depend on the kind of minister and the kind of marquis.

The Church having become impossible for "doubting Thomas," what next could he turn to? There was teaching open at that time—open to every old soldier who had lost a leg, to all the halt and the lame and the blind who had muscles left for the effectual use of the taws; and there was literature open to every one who could purchase pens and paper, and find a patron or a publisher.

Through Sir John Leslie's recommendation, Carlyle, at the age of nineteen, got the mathematical mastership in Annan, with a salary of about £80—not a bad beginning for a lad of that age, with a quiescent disposition and a capacity to observe the tenth commandment. Then, by the same influence, he got the classical and mathematical mastership of Kirkcaldy Academy, owing to an arrangement brought about by the desertion of a part of Edward Irving's patrons who disapproved of his excessive severity. He went there—at least he was taken there—to be rival to Irving, who had shortly before been set up in a private academy to rival that of the burgh; but Irving and he (Irving being a native of Annan, and educated there) turned out the most intimate of friends,—rivals in nothing except, it may be, a little mild flirtation over æsthetic tea, and also, I am sorry to say, in the use of the rod; for I learn through a Kirkcaldy gentleman who was well thrashed by both of them, that they were both equally energetic and zealous in that somewhat savage department of human industry, Carlyle to the last believing in the liberal application of the "beneficent whip" to all sorts of blockheads, whether they had thick oily black skins or softish white ones. Excellent teachers, I believe, they both were, not to be surpassed in knowledge and in earnest desire to impart it, but severe with a severity that would not be tolerated in these humaner days.

Two sessions spent in Kirkcaldy led him to abandon the profession of public teaching in disgust. From his letters and his reminiscences, it is plain that he rather liked the people of Kirkcaldy, finding in them more kindness and less conceit than he had found in Annan, but that he felt driven to the conclusion that teaching boys in a school, with its thankless unhonoured drudgery, was a trade that he could not

spend his life in. In Kirkcaldy his own education
had been progressing. He had begun to try to learn
German. He had devoured Edward Irving's library
out and out, reading, for example, Gibbon's 'Decline
and Fall' at the rate of a volume a-day—not without
admiration; for in 1833, on Emerson's visit, as a hero-
worshipper, to Craigenputtock—"first visit of the kind
since Noah's Deluge "—he spoke of it to him as "the
splendid bridge from the old world to the new." He
had, besides, begun to experience dyspepsia, or, as he
expressed it long afterwards, had come to know practically of that "infernal arrangement called a stomach,"
which tormented him occasionally to the end, as it does
many who live to extreme old age, and who are compelled to be strictly moderate in eating. I infer this
from a story that came to me from the schoolmaster
of Kilconquhar, in that time, as also in my early college days, Mr M'Laurin, the father of the late Rev.
James M'Laurin of St Luke's, Edinburgh. Kilconquhar
M'Laurin had been in conversation with Kirkcaldy
Carlyle, and the latter was grumbling very copiously
and giving vent to a great deal of wild despair.
"Hoot, man!" says M'L., "cheer up! you'll see your
books sitting on the shelves alongside of Newton's
yet." "Ah!" rejoined the dyspeptic, "I would prefer
a sound stomach to a' the fame of Newton."

Further, in the way of education, and in addition to
Gibbon, and German, and gastric irritation, I think he
fell in love. There was a Margaret Gordon in Kirkcaldy, a native of Nova Scotia, orphan niece of a

widow, Mrs Usher,—a handsome young lady with wit as well as beauty; and it is plain enough that Carlyle fell in love with her, and that Irving was on the verge of it, and but for his engagement to Miss Martin, minister of Kirkcaldy's eldest daughter, would have been over the verge. This Margaret Gordon is the Blumine of 'Sartor Resartus,' treated as the foundation for a mythical flower-goddess. Blumine is dark, but Margaret was fair and "good-looking"; but more about her appearance I have failed to pick out of an old lady-friend who knew her in those days, as well as Carlyle and Irving. Margaret's letter bidding Carlyle "a long, long adieu as a sister," is in part quoted in Froude's Life, and it shows Margaret to have been no common personage; exhorting Carlyle to lay aside his scorn of men, and saying, like a daughter of Miriam, "Genius will render you great. May virtue render you beloved!" and withholding her address, "because I dare not promise to see you." The kiss that made the Teufelsdröckh immortal is probably mythical, and the marriage of the fickle fair to the wealthy suitor is certainly mythical. It was years after before she married a gentleman, then or subsequently M.P. for Aberdeen, next Governor of Nova Scotia, and a Knight. His name was Bannerman, I have learned privately; and for aught I know, she may be still living as Lady Bannerman.

Out of Kirkcaldy the scene shifts to Edinburgh, with the means of livelihood limited to a little saved money, about £90 in all, the chance of private

teaching and of literary work. A guinea a-month
for an hour a-day's teaching was not bad pay
for that time, but it probably was not easy to get.
What the first literary bit of work of Carlyle may
have been, is nowhere stated. Perhaps it was too
insignificant to be worth mentioning, or even remembering, though it is not likely he or any one else
could have forgot his first appearance in print. Sir
David Brewster, then Dr Brewster, editor of the
'Edinburgh Cyclopædia,' with his fire full of literary
irons, some of which burned his own fingers, was, I
cannot help thinking, his first introducer to literature.
He gave him Cyclopædia articles, biographical and
geographical, to write at small pay, what he calls
oftener than once "bread-and-water wages," and
£50 to translate Legendre's 'Elements of Geometry'
from the French. That is a capital book, published
by Oliver & Boyd in 1824, but I doubt very much
if ever £50 was realised by the sale of it. I have
seen but two copies of it—one in St Andrews, the
other in Edinburgh. Carlyle's name does not appear on it, and it was told to me in St Andrews long
ago, as a secret hardly to be whispered, that he had
translated it. Tait the publisher, also, must about
1820 have taken Carlyle by the hand a little, though
in what way I am unable to trace, the magazine
bearing his name not being started till 1832; and
for ten years Tait continued loyally to admire him, in
a way that most young authors would be rather proud
of especially on the part of a publisher; but I see that

Carlyle, in the 'Reminiscences,' commemorates him merely as " bookseller Tait—a foolish, goosey, innocent, but vulgar kind of mortal."

Fortunately fate did not leave Carlyle to Brewster's bread-and-water and Tait's small-beer. The deliverance from bread - and - water came to him mainly through Edward Irving. The two had deserted Kirkcaldy and schoolmastering together, but Irving had both money and friends, whereas Carlyle was rather scarce of both. Irving, however, had not got a church; he had only got engaged to a minister's daughter, when a patron's might have been of more use to him. However, Irving was steadily reading and thinking, and trying to arrive at a pulpit style, modelled on that of the old English Puritan divines, and to put into his sermons what could keep his hearers awake, and perhaps elevate their thoughts a little after Sunday was over. Somehow Dr Chalmers, then in the noon of his fame at Glasgow, heard of him, heard him *incog.* in Dr Andrew Thomson's in St George's, Edinburgh, and engaged him as his assistant. Then, after three years' Glasgow popularity, he was translated to the Caledonian Chapel, London, and there reached the mountain-peaks of unexampled fame as a preacher, with peers and peeresses crowding his church,—for a time. His fame, though deadly to himself in the end, was of essential service to Carlyle. Irving's London influence got for Carlyle a tutorship in the Buller family worth £200 a-year, Charles Buller, afterwards a distinguished M.P., being one of his pupils; got a publisher to pay for his 'Life of Schiller' the sum of £100; introduced him to Fraser, of 'Fraser's Magazine,' who was one of his regular hearers; introduced him to Mrs Basil Montague, whose daughter, Anne Skepper, became mother of Adelaide Proctor the poetess, whose father, best known as Barry Cornwall, introduced Carlyle to Dean of Faculty Jeffrey, the editor of the 'Edinburgh Review,' the most valuable of all the introductions given to Carlyle except one, and that one also was given by Irving—I mean the introduction to Jane Baillie Welsh, who became Mrs Carlyle.

Edward Irving had been a teacher at Haddington before he went to Kirkcaldy, and among his pupils, and perhaps the brightest of them, was the daughter and only child of Dr Welsh, the principal medical man in the district, the owner of a little estate in Dumfriesshire, which had been in his family, it was believed, from the time of an ancestor who had married a daughter of John Knox. Edward Irving taught Jeannie Welsh Latin and mathematics, and a variety of other conscious academic knowledge; but they somehow, in the course of studies and of years, taught each other unconsciously a little bit of non-academic knowledge—they fell in love. Without any positive declaration, they had become to each other dearer than they knew. From Haddington Irving went to Kirkcaldy—to a new private academy starting there; and forgetting, or supposing that he could forget Jeannie Welsh, he philandered with Miss Isabella Martin, eldest daughter of the parish

minister, and rashly engaged himself to her. Still he
visited Haddington occasionally, advised Miss Welsh as
to her studies, her readings, and her literary efforts—flit-
ting round and near the flame, as Abelard, and Jonathan
Swift, and other wise, but not entirely wise, men have
done. In one of his visits from Glasgow, in 1821, he took
Carlyle with him as talking and walking companion to
Haddington. They had three or four evenings' talk
with Miss Welsh, then aged twenty, and her widowed
mother, who was a faded beauty and an affected
poetess. Thereafter Carlyle acted as a second literary adviser, sent her books to read from Edinburgh,
and called for her there when she came to visit her
"Uncle Robert," a legal practitioner in Northumberland
Street, and "old Mrs Bradfute" in George Square,
and drifted into a literary, more or less confidential,
correspondence with her. Four years of letter-writing
passed away, in which Miss Welsh pushed away from
her suitor after suitor—some admiring her wit and
learning, some her face, and some her fortune. Irving
migrated from Glasgow to London, there became
splendidly popular, and the not too willing husband
of Miss Martin, who would not let him go, whether
he blessed her or cursed her; and Carlyle remained
the steadfast admirer of the accomplished heiress—
faithful to the end, and in the end successful, after
some of the usual obstructions to the course of true
love, common enough, but wearing an original aspect
in the letters of this original pair. She had intellect
enough to recognise his genius, and to discover the

possibilities that lay in him and before him. Not a common kind of heiress she who, herself gifted with physical graces which officers and dandies and ordinary fools could admire and volunteer to marry, could receive with toleration, not to say respect, the attentions of a mason's son, an ex-schoolmaster, without office or salary, or any sure or visible means of livelihood; could brave the ridicule which relatives and acquaintances would be likely to have copiously ready for her and her eccentric and impecunious suitor; and could marry him at last, after telling him flatly that she did not love him and would never marry him.

Of all the wives that ever fell to the lot of men of genius, I think her somewhere about the best. She is the only wife of a man of genius known to me who ever gave her husband positive help to do his life-work, —who guided, who stimulated, who encouraged, who criticised without flattery and without fear, who acted the part of a guardian angel so effectually in fine instinctive guidance as to what should be done and what left undone. There is a subtle indescribable female delicacy traceable in his books, and I ascribe that delicacy to the influence and positive criticism of the lady who was truly to him a helpmeet, and whose insight really discerned prophetically what he could do, and actually helped him to do it. All honour to her! At least whatever we accord to him she is entitled to share it, for without her his life might have turned out comparatively barren or a failure. Most men of genius have got on in spite of their wives; and of these I call to witness Shakespeare, Milton, "the judicious Hooker" (judicious in all affairs but marrying), Sterne, Sir Walter Scott, Byron, Hazlitt, and ask you to note how much more fortunate in matrimony Carlyle was than any of them. Whether she was equally fortunate, I do not pretend to determine. Mr Froude is at pains—rather too great pains, I think—to hint that her married life was unhappy, and that Carlyle sacrificed her health to his convenience and selfish ambition. She, it seems, had been heard to advise some lady or other, "Never marry a man of genius," and to nine hundred and ninety-nine women out of every thousand that is excellent advice; but the value and meaning of that advice depend entirely upon the person to whom it is given. Also she had been heard to say, "I married for ambition. Carlyle has surpassed my utmost hopes, . . . and I am miserable." Well, to that I answer, *if* she married for ambition *alone*, she could expect nothing better. No one can extract enduring happiness from ambition; and as we sow, so we must reap. My own candid conviction is, that neither of them was very happy, in the ordinary sense of that term. They were so constituted mentally that they could not be; but I think they were really happier together than they could have been apart, and that their lives were of greater use to mankind spent as they were than it is at all probable they could have been otherwise.

Suppose she had married Irving, and that Miss Martin had been left free to inveigle some other young

unsophisticated probationer, " there would have been no
tongues" perhaps; but what could Edward Irving have
done more or better than he did? I think he managed to tell all that he had to tell, and that no aid
from a logical, sceptical, although poetical wife, could
have been of the least service to him—that, in short,
it is far from unlikely that Miss Martin, believing
all things, hoping all things, really aided him to
deliver his message to his unsympathetic age—such
message alone as he could deliver—and that Miss
Welsh would have repressed it, and shut him out
from the only fame and effective well-doing possible
for him. She would have perhaps saved him from
the imputation of insanity and of humbug, but she
would have saved him equally from the reputation
of being a prophet, and the chance of being remembered as the founder of a sect of Christians who
remain sincerely faithful in a faithless age. And then,
what would Carlyle have done without her? He
was a Calvinist of a kind; and if ever a predestined
blessing fell upon him it was his wife, " his Eve, who
made all things beautiful around her"; and let Mr
Froude and other open or covert advocates for treating
women as useless angels say what they may, I don't
see, and cannot conjecture, where else she could have
found her paradise, which was bound from her nature
to be, not a paradise of enjoyment and do-nothingism,
but of renunciation and unrest. Far, far behind her
and her chosen Adam lay the Eden of old and its
single serpent, dropping temptation into the ear of

half-happy idleness. They had serpents of their own
to tread upon and strangle, and no desire to look back
upon the gate with the flaming swords. They had
realised, as if from a personal revelation, as clearly as
if told by myriads from the dead, that they had no
business in God's universe except to work, and no
access to composure or perfection except through
suffering.[1]

---

[1] The publication of Mrs Carlyle's letters, edited and annotated by
her husband, has afforded fresh and fuller materials for forming an
estimate of her, of him, and, if it be of any consequence, of Mr
Froude. It has confirmed my convictions, expressed or hinted,
in regard to all the three and their relations to each other, and
has, if it has induced any definite alterations, led me to think her
a brighter, cleverer, happier, more affectionate woman than I had
previously thought her. As for Mr Froude, it is difficult to understand what he aims at. Is it to glorify her at the expense of her
husband, or truth and the domestic joys of dullards at the expense
of both ? Is it to point out the dark parts of Carlyle's character, so
that there may be in it the proper proportion of light and shadow ?
Most saints and prophets have an *advocatus diaboli* appointed for
them after death, but it would appear that Carlyle nominated his
own by will. Whatever the motive, Mr Froude makes no attempt to
conceal or palliate Carlyle's infirmities. He had ample charity for
Henry VIII., but Carlyle was not subject to the same kind of frailties. At least he permitted his wife to live and write letters. No
doubt Mr Froude hints that he was a heartless, inconsiderate tyrant;
and a vast mob of newspapers, led by the 'Times,' improving upon the
confidential hint of the *advocatus diaboli*, had a wild shrieking outcry
about want of feeling, selfishness, cruelty, and the inconsistency of
preaching the right and practising the wrong. Such a quantity of
fatuity or hypocrisy, or both, was probably never written about any
husband and wife ; and I can fancy that, if properly reported on the
other side of the Styx, it might create not a little contemptuous
merriment there, especially on her part. Whatever shallow, weak,
false, or malignant men may say in newspapers, I say that no letters
ever written by a woman show more personal independence, more
fearless freedom of speech, more intellectual vivacity and sympathy,

The marriage of this singular pair was celebrated at Templand, on 17th October 1826—Mr Froude says, in the parish church; but that, I feel sure, must be a mistake, for until the Rev. Dr R. Lee reintroduced the fashion some twenty years ago, there had been no marriages in Scotch parish churches for a century. He was then close on thirty-one years of age, and she was twenty-five, having been born 14th July 1801. His acknowledged work up till this time had been translations of Legendre's 'Geometry,' of 'Wilhelm Meister,' of a volume of short pieces from Tieck, Musæus, and Richter, entitled 'German Romance,' of articles chiefly biographical for Brewster's 'Cyclopædia,' and of the 'Life of Schiller' first published in the 'London Magazine.' For some months after the honeymoon, he had nothing to do except read, and meditate, and mope. By February 1827, he had the letter of introduction, formerly mentioned, to Jeffrey from Barry Cornwall, *alias* Bryan Proctor. This he did not deliver for a month or two, remembering that a contribution volunteered

and less consciousness of the pressure of despotism, either domestic or social. Few wives have been so independent of their husbands and of Mrs Grundy. No doubt many female fools have been happier, or at least less miserable, after their kind. She too, clever as she was, could torment herself: she was jealous of Lady Ashburton—the intellectual, the beautiful queen of the best of the mind of London, and who, but that she was a kind friend to both, was a "heathen goddess" to both of them. Jealous! What wife of literary man, out of Church orders, in or near London, ever had such slight cause to be jealous? What other woman's life ever realised so many splendid expectations? Only one was wanting—she was childless; and such are the compensations of life, that those who suckle fools can condescend to pity her.

by him to the 'Edinburgh Review' six or seven years
before, had been left with Jeffrey's valet, and neither
acknowledged, nor inserted, nor returned; but at last
he plucked up courage, and saw the little great man
—not then, but soon to be, Dean of Faculty—sitting
in his chambers in George Street, among ill-bound
tattery books and law papers, and five pairs of lighted
candles, and had twenty minutes of "successful" talk
with him. Thereafter Jeffrey and his wife called at
Comely Bank, No. 21, for the Carlyles. Jeffrey discovered that Mrs Carlyle was some far-off Scotch
cousin, the exact lines of the relative pedigrees being
still rather hazy; but in noonday clearness he saw that
she was a clever charming woman, and he straightway
plunged into a course of romantic admiration, not to
say affection, for her, which lasted for years, and
greatly deepened his interest in Carlyle. To be a
lawyer, Jeffrey was a very kind-hearted genuine
little fellow, with a moderate amount of charity, very
little faith in anything or anybody, next to no hope,
and he could appreciate original genius only in a kind
of way, after the world had, by its collective vote, decided upon it; but I cannot repress the suspicion, that
had it not been for Mrs Carlyle and her intellectual and
personal fascinations, Francis Jeffrey never would have
done anything for Thomas Carlyle, until perhaps he had
gone to an early grave like Burns, and then he might
have expended a few pathetic platitudes upon him
and his sad fate. However, after Proctor's introduction, and the call at Comely Bank, Carlyle was *invited*

to contribute to the 'Edinburgh Review,' the function pointed out to him being to Germanise the British public. His first article, a short one written hastily in a week or two, appears in the July number for 1827, and is on Jean Paul Richter. Thus was begun his seven years' contributions to the Reviews, which now form the four volumes of his 'Miscellaneous Essays,' and contain some passages of his writing, and some nodules of his thought, second to none in weight and significance. Thus was accomplished his introduction to the higher walks of literature through the combined influence of Irving, Proctor, and Jeffrey.

The story of his relations with Jeffrey is told in his 'Reminiscences' in an interesting, not unkindly way. Carlyle is accused of uncharitable depreciation of nearly every literary man he came in contact with; and there may appear to be some ground for the accusation in the minds of those shivering creatures, so plentiful in the world, who are afraid of the naked truth. But as to Jeffrey, I may be permitted to say that, so far as I am concerned, Carlyle's account of him has raised him vastly in my estimation. I knew him previously from the collected Essays, with their wide but shallow learning, prim dignity, graceful turns of style, elegant utterance of uncontroverted truth, and playful melancholy, and from his opinions as a judge, which I hear sometimes sneered at by legal men, mere tradesmen some of them, barely worthy to tie his shoe. But from his Essays, and not less from his judicial opinions, I fail to gather that he was a great strong man; I

gather that he was only a little lively one, fit to pass for
an apostle or a demigod only in an age of decomposition
and corruption and ruin, that was decidedly deficient
in the apostolic and the godlike, that was rich only
in eatables and drinkables, and sweetmeats, and self-
conceit. From Carlyle, however, I can gather that
there were elements of real genius in Jeffrey, as also
of real human kindness, nobleness, and love, generally
of truth and goodness, or such plausible substitutes
for them as would pass muster for a week or two, in
the absence of any test of what is really not counterfeit. Jeffrey's greatness is now, even in Edinburgh,
very much of the nature of a tale that has been told.
His lucubrations, once so brilliant and celebrated,
which girdled the planet with his fame and ruled the
literary opinion of Europe, are now unread, and in
another generation he will be all but forgotten. If
remembered at all, he will be remembered as the friend
of Macaulay, of Sydney Smith, and of Carlyle, and
longest and most honourably by what Carlyle has
written about him. Little though he recked it, his
last title to withstand oblivion will be his kindness to
this stiff-backed, stiff-necked, wrong-headed German-
ised man from Annandale, whom he accused of being
impracticable, a sectary, a mystic, "dreadfully in
earnest," a visionary, and could not quite trust or
patronise, perhaps from a kind of dim half-conscious-
ness that he was far greater than himself.

Up to his meeting with Jeffrey and introduction to
the 'Edinburgh Review,' he had failed to find any

steady occupation worthy of him, and fit to call forth his intellectual powers. He had tried tutoring, school-mastering, translating, magazine-writing, and he read one or two pulpit or *quasi*-pulpit discourses by way of passing the student's curriculum for the Burgher Church. He had thought of being an artist and an engraver, and he actually attended Baron Hume's lectures on Scotch law, in the hope, I suppose, of passing as an advocate. But he could not endure either Scotch law or Burgher theology, beyond a few months' trial; even Baron Hume, the greatest of Scotch law professors, had been unable to awaken in him any interest, or secure for himself and other lawyers a more favourable opinion than that they appeared to be " mere denizens of the kingdom of dulness, pointing towards nothing but money as wages for all that bog-pool of disgust." He even thought of being an engineer, and had, no doubt, mathematics to set up a score of engineers, with their little bits of calculations and rule-of-thumb formulas; and after he had begun to wrestle with the French Revolution, and was finding it " shapeless, dark, unmanageable," he again, in his desperation, recurred to what he calls " the old primitive Edinburgh scheme of engineership." But somehow his guardian angel guided him better, Destiny having assigned him work in the building of bridges that are proof against the hurricane, and stretch from era to era.

A home for the new-married couple was nearly as difficult to get as something to do in it and wherewith to keep it. Comely Bank, No. 21—a smallish main-

door house, still standing in habitable order—was the
first married home of the Carlyles. Then, after eighteen
months' trial of it, doubts as to the means of keeping
up his modest establishment there of a dog and single
servant, and contempt for Edinburgh—which he wrote
of years afterwards, after his last long visit to it, as "a
wretched infidel place—not one man that could forward
you, co-operate with you in any useful thing. Scarcely
one I could find (except Sir W. Hamilton) that could
speak a sincere word"—set him off to live on his
wife's estate in Dumfriesshire,—far enough away from
wicked and insincere people, there being nobody to
speak to nearer than the parish minister of Dunscore,
as he told Emerson, and he was "sixteen miles" distant. At Craigenputtock — hill of the puttocks (a
species of hawk), and also of the moorcock—he lived
six years, and there wrote the most of his four volumes
of 'Miscellanies,' and manifestly thought out his final
views of Man and the Universe, and the Maker of them,
many of which are embodied in 'Sartor Resartus,' also
thought out and written there, during a period of nine
months, which were darkened and inspired by the
breaking down from consumption, and by the death, of
his dear sister Margaret, and his own perennial melancholy. From the "whinstone fortress on the moor,"
where he could live on oatmeal and other home-pro-
duce, and pay his way completely for £100 a-year, he
set out for London—in part wearied of solitude, in part
driven to seek work, because the publication of 'Sartor
Resartus' piecemeal in 'Fraser's Magazine.' had rather

made publishers chary of his wild conglomerate English style, and wilder views, most of them apparently agreeing with the reviewer who denounced 'Sartor' as "a heap of clotted nonsense." His London home, after some weary weeks' search among unlet houses by him, was fixed at 5 Cheyne Row, Chelsea, to which the arrival from Craigenputtock took place on 10th June 1834. Then by-and-by, after much reading, moody meditation, unsatisfactory abortive efforts, he began the 'French Revolution,' having about £200 between him and starvation, and finished it in about eighteen months. The publication of the 'French Revolution' lifted him at once into the front rank of living literary men, silenced the buzz of small critics, and relieved the doubts of dull publishers—who, as a rule, cannot trust themselves to publish anything that will not be acceptable to the taste of commonplace women and the keepers of circulating libraries. The rest of his work was done in 5 Cheyne Row, the only migration there being from the ground-floor to the attics, all the upper storey being converted into a library, in which 'Frederick the Great' was written, amid a multitude of German books, and a great variety of stoves and other heating apparatus, most of which failed to keep him warm at his tedious, dreary task of some thirteen years or thereby, in which his toils, cares, and curses were extraordinary even for him. The first two volumes of Frederick were published in 1858, and the last two in 1865. In the course of it he had re-solved, and re-resolved, many a time, that he would not undertake any other large work—and he adhered to that resolution.

Shortly after the publication of the last of Frederick, he was most properly and opportunely chosen by the students Lord Rector of the University of Edinburgh. The election was in November, and next spring he came to address the students after the manner of Lord Rectors. On 2d April 1866, he appeared on the platform of the Music Hall, which was crowded in all its parts. Brewster, his ancient employer in bread-and-water literature, was there as Principal, also in splendid official robes. On the platform were to be seen Dr R. Lee, with his quick pale face and restless blue eyes; Professor Blackie, with his long, thin, white locks, big stick, and spasmodic airy restlessness as if of a half-tamed squirrel; Huxley, who had just been made LL.D., and been hissed by some of the less polite but more orthodox students as he came up to receive that honour, looking specially beetle-browed and sulky; Professor Tyndall, who had come almost like a son to take care of Carlyle, wearing the appearance of a clean-made, tall, athletic joiner; Dr Rae, the Arctic explorer—a burly, grizzly, curly, soldier-like figure; Erskine of Linlathen — a mild, full-eyed, tottering shadow of an old man, one of the Rowite heretics who believed in Edward Irving and the permanence of the age of miracles, but who doubted the perpetuity of hell; and a host of others, who had come to receive degrees, all mixed up with local celebrities, who looked

C

brilliant enough that day, though they have faded from memory.

I saw him twice on the occasion of this Edinburgh visit. I heard him deliver his address, keeping eye and ear wide open; and I had the honour of an introduction to him from his brother, Dr John, as I met them accidentally on the street. From my own observation and that of others, I can tell in a general way what like he was to look upon and listen to. He was no dandy, but he was still less of a sloven. He was dressed with great care and neatness—his whole raiment of good strong not very fine black cloth, and shaped not quite unfashionably, but with Puritanic plainness, according to Dumfries rather than London tastes and ideas. I could infer, from what I saw, that he made dressing, like everything else, a matter of conscience, modified a little by contempt for useless fashion and its styles. His features were such as you can see represented fairly well in most portraits of him, though some of the earlier sketches seem scarcely credible—such as that of 'Fraser's Magazine,' which has in it too much of the prim schoolmaster and potential prize-fighter. The grandest likeness that I have seen or heard clear word of is a bust by Woolner, belonging to Mr Charles Jenner. Most of his likenesses give the expression of an intense melancholy, which I never distinctly saw in the flesh, unless, perhaps, when he was sitting in his theatrical Lord Rector's dress, before he rose to speak in the Music Hall. Embarrassment, diffidence, determination, were the

feelings visible in his face as he began to speak, and
these passed into sadness, sorrow over the long ago, the
never more of his college days; fatherlike kindliness
to his young hearers; quiet scorn for talk, for money-
making, gold-nuggeting, and other pursuits of this
frivolous, materialistic, atheistic generation. From the
heart to the heart he spoke, slowly, gravely, kindly—
without a gesture, without an effort—in the accents of
his native Annandale, the weightiest, freest, easiest,
deepest talk I ever heard, revealing a modest, deep,
stoical, widely cultivated, conscientious man, grateful
in a sincere, not in the least gushing sort of way, to
the lads who had loyally risen up to do him — a
prophet—honour in his own country while he was
still on this side the grave; but manifestly indifferent what they or others might think of him,
and apparently not unconscious that, now that his
battle had been fought and his life was nearly over,
the good opinion of Edinburgh College lads, and of
Edinburgh people generally, was, though pleasant
enough in its way, of next to no consequence to
him. To a phrenologist, I think his head must have
been disappointing, and a puzzle for, if not a confuta-
tion of, his science. It was a head of that type which
is found in the mystic, the half-mad prophet, the
religious visionary. It contained the accurate symbols
of his mathematical and metaphysical power, but it
did not in the least disclose any sign of powers for
the closest observation in detail and the most extraor-
dinarily tenacious of memories. Emerson, in 'English

Traits,' speaks of his "cliff-like brow," and that phrase
is accurately descriptive.   George Gilfillan used to tell
me that Carlyle's eye was his only remarkable feature,
and to talk of the wild, fierce light that glowed and
glared in it, and of its restless throbbing.   Seen from
a distance, it looked a dark, piercing, defiant eye, deep-
set among shadows; seen near, it looked keen, searching, questioning, but not really dark—its colour being
light brown or a sort of brownish grey.   Sir Walter
Scott saw Burns once, and records that his eye "positively glowed."   I could not say that of Carlyle's.
Neither his eye nor soul could glow like that of
Burns; but I rather think there was more cold, dry
light in it, more illumination to work by and explore
dark places, but less wild heat to set human hearts
on fire.   Taking the body to be a visible revelation
of the mind — the temporary home of the spirit,
shaped for it and by it, and reacting upon it day by day,
—I should say that, to the best of my thinking, Carlyle was not equal either in sheer intellectual strength
or versatility to Burns, or even to Professor Wilson.
Both outwardly and inwardly, these two came nearer
to the godlike Apollo—to the highest ideal manifestations of the highest mental gifts in the most noble
embodiment.   And in their works, too, I think I can
see glimpses of sunnier, loftier summits than he ever
reached, surer signs of the unseen power that can stir
mountains — ay, even the great world itself.   But
nevertheless he did ten times as much work in point
of *quantity* as both of them.   They amused themselves

picking flowers by the wayside, looking into bright siren eyes, giving and taking pleasure as if it was not entirely wise to renounce all enjoyment in this world, resplendent with beauty, and hung amid stars, and ringing with lightsome jests and laughter. But he, strong in his devotion to *Entsagen* — in his renunciation of pleasure, mere pleasure, in every form— toiled on drearily, wearily, finding existence tolerable only in toil, and no prospect of heaven here or hereafter, which was not conquered by unflinching effort and a scorn of all the pleasure that earth or even heaven itself could offer.

The Germans are said to teach and practise "plain living and high thinking"; and in this matter I fancy Carlyle was at least a German, probably more than a German. I don't suppose that he did or could eat raw herrings and garlic, and suchlike delicious cheap German luxuries, but he certainly lived on the plainest, cheapest fare. The staple of his food was oatmeal-porridge morning and evening. On the subject of Scotch Presbyterian oatmeal, Dr Begg himself is [1] not more puritanically perfect. When in London in May 1834 house-hunting, he records as follows in his fragmentary but most veracious journal: "Dine with a

---

[1] Now, alas! was. He died 29th September 1883. One of the most notable and active Scotchmen of his day, he used publicly and privately to recommend the old national fare, and himself supped on porridge every night when at home. He was a preacher of thrift and patriotism; and though a Tory and a Free Churchman, and a hater of organs and all new-fangled notions and instruments, he was really a sincere, excellent kind of man, intent on doing good, and actually accomplishing a great deal.

dairyman on bread and milk beside his cows—a most interesting meal; charge, three-halfpence, I having furnished the bread. Gave the man 6d. because I liked him." A dinner which will remind you of the early London frugal meals of Samuel Johnson.

About three months later (1st September), in a letter to his mother communicating that the writing of the 'French Revolution' was actually to be begun instantly after the letter, he specifies the "freight of eatable goods" required from Annandale to keep him living in the meantime, while he was toiling through this valley of the shadow of guillotine, which you will forgive me quoting, as it tells more about his dietetic habits and economics than any other bit of writing I have come across:[1]—

" Here is the list of our wants, as I have extracted it by questions out of Jane. First, sixty pounds of butter, in two equal pigs (the butter here is 16d. a pound!); secondly, a moderately sized sweet-milk cheese; next, two smallish bacon-hams (your beef-ham was just broken into last week, and is in the best condition); next, about fifteen stone of right oatmeal (or even more, for we are to give Hunt some stones of it, and need almost a pound daily; there is not now above a stone left); and after that, as many hundred-weights of potatoes as you think will keep (for the rule of it is this: we take two pounds daily, and they sell here at three-halfpence, or at lowest a penny a pound, and are seldom good): all this got ready and packed into a hogs-head or two, will reach us by Whitehaven, and we will see how it answers."

[1] Froude's Life, vol. ii. p. 454.

"Eat not too much" was an advice given to Swedenborg by some angel, black or white, I am not sure which; but it does not signify, as the advice was good, coming on the back of a nightmare after some heavy London supper. Carlyle did not need this advice; he was always most moderate—moderate on the excessive side in both eating and drinking. No man could do the work he did and live so long who exceeded in anything, except, perhaps, tobacco. And I am afraid he did exceed a little in the consumption of that particular weed, consuming I know not how many ounces a-week, but smoking pretty diligently—not expensive cigars, though he was sometimes prevailed on to take one by a friend, but common tobacco out of a common short "black cutty-pipe." I see that he stipulated with his bride for leave to "*smoke three cigars*" in the carriage on their way to Edinburgh after the knot was tied; but I have heard of the "cutty-pipe" from George Gilfillan and other eyewitnesses. He often mentions the pipe himself; but whether long or short, black or white, he does not say: it was, I believe, whatever was readiest.

The order of his working-day varied at different places. In his father's house he was sometimes awakened for study at five in the morning; and too often in his after-life he did not require to be wakened at all, for a barking dog, or a noisy cock, or mere nervous excitement, often kept him awake for a week or ten days at a time. By 9 A.M. in his Chelsea working-days he was generally breakfasted and at his desk—an old mahogany article made for his father-in-law, and left as a legacy to Sir James Stephen. He wrote, or tried to write, until 2 P.M.,—writing all his books, I think, with his own hand most carefully and neatly, and attending to punctuation with uncommon care. About two he went out for exercise on horse-back, and might be seen in the afternoons riding in Rotten Row, a queer-looking apparition among the gay crowd of horsemen and horsewomen, with garments far from gay, slouched wideawake for one item, well drawn down over a terribly grave visage, dark with the shadow of deep, sad, far-away thoughts. His afternoon ride over, he sought the company of his wife in the drawing-room, and heard in her sharp swift style the notes she had gathered from callers and otherwise in the course of the day, he sitting the while on the hearthstone, with his back to the jamb, so that the smoke of his pipe, the door standing a chink open, might go all up the chimney and keep the drawing-room free from tobacco-taint. Dinner was generally of one course, and never late; and in the evening there was reading, either by way of amuse-ment or of preparation for the composition of next day. A most regular, orderly, self-denying, method-ical way of life—not the kind of life that a mere student of his books would be likely to ascribe to him. He was most punctual in everything, kept all his letters that were worth keeping, wrote an enormous number of letters that will bear not unfavourable comparison with any in the language, was saving of money and of time, which is the substance of life. Many a request of young hero-worshippers for a specimen of his hand-writing did he kindly answer, quoting generally a verse from the Bible, or of the Koran, or of some old Scotch song. To visitors, especially Yankee visitors, who wished merely to see him as a lion, he was often not so civil. They occasionally caught a little more of the lion than was quite pleasant to them, roaring at them as blue-bottles buzzing about and bothering a man at his work, and de-nouncing the Americans, notwithstanding their rampant admiration, as having performed hitherto no feat in his-tory except having begotten, with unexampled rapidity, 18,000,000 of the greatest bores the world ever saw.

Of his works much might be said, if it were useful to say it, which, I am afraid, it is not. I am not going to criticise his books in detail, but I do most strenuously advise all interested to read them. After that has been done, but not till then, detailed criti-cism may be appreciated, and perhaps a little light gathered out of it. There are some, I daresay, who think his books not worth reading, and there are many who will extract little amusement and no edification from them. The fashionable gospel of "getting on," the liturgy of mammon-worship, the psalms of victo-rious wealth, the atoms of useful knowledge forming the vaunted "ologies" of the day, are not to be found in them. On the contrary, there is plenty of scorn of all these things, indeed of everything that does not tend to the spiritual enlightenment and development of man, and the lifting him high above the gratifica-

tions of appetite and of vanity, feasts of fat things and
of rich wines, opera music and its illuminated flirta-
tions, parliamentary eloquence and statecraft bribery,
aristocratic idleness and double-barrelled game-pre-
serving, the cheers of 27,000,000 mostly fools, the
hallelujahs of flunkeys.

I advise you to read his writings, not to help you
to arrive at happiness, but to help you to arrive at
wisdom. If you do not care for wisdom, do not waste
your time over his pages. If you seek amusement
chiefly, go to Sir Walter Scott, where you will not fail
to find real instruction also; or to Dickens, where you
will get entertainment in the farces of existence, and
instruction in benevolent humbug. But when you go
to Carlyle, recollect you that " he who increaseth knowledge increaseth sorrow." Carlyle's books are really
sad books, terribly true as to the deeper, blacker
shadows of existence, and among the saddest I know,
not excepting Thackeray's, although in both there are
wit and laughter shining through clouds and tears.
The utility to be found in a study of Carlyle is,
in the *first* place, in the moral field, where all the
virtues flourish unstunted, unblighted, though over-
topped, and it may be sometimes hidden, by hatred
of vices, and in particular, by abhorrence of lies; and
in the *second* place, in the accurate knowledge con-
veyed in regard to many things deeply interesting to
a modern man or woman—modern history, literature,
politics, religion,—in short, in regard to all the relations, physical and mental, of modern society.

Herbert Spencer has a book called 'Social Statics';
and if you want to find a description of social forces
and phenomena, given as a mechanician or a mill-
wright would give them, you may with profit study
that book. Indeed you may study it with profit if
it were only to learn how little satisfactory light can
be obtained from engineering theories of the universe
and man—man singly and man in organic masses,
flung together by evolutionary or other mechanical
process. But if you really want to arrive at the
dynamics of modern society and of the modern civilised world, upon the theory that the universe is not
a dead machine, and to find yourself abreast of the
foremost thought of this age, you *must* read all Carlyle's books. Nowhere else, if you devoured libraries,
will you learn so well, and so clearly and distinctly, to
understand the circumstances that environ you—circumstances touching duty, government, conduct of life.

'Frederick the Great' is six volumes of toughish
reading, though, in sketching characters and describing battles, more entertaining than any romance; but
it puts before you the whole panorama of European
history, indeed of the history of civilisation in last
century up to the time when newspapers began to
take charge of European history, and tell the story
of it by small instalments, according to their insight
and integrity. It is a shaft bored through the strata
of European history for eight or nine hundred years
before Frederick. If it does not disclose many veins
of silver or of gold, that is not the fault of the borer.

If it does not let the reader see pretty well where he now stands in European history, that will be his own fault. The sense and the pretence of modern politics are to be seen there in full operation, also the mysterious caw-cawing and hoot-hooting of diplomatic owls and other doleful creatures, the insane plunging into war for such delusions as the balance of power, also the growth of our colonial empire, the growth of our marvellous National Debt, and the mad wicked wars and warlike projects upon which the money was spent. The French Revolution also throws a light upon the latter half of last century; but it is a lurid light, as if of volcanic fires and of burning cities, telling, as interpreted by Carlyle, the old, old tale of inspired prophets, that idleness, vice, lust, selfishness, wickedness, cannot last for ever, even in this world, but will, sooner or later, call effectually down upon themselves inevitable destruction.

An unhappy, accursed century the last, according to his view of it, though not much worse than the present, in which the world-phœnix is beginning to put on its new feathers, under the still unextinguished funeral fires. To older centuries he turns for examples of what God's world ought to be; to the age of Cromwell, last ruler of England, who believed alike in the efficacy of cold steel, dry gunpowder, and the dogmas of the Puritan faith; to the age of Abbot Samson, the elect of Bury St Edmunds and Henry II., some 700 years ago, managing his great religious house and its revenues with integrity and industry, when Edinburgh was but a village clinging to the ridge between two lochs, under shelter of the Castle, and straggling down to the Abbey of Holyrood, then newly built and endowed by the pious generosity of David I.—St Mungo still ruling in Glasgow, James Watt slumbering in the deep of time; and persistently contrasting "Past and Present," not merely in the most interesting and profoundly suggestive book bearing that name, but in 'Chartism,' 'Latter-Day Pamphlets,' and all his historical writings, reverently pointing out the sincere belief and active virtues which, like salt, saved it from corruption, and bitterly contrasting these with the sham beliefs, and selfish pursuits, and godless beaverism and Mammonism of the present, with which we are entertaining ourselves on our way to fiery purification or total extinction.

Although I have mentioned 'Frederick the Great' as holding a high place in point of utility,—for a student of modern political empire, its development and distribution—I should say the highest for showing how existing European States have grown up and hang together, and carry on their business of ruling mankind, both internally and internationally,—yet I would not advise any student of Carlyle to begin with 'Frederick,' because to read it intelligently requires a familiarity with his style, with his views of the laws that govern the world, and of the necessarily inevitable failure of pleasure-seeking, power-loving rulers and legislators to understand and to apply these laws. I would recommend a beginner to try some of the essays first—

say Burns, Dr Johnson, any one whose title excites
curiosity, and of which the subject is already somewhat familiar; the Lectures on Hero-worship, which
are intended to be popular, and were originally delivered *extempore;* then the 'French Revolution,' which contains many varied literary styles, effects, descriptions,
portraits, profound meditations, and is generally
thought the greatest of his works; or 'Sartor Resartus,'
which contains his philosophy, practical and speculative, in small compass, and was by himself reckoned,
quite rightly, I think, the most valuable of all his productions. 'Sartor' will require and will repay several
meditative perusals; and the 'French Revolution,' in
some passages, reflective and descriptive, nearly as
many. So also with most of the interjected meditations among the 'Letters of Cromwell,' which book was,
I believe, Dr Chalmers's favourite, from considerations
which will occur to the thoughtful reader. The
'French Revolution' was Jeffrey's favourite. It and
the applause it created conquered his aversion to Carlyle's literary style and transcendental notions—after
it was too late for both of them. Very few writings
of this century require such steady attention, so frequent pauses of reflection, with the finger between the
leaves. And yet, in my experience, they are not so
exhaustive and productive of mental strain as the
pages of Macaulay, which tend to be, after long reading, like a series of feasts confined to mince-pies and
maraschino. The only writings known to me which
are so little tiresome, and not less profound, are David

Hume's and Sir W. Hamilton's in prose, and Byron's both in prose and verse.

Regarding Carlyle's place in literature and in wide-world influence, opinions vary enormously. Some men, not void of sound judgment, think him an impracticable visionary, whose discontent with everything was due to overflowing bile; whose denunciations of cant and insincerity and dishonesty are as vain, and nearly as groundless, as the ravings of bedlam; whose pages are not worth reading, except for the purposes of excitement or contradiction; whose English style is not drawn from the pure wells of English undefiled, but is a heterogeneous jargon of English, Scotch, French, German, and Carlylese, neither intelligible nor elegant. Though I can recognise a slight tincture of truth in such opinions and vituperative criticisms, I cannot say that I either sympathise with them or think them worthy of serious refutation. According to my estimate of Carlyle, not arrived at without reading the bulk of his writings over and over again, six or seven times some of them, I judge him to be among the greatest, if not the very greatest literary man of his time, and worthy to hold a high place among the literary men of all time; and I do not know of any literary man, except Voltaire, who ever exercised so great an influence on his age. But Voltaire's was by no means so wholesome an influence, being all but entirely destructive, and destructive of much that the world is interested in preserving. I find in Carlyle the highest eloquence—

strong and crabbed, it may be, like oaken boughs
moulded by storms—and the deepest insight, piercing
through the weak points of individual character, the
rotten parts of social organisation, and divining the
future from an accurate knowledge of the present and
the past. I find in him an instinctive force of perception, an eye and a respect for fact seldom exampled, never surpassed, and a correlative power of
representing the actual in language,—the intuitive
power of a man who has resolved to know the truth
and nothing but the truth, to reject the tempting
vestures of fancy, to postpone the beautiful to the
true. And I find further, as part of the mental equip-
ment of a votary of truth, a memory of unexcelled
range and tenacity—a memory that took in facts
correctly or not at all, and retained as if cut on steel,
after long years, the exact results of the exact observation made by a clear eye and an unflinching conscience. I find in him an enormous amount of *vital-
ised* learning in all branches of human knowledge,—not
the barren dusty knowledge of the pedant, not the mal-
odorous results of the laboratory or of the dissecting-
room (though he was by no means ignorant of physical science, or unfit to extend its borders), but learning
touching all the great movements of human thought,
all the great factors of human progress, whether
speculative or practical, secular or sacred, all the great
feats of individuals or of nations. I find him to be
very serious, an intense lover of right, a still more
intense hater of wrong, one of the most melancholy

of men, but also one of the fullest of humour, fit to awaken convulsions of laughter, like Rabelais, Dean Swift, and Smollett.

Yet I am not quite blind to his imperfections. I do not say that his latter English style is perfect, but I say that it is a suitable vehicle for Titanic disrupted thought. I can see perfectly well that his pages abound in exaggerations and contradictions, that from his books no logical system of philosophy of any kind can be extracted, and that if he were to be attacked as John Stuart Mill attacked Sir W. Hamilton, great havoc could be made among his sibylline conflicting doctrines. I further see the scope for ridicule that can be found among them, the laughable burlesques that can be made of his style and his ideas, or recognisable caricatures of them. I know how he has dealt with Voltaire, playing kindly with him and his monkey-tricks, and his ladies and their cards, paint-pots, and bandboxes, giving him the highest honour he can award to any mere destroyer, and dealing mercifully with his disregard of domestic virtues and his mean shifts to acquire money and fame. But I can also conjecture in a dim way how Voltaire might have dealt with him had he had a chance, and that out of him he could have found materials for a satirical caricature not inferior to Dr Akakia and Candide ; for Maupertius and Leibnitz, to say the least, did not lie more open to the shafts of a skilful unscrupulous satirist.

Nearly every great literary man has disciples, who listen to him, follow him, believe in him, imitate his

D

style of thought, probably also his style of expression,
appropriate and repeat his ideas, pulverise them for
and disseminate them among the multitude.   Scott
and Byron were leaders of hosts, and their influence
can be traced in the pages of each other, and of almost
all contemporary writers.   So, too, with Carlyle, and
to an extent never exampled before in any writer of
prose.   His influence can be distinctly detected in all
modern literature, from the writings of Browning and
Tennyson down to sermons, popular lectures, and half-
penny newspapers.   The region in which he exercises
least *direct* influence is that towards and against which
he shot most of his bolts, and that is the region which
controls the government or no-government of this
country.   But yet here, too, he has not been without
effect. The prophecies of the 'Latter-Day Pamphlets,' so
terribly fulfilled in the bungling and preventible misery
of the Crimean war, were not lost upon the managers
of the expeditions to Abyssinia, to Coomassie, and that
of the other day to Egypt.   Nor has nepotism, and the
various forms of bribery of which it is the symbol,
flourished so healthily as it did before the simooms of
his scorn struck and shattered it.   Public examination
has been resorted to to keep dunderheads even out of
the army, no matter whose nephews they may happen
to be.   Public competition has been tried as a means
of getting the best public servants; and if not an entirely perfect plan (as what human plan can be ?), it is
better than bribery in any of its many various open
and covert forms, and it does help poor men's sons to

rise with certainty to a level where they can be of use
to society, more surely than is possible by begging,
sneaking, tuft-hunting, or fussy electioneering. And I
daresay, since the date of Model Prisons, the condition
of scoundrels has not been quite so comfortable as it
used to be, and there has been a good deal less of what
he calls "that sugary disastrous jargon of philanthropy." No doubt his fierce denunciations in the
meantime have fallen far short of their aim in many
points—I am sorry I must say in most; but his words
and thoughts are winged, and if the truth be in them,
the right mark, the right chink in the harness of corruption, will be struck in their flight through centuries.
In spite of his warnings and the faith that America
placed and still places in him, their "domestic institution," as Americans called it—negro slavery—was suddenly, not gradually abolished; but whether he or the
politicians of the North, spurred as they were by the
exigencies of civil war, saw deepest into what was best
for both black and white, is getting expounded by an
experience which threatens in a few generations to
thrust the negro back to Africa or into extinction.
And indeed I am afraid that America, notwithstanding of its professed discipleship, is much more corrupt
than England—bribery of a pretty open, unabashed kind
being one of its surviving domestic, or rather social institutions, an institution incurably accursed, which slavery
need not necessarily have been, though, I suspect, a
multitude of unconscientious masters had made it so,
and secured the vengeance of a just Heaven for them

and theirs. But let me say, the penetrating insight which educed the prophecies of the 'Latter-Day Pamphlets' is not unworthy of close attention, and, it may be, of a little reverential respect. That insight may be a guide to England against many dangers, even though the state of society is such that its warning cannot be directly and immediately acted upon. Human society is fluid, but it is also solid. Its fluidity is seen in the centuries, its solidarity also, but especially in an attempt to alter laws or customs or institutions except step by step. The gradual evolution of the physical world is a necessity also in the political, unless the rights and interests of individuals are to be sacrificed. Spasmodic reforms are incapable of being dissociated from the evils incident to all sudden social changes, such as have been illustrated by negro emancipation and in the revolutions of France. Carlyle knew this well enough, but he thundered at the walls of all manner of unreformed, corrupt Jerichos as if he expected them to fall to-morrow. And here it is that his political blasts and counter-blasts require to be read and pondered with qualifications. Perhaps they will have taken full effect two or three centuries hence; but they cannot work themselves out in one generation, or even in two or three. That perfect liberty is an impracticable dream, that democracy is the government of a mob mostly fools, may be true; but what boots it, when it has been plainly predestined that the problems of democracy *must* be worked out practically, that we are in the rapids of the democratic Niagara without power

of return ? There is no use winking at the inevitable,
and just about as little in railing at it. The government of the wisest would be the best, if it could be
obtained; but being unattainable, we must be content
with the least objectionable substitute which can be
got, and that is, in this current age, the will of the
majority. Whether that is to whirl us back again to
despotism, as happened to France and old Rome, or to
send us over the precipices, we cannot know. Carlyle in-
clines to the latter opinion, and holds that the prevailing system of governing by canvassing, caucuses, beer,
ballot-boxes, and well-disguised multiform bribery, is as
certainly doomed as was the world before the Flood, and
that the hopes of mankind, in so far as government is
concerned, lie first in acknowledging that the wisest
ought to govern, and next in finding him out. We
are now trying the plan of putting these problems to
the vote, as the old Romans did, and as our George
Buchanan, father of all modern Chartists and refor-
mers, resolutely maintained ought to be done; and
perhaps success may arrive as George Buchanan hoped,
but as Carlyle does not in the least believe, after considering three centuries more of teaching by experience
than Buchanan had the chance of perusing.

I am not here to meddle with or expound any
current political creed. Carlyle was neither Whig
nor Tory. He was more Conservative than the Tory,
and far more sweepingly Radical than the Whig.
The right to govern was in his eye a sacred privilege
conferred by Heaven, and not to be purchased by

bribery or distilled out of ballot-boxes; but the right
to go idle, and shoot pheasants, and pretend to govern—
that, in his belief, had not been conceded to any man,
and could not be pretended to be exercised by any
other than a stuffed clothes-screen without conscience
or soul, further than what may be required to save
the expense of salt. No right could he recognise
which was not linked and weighted with a duty. The
man, or the class of men, who could sit with folded
hands, who would not strive to work the pressing
work of duty, he held ought not to exist, and must,
according to the inexorable laws that govern this
world, sooner or later cease to exist. Still, some of his
brightest hopes for this country rest on its hereditary
aristocracy. " The Peerage " is by no means contemptible in his eyes. He recognises in it generally a
higher sense of honour and of duty, and more noble
qualities, than are to be found in mere lucky scram-
blers after money, or political schemers, or parliamentary talkers, and all such stump-orators and windbags.
How to dispense with these, however, he has not made
clearly practical anywhere, nor has he any feasible
substitute to propose for that " constitutional talking-
machine "—the House of Commons; though he de-
claims as if he would, without compunction, dip it
into carbonic acid gas.

His politics are not practical, at least as yet. But
there is a speculative truth in them difficult to gain-
say—a truth which must sooner or later undermine a
great deal of the political insincerity, pretence, corrup-

tion, incompetence, and dishonesty of the present day. The democracy which is coming will have vices of its own, but it will be terribly intolerant of non-democratic vices, and of all the ancient divine rights that have neither right nor divinity left in them. Woe be to the people that cannot profit by the fiercely earnest denunciations and vaticinations of this modern Jeremiah! Yet if they had happened to disregard or even stone the prophets, they will be just like other peoples whose vices have stirred the voice of prophecy. But, to do them justice, be it recorded of his contemporaries that they listened to him with a reverence and attention seldom if ever accorded to any seer on this planet before. Though unable to discern fully the practicality of his teaching, they recognised its moral worth and fire, and were not entirely blind to its potential force—both destructive and regenerative—when the right time came for renouncing the old and adopting something new.

The main secret of Carlyle's greatness, to the best of my deliberate thinking, lies in his religious creed. In an age of doubt and practical atheism, and belly-worship, and mammon-worship, and devil-worship, he actually believed in GOD, the God whose creature he was, whose servant he was bound to be, and whose judgment-seat he could not escape and dare not think of escaping, and whom he recognised to be pre-eminently the enemy of lies—lies whether spoken by the tongue or acted in the life. I do not think that, among literary men for 1000 years, I can recognise

a more sincere and intense believer; and I see, it may
be through mists of prejudice or through a glass darkly,
that he takes rank in the matter of real, earnest, religious faith with Dante, with Milton, and with Spinoza. Like Dante, he may have had little sunshine in
his faith, little hope, little joy; he may have walked in
hell, and peopled it with his enemies; and indeed I
rather think, in that particular, his Rhadamanthine zeal
would have transcended even that of Dante. Like Milton, the tragic wail of his 'Paradise Lost' may affect the
human heart more, far more, than his faint glimpses of
a 'Paradise Regained'; and like Spinoza, his *unica
substantia*, his supreme and infinite essence—out of
which all things proceed, to which all things return
—may be but dimly discerned as a personality,—
may be but touched by the groping finger in the
unfathomable night, but is accepted as the certainty
of certainties, as well as the mystery of mysteries, not
to be worshipped by the lips merely (if at all), but to
be reverenced in the heart of man as the ultimate
holy of holies upon earth, and to obtain, as the only
acceptable service, the lifelong consecration to duty
and truth of all His children. All these men were
in a sense inspired. The spirit of the Universal All
had penetrated and possessed them. They were all
heretics—even Milton, who was the most orthodox of
them. Their creeds are all unwritten, except here
a little and there a little, never to be written
out completely in the ink and dialects of time;
open to criticisms, to scoffing it may be, to the

scowl of bloodthirsty inquisitors, but having all
the one crowning virtue of a creed, that they
were fully and sincerely believed, and unflinchingly
carried into life and conduct.   Professing a creed with
the lips is one thing, practising it is an entirely different thing.   Show me a man who prefers a personal
interest—be it the interest of his Kirk—to truth and
justice (and such a man can too easily be found), and
I tell you that that man is practically an atheist,
however often he may have signed the Confession of
Faith, however frequently he may have recited the
Athanasian Creed.   I tell you further, that the "green
bay-tree" of blind selfishness, which he nourishes with
falsehood and stolen waters, has a worm at its root, and
will go like the prophet's gourd, leaving him at last
in shelterless surprise.   You may at your leisure consider the ways and the fate of such men.   You will
recognise them not merely in Churches and trades,
but in literature, which is also a kind of Church not
as yet roofed in or fenced with theological standards
and ordination vows, but open to the ministration of
street-preachers, some of them ragged and sincere, a
good many of them with better coats than principles—
the prevailing principle at present being to manufacture what will sell.   One result of Carlyle's creed and
its correlative sense of duty was, that he never wrote
anything merely to sell.   Unlike some newspaper editors
who, as he scornfully describes, gird themselves up night
after night to thrash the same old straw over and over
again into smaller and smaller dust, or to fabricate

new partisan falsehoods; unlike some political pleaders who look in each legislative change for the pecuniary advantage of a class, probably their own class; unlike some occasional inspired bagman who raves about a calico millennium,—he tried to publish the truth as he had ascertained it, wholly regardless of class interest, believing that in the end the truth will, when weighed in the balances, not be found wanting, and will be the best, not for one class, but for all classes.

That love of the truth which, according to ancient promise, "makes free," breaking the fetters of gold and silver, and brass, and craven fear, and carnal sensation, made him also great, lifting him out of the trammels of slavery into the bright open sunshine of the temple of the Universal All. Out of his love of truth arose his devotion to the fountain of truth, his antipathy to the Father of Lies in all his manifestations in men and multitudes. Definite creed he had none—none that could be expressed in Westminster Standards taught by his father and the teachers of his youth, or in Thirty-nine Articles whencesoever collected. It was definite only in its negatives. But it was real, nevertheless, at the very heart of it. Whether it was theism or pantheism he would not have undertaken to tell, and I cannot. It stretched away from the unspeakable to the unthinkable, to the infinite. It had no liturgy and no hymn-book. *Laborare est orare* was the only saintly maxim which he could completely appropriate. But his creed was real, nevertheless. Never hermit or devotee was more thoroughly possessed and penetrated by a religious creed. At the centre of his life it burned like vestal fire, irradiating his whole being with the light that never was on sea or shore, ever generating that imperious moral force or sense of duty that gave him his power—that, so to say, spoke through him, and sent his ·burning words and thoughts over the world to raise conflagrations and to give illumination and vital heat for ages to come. True it is, his intellectual powers were of the highest order, and approached to genius, or actually reached it—in every field except the poetical; an intellect fit to be the ally and rival of Kepler, or Newton, or Napoleon, or Hume—to rule States, to lead armies, to do whatever requires the greatest force of the practical reason, whatever is most difficult for man, except the construction out of nothing of the aerial fantastic kingdoms of a Shakespeare, a Dante, a Milton, or a Goethe, or the crystallisation of the floating spirit-melodies to be found in the verse of a Burns, a Wordsworth, a Shelley, or a Tennyson. He was not truly a poet, though most of the elements of a great poet lay inarticulately in him. They are there, the poetic gold, the poetic silver, the poetic iron (the latter in plenty); but the fire from heaven that might have melted them has never come, and they are flung abroad only half molten, as if scattered by an impatient volcano that had wearied waiting for the full influence of the central fire. Contrast his writing with Byron's, and you will better see what I mean. They had much in common mentally, and in particular

the same restless discontent, the same scorn for the
contemptibilities of human life, though Byron had not
classified them with the same care as Carlyle did.
But see in Byron how thoroughly the material is
molten, and how it flows in melodious " Childe Harold "
cantos! how it coruscates and leaps upward in the
" Giaour " and the Hebrew Melodies! how it eddies,
and laughs, and scorches, and abolishes in the stanzas
of " Don Juan "! See, moreover, how little has come of
this splendid poetic endowment for want of a religious
faith, the faith that can move mountains which it
cannot melt! And see, too, how this faith irradiates and
preserves .the mild pieties of old Cowper, the aspirations of dreamy Coleridge, the nature-hymns of Shelley,
the heaven-scaling meditations of Wordsworth, the
hopeful interrogations of Alfred Tennyson! Fortunate
above all these is Carlyle in inténse strength of conviction, and therein was concentrated all the rest of
his strength. He believed in God,—that God made the
world and him; that He had sent him here not to
gather flowers on sunny afternoons and be happy, but
to work while it is called to-day, without haste, but
without rest; that He had given him a message to
deliver to his age, and ordained him to that end;
bound him to poverty, to incapacity to steal or to beg,
to continuous ill-health, shutting him out from most
of the distracting, debasing enjoyments of the flesh;
dooming him to melancholy days and sleepless nights;
scourging him with bodily miseries, and many cares
outward and inward, and binding him as if by the iron

of fate to his appointed task as the *one* thing he could
do in this world except die and go as a deserter from
his post, his work undone, his generation unwarned,
and the fires of devouring destiny bursting under their
feet. Ordination vows he had none to keep or to
break; but he was ordained, nevertheless,—ordained,
like all great men, to bear the torch of truth into some
part of the realm of night, and guided along a way
that he knew not by the touches of unseen hands,
and the repulse of impenetrable iron bars. Conscience
shut the Church door against him; honest pride ejected
him from the school. A demon of disgust warned him
away from the portals of the law and its selfishness
and insincerity. Poverty severed him from his first
love, and from much else in a world where Mammon
is so reputable a divinity. And yet he was not alone
or without guidance or help. More affectionate, encouraging mother no man ever had, nor a more faithful, helpful, sternly kind father; a wife more noble,
more fit, never fell to the lot of man of genius. Few
men, especially surly men, have had such a troop of
devoted friends. But self-help is God-help, really the
only available God-help; and he had for the most part
to walk abroad under the silent heavens silent and
alone. Still the stars were there, shining over him,
pouring consolation from their serene immeasurable
depths over his temporary troubles; and the moral
law within teaching that there was no trouble of any
moment for him who unswervingly steered towards
the right. So he walked and worked, as ever in the

great Task-master's eye, toiling with a fervour, almost
a fury, unknown to sluggards or to slaves, one of the
most industrious, conscientious, God-fearing, and yet
unhappy of men.   Unhappy he was, like Milton,
Dante, and the Hebrew prophets of old, but, like them,
believing that he was commissioned of Heaven to denounce the wickedness of earth,—not in the least to
seek for pleasure in it,—to rekindle once more the
altar-fires in the heart of man that point upward to
the throne of the Supreme, and to spread conviction
that in the doing of duty alone, in the renunciation of
carnality, sloth, selfishness, lies the single straight path
to happiness here or hereafter.

HOROSCOPE

A HOROSCOPE OF BRITAIN:

OUR AGE—ITS DOINGS AND DRIFT.

———◆———

OF that strange encompassing phantasm Time, so essential to all we have been, all we are, and all we hope to be, what point draws our gaze towards it with intensest force? upon what tract of its invisible extent are our thoughts most apt to wander? Is it upon the past, with its completed labours, subjugated difficulties, forgotten cares, friendships grown icy or carried to the grave, the shed rose-leaves of childhood, the withered violets of life's spring? Is it upon the present, where every day has its measure of care, every step its possibility of battle, even sleep its distractions and confused welters and worries, its monsters and tyrants, its weapons that decline to wound, its explosives that will seldom burn? Do we not rather steal away by fancy's flowery bypaths to the delectable mountains and happy valleys, Goshens flowing with milk and honey, Edens with no fruit of mortal

E

taste, planted afar in the dreamland of the future and
of hope ?

> " Man never is, but always to be blest."

He is afflicted with

> " The desire of the moth for the star,
>   The night for the morrow ;
> The devotion to something afar
>   From the scene of this sorrow."

He will listen to almost any voice that offers to soothe
his present afflictions by balm drawn from the future.
Therefore he has listened to astrology, to augurs, to
soothsayers, to fortune-tellers, to magpies, to ravens,
and to clergymen or madmen professing to open up
the hidden things of the prophets and the seals of the
Apocalypse. Stœffler, an astrologer, in 1524, from the
conjunction of three planets on the watery sign, foretold
·a universal deluge, and threw all Europe into conster-
nation. Noah did not secure one hundredth part the
attention or credit, nor did our own Dr Cumming
when he fixed the end of the world for 1865, though
he too was well paid for his dogmatism about futurity.
But the world somehow has survived him and Stœffler,
and almost the memory of both, and a vast procession
of coming struggles, Zadkiel almanacs, prophetic he-
goats, and other apocalyptic and mythological machinery. Mankind, in so far as civilised, are awakening to
the conviction that in order to forecast the future, it
is necessary to know the present time and the forces
at work in it, as also to recognise the prophetic relation

of cause and effect, and the mode in which divine law evolves one era from another.

The prophetic eye that does not look along the line of cause and effect has in it either the sly, knowing, winking cast of imposture or the glare of madness. The prophet, like the astronomer, requires to plant his telescope upon solid ground, otherwise the oscillations and tremors of himself and his instrument will give rise to wonderful conclusions. From truth only can we infer truth; from guesses, guesses; from oracles that may mean twenty things, anything, according to the taste or whim of the interpreter. Let us prefer and rest upon the truth—a grain of it will give us a better starting-point than Andes of hypotheses or the shaky tripod of a pythoness. We shall find it pure in reason and conscience, slightly alloyed with fable in the observations of external experience, and in history, which is the record of the experiences of sections of the race. From experience, moral, intellectual, historical, we can infer truth; from our own experience we can look out with confidence upon that of others—

> " For all experience is an arch wherethrough
> Gleams that untravelled world whose margin fades
> For ever and for ever as we move."

We can look back upon the past and consider how one era evolves from and is conditioned by the possibilities of another, round upon the present and consider how it grew out of the past, also how the future may grow, indeed, must grow out of it, as the plant from the seed.

Metaphysical delineations of the great world-plan by
the great of the world's sages are not awanting: in
history we can faintly trace the causes of the rise and
fall of nations; by reason we can solve, at least pro-
visionally, the riddles of circumstance; from conscience
we can anticipate the judgment of heaven, for it is
God's law written in our hearts.   But, alas! history is
obscure, often fabulous, and oblivion is ever wasting
it.   Reason has its limits, and knowledge too, and
neither reason nor conscience has materials to decide
upon without knowledge.   The longest vision meets a
horizon; the eagle's wing cannot transcend the atmosphere in which it floats.   Verily, it is difficult within
the compass of nature to find an emblem for this
mysterious mankind in its journey through blank space
and time.   Let me ask you to listen to this apologue,
and apply for yourselves what it suggests.

On a coral rock, white in the bright sunlight, fringed
with white breakers, strewn with the wrecks of vegetation and of fleets, sits a solitary sea-bird, wearied, with
drooping wing.   Under it is the substantial masonry of
thousands of myriad-strong generations of insects, "the
home and the mausoleum of its architects"; around it
the restless, frothy, troublous billows and the far-drifted
spoils of the tempest; behind it the uncounted miles of
its invisible journey and aerial track; before it the
green ocean-waves bounding from their rock-foundations
five miles deep, and the ever-fleeting horizon kissing
them afar.   Short breathing-space granted, and away
it must, for the sun is sloping to the west, the impa-

tient winds are blowing, the ocean's bosom is rising
and heaving to the hidden moon, to bury under the
waters the place of its accidental and welcome rest.
Not far different is it with mankind.   Under heaven's
sunshine it rests, or seems to rest, over the accumulated conquests and labours of countless generations;
around it the wrecks which history has saved from
the edacious Lethe of years; behind it the acted and
nigh-forgotten past; before it the unsounded abysses
of time; around it the swelling tides of destiny—swelling not under planetary but providential influence,
and with urgency murmuring " onward, onward, ever
onward."   For Providence is our moon at noonday,
moving by irresistible influence the tide of ages, itself
unseen.   Yet not quite identical is it with mankind.
Mankind has reason for a chart-interpreter, conscience
for a compass, duty for an inobscurable pole-star, and
faith in a land of promise and of hope, indefinitely
distant, but nearer as the infinite years evolve.

   Surrounded by mystery, we feel the never-failing
force of the solemn and wise admonition of the St
Gilgen's memorial-stone: " Look not wistfully upon
the past: it comes not back.   Improve the present:
it is thine.   Go forth into the shadowy future without
fear, and with a manly heart."   And as we gaze forward among its shadows, let our vision be strengthened
and regulated by those powers that raise us superior
to the sea-bird,—Conscience, Faith, Reason,—and let
it be under the conviction—a conviction that lies at
the root of all rational effort to forecast the future—

that the only lines of light that go direct and unbent
through all time are the Creator's immutable laws.
Seed-time and harvest, summer and winter, day and
night, birth and death, succeed each other. They, and
a host of other sequences, are regulated by those known
and invariable manifestations of providential agency
which attest the unity of the creative mind—to interfere with one of which would disturb the settled order
of the universe. Similar laws, it is all but certain,
regulate the life of man on earth, and the relations of
human societies; but they are extremely obscure, and
only a general statement can be hazarded from all we
know of them. It may be expressed in this vague
proposition: Nations rise and fall by the combination
and coexistence of three classes of forces—(1) physical,
(2) intellectual, and (3) moral; and of these the moral
is the most important, and in its weakness or strength
is the index of social weakness or social strength. The
same thing is true of individuals. They make way in
the world by physical, intellectual, and moral powers
—even ladies, who depend, or used to depend, chiefly
upon passive graces, beauty, modesty, and the like.
Allowing that modesty which is so amiable to blush
undisturbed, consider, if you please, how essential a
moral bias is to a man's success. Suppose he has
been stinted to a feeble intellect, a full purse, and
great animal strength. He is a mere human bullock,
fit for a heathen sacrifice, likely to knock out his
scanty brains, and riotously toss and gore peaceable
members of the community. Suppose he has intellect

without conscience: then he becomes an adept in scoundrelism; cheats all and sundry, and himself at last; is distrusted, detested by all; is a Rush, or a Palmer, or a Pritchard, and ends in a hempen cravat or in penal servitude. The three are requisite. Without a moderately tough weather-tight body, the journey of life is not comfortable, and seldom long; without intellect it is full of crooks and blunders; without morality it is all muddy and filthy, fit for the hard scales and hard heart of an unsocial crocodile. And the parallel indicated by these extreme hypotheses holds with nations. Man cannot exist comfortably except under certain physical conditions. He must have food, moderately pure air, a climate that will neither dissipate him into gas nor freeze his blood. He cannot exist comfortably without some intellect, to open up for him the mysteries of cooking, tailoring, delving, pilfering, or the like. He cannot exist in society without some idea of moral responsibility. Not even a band of robbers could be held together for twenty-four hours without intellect to guide and morality to restrain. Thus a sense of equity comes last to render man fit for society—to raise him, as it were, to the social level; and the sense of justice disappears first when nations are perishing, not by external violence, but by internal decay. Total unrighteousness brings down infallibly the fate of Sodom; the ground burns under the feet of injustice and unbridled vice; if there be not ten just men in a state, woe be to it. Its acquired momentum may carry it

along, but only for a little space, as a deer, stricken
through the heart when at full speed, staggers into
slowness until the force of its velocity be spent.

Ask Conscience "how the world ought to be governed?" It answers, "By Justice, and not otherwise,
though the Omnipotent were to will it." Ask Reason.
It answers, "By Justice, or not at all. Justice and
true expediency are one. Tyrants, single-headed or
many-headed, may pervert and obscure the right, as
fogs seem to twist the stars from their positions, and
obliterate them; but the stars outlast the fogs, and
justice expelled often and again, returns often and
again accompanied by retribution fiercer than itself."
Ask History, after Reason and Conscience (witnesses
in whom you can confide before all others) have prepared you for apprehending its testimony. It will
answer in small whispers, distinctly audible through
ages of superstition and unbelief: "The great world
tribunal stands in the centuries far away; judgment is
seldom executed speedily, for that work can bear delay
which has eternity for its completion; but judgment
comes at last, and its aim is sure, though its path of
striking be the zigzag of the forked lightning."

All human experience, subjective and objective, tes-
tifies that equity is the single keystone of the social
arch, absolutely essential to its permanent existence:
remove it, and the whole structure totters and tumbles
into confused ruin, destructive alike to the just and
the unjust. And, over all, that the fabric be not swept
away by the frothing, raving, stormy sea of human

passion, rises religious faith, solemn, beautiful, divine, pointing spirewise to the "great white judgment-seat, and Him that sits thereon," dispensing justice to the ends of the earth. Never yet did a people rise without religious faith, which could guide them in this life, and carry their hopes and fears beyond it, going before them like a pillar of fire into the darkness of futurity; never yet did a people fall without having lost their guardian faith, and along with it all reverence for justice, and those virtues which centre on it.

The history of Rome is a grand practical demonstration of this truth. Romulus gave sacred rites and laws to the robber-horde, to whom it had been assigned to inhabit the seven hills, glory in the name of the " she-wolf's brood," and with short swords and steady belief in destiny to subjugate the world. But the old creed became an incredibility and political machine, with its temples and augurs; the patrician rich oppressed the plebeian poor; the poor cursed the rich; corruption grew; and the luxury which conquered Hannibal after the short swords had failed, in the course of ages conquered Rome herself. Out of her had fled for ever the patriotism that stood with Horatius on the bridge, and consigned Curtius in his armour to the yawn of the forum. Self-abasement had made her kneel before she fell; and when the Goths and Vandals came to strip her of her queenly ornaments, she was the shadow of her former self. Her people had lost bravery and virtue—that courage which rests on conscious rectitude. She was like a great old tree, the product of

centuries, that had lost occasional branches by the
storms of fate, and yet seemed little marred, but was
all the while decaying inwardly and unseen, so that
when the barbarian force was applied to crush her,
from the bark to the core passed out of rottenness into
ruin. The crisis came in the fulness of time. Then
over her domestic vices, worthy of a second Sodom,
her oppression of provinces, her aristocratic idleness
and extortion, her democratic wrongs and debasements,
swelled the still small voice of justice into the blare of
a trumpet of doom, levelled the throne of the Cæsars,
and shivered the gorgeous sceptre of the Seven Hills.
So had it been of old with the cities once so famous,
then and now desolate—Nineveh, Babylon, Palmyra.
Intoxicated with the wine of victory, they forgot justice, they forgot mercy, they forgot God. They fell,
therefore; and tribes that know them not are dwelling
in tent and hut amid the mighty ruins.

"Shall not the Judge of the earth do right?"
Shall we not infer that injustice cannot live in Britain, since it has never lived in any country under
heaven, but has proved the ruin of every country that
had not the moral acuteness to detect it, the moral
courage to cast it out? If conscience, if revelation, if
history do not deceive us, we have a moral criterion
which we can apply to existing institutions, customs,
laws. If any one of them is immoral or unjust, there
is no room for doubt about it and its effects. It is
destructive until it be destroyed. Equity is the necessary bond of society; all else is contingent and empiri-

cal, to be managed according to circumstances, and the ability of legislators to grapple with them, and unloose their Gordian knots or cut them. But here occur atheistic moralists—lawyers and legislators, some of them—who say, or think, or act as if they thought, that there is no such thing as justice, that it is all a matter of convenience, of expediency, of temporising, of compromise. Nations have held the same dogma, and where are they now? I assume, as an axiomatic principle, that "the Great Soul of the world *is*, and *is just*," —a principle corroborated and consistent with all truth whencesoever drawn, if correctly understood. Right is immortal, and the roll of centuries serves only to establish it; in it certainly and chiefly lives the spirit of prophecy, for the laws of God are true and perpetual, and sooner or later they burn up all who disobey.

Firm in these convictions, let us turn to Britain, and see what she is, and what she may be ·expected to be. She was peopled originally we guess not how or when. She was invaded and governed by Romans, Saxons, Danes, and Normans in succession, and her population and arts of civilised life grew from the union and communion of races. Once blessed with inhabitants, she fed them by the productive force of the earth and the waters, defended them by her stormy shores and inaccessible cliffs, kept them awake and active by the stimulating force of her cold climate, intolerant of the indolence of tropical regions, and was a home in which they could live—perhaps comfortably—a sphere for the development of their physical and intellectual

powers, imperatively called into exercise in warfare
with wolves, the marshes, and the elements.   Various
kings led them to battle with various results; thousands of them joined in the Crusades, conquered at
Ascalon, left their bones in Palestine, or returned in
handfuls to civilise their kindred with the invaluable
knowledge gathered in strange and more favoured
countries.   Simple John of England was forced to
grant the Magna Charta which contains a mustard-
seed of civil liberty; and Edward I., desperately in
want of money to make war upon Wales, France, and
Scotland, had to create the first House of Commons[1]
as an instrument of tax-gathering.   A self-willed, imperious Henry VIII. and his Amazonian unamiable
daughter Elizabeth freed Britain from the fatherly
attentions of the Pope, when the old man of the red
stockings fell into feeble or mischievous second-child-
ishness, not without strenuous co-operation and violent
Calvinistic eloquence on the part of our own brave,
far-sighted John Knox. The Puritans of England and
the Covenanters of Scotland fought and won the
battle of religious liberty, and William of Orange was
imported to announce the victory with official splendour, after they had borne the burden and heat of the
day.   Scotland and England at last were one, Ireland
gradually joins, and the sputter of Scotch rebellions
over Britain is at leisure, with a constitution becoming
free, an enterprising people, and several special physical advantages, to enter upon a career of commercial

[1] 1295.

and mechanical industry not yet rivalled in the history of civilisation.

Centuries after the discovery of the magnetic compass had freed the mariner from the necessity of creeping timorously along the sea-coast, after America had been discovered, and the passage by the Cape to India, there was needed (to take the place of the ancient emporia of trade on the shores of the Mediterranean) a market-place accessible to the ships of every country, safe from the incursions of depredators, and large enough to be a workshop for the world. About the period of the French Revolution, it so happened that Britain satisfied the required conditions. It had deep water around its shores for the approach of ships, deep river-mouths and sheltered creeks for harbours ; and its navy, manned by bold hardy tars, could protect it from invasion. It had large towns, considerable liberty for its subjects, the culture and inspiration of a noble literature, and above all, (why, we know not) the intellectual, practical, enterprising Anglo-Saxon race. It had iron and coal abundant, wherewith the ingenuity of that race could devise and manufacture tools. And at the right time, when France was undergoing volcanic reforms, several members of that race were constructing instruments of a deeper revolution and more lasting reformation. In succession, Hargreave invented the spinning-jenny, Arkwright the spinning-frame, Crompton the spinning-mule, Watt the steam-engine, and Cartwright the power-loom. Half a century later came Stephenson,

the inventor of the locomotive, as also the inventor
of the electric telegraph, whoever he may be, these two
annihilators of distance. Greatest of these is Watt.
He made possible cotton-spinning, railways, steam-
boats, and steam printing-presses, and is the Alexander
of the conquerors of material nature. He is the chief of
those poets whose Parnassus is of iron ore, and of coal,
the rock-imprisoned fossil sunshine of extinct millenni-
ums. He is the true hero of Carlyle's unwritten and
unwritable epic of the age, which, he says often and
again, is no longer "arms and the man," much less
"shirt-frills and the man," but "tools and the man."
Not even Achilles, fortunate in his Homer, had so many
noisy rhapsodists chanting his exploits as James Watt.
What a whirring of spinning-mills, what a snorting of
locomotives, what a dinting of Nasmyth steam-ham-
mers, what a clatter of steam-looms !

So here and now we have Britain grown to be the
queen of those huge bee-hives of modern industry,
wealth, and civilisation,—the busiest workshop of the
world, the finest market-place ; holding, therefore, the
foremost position in the world's business in this industrial mechanical era, with an unexampled accumulation
of material wealth, with an unsurpassed supply of
practical talent, and with an open sense of private and
public virtue which, notwithstanding of many lapses
from a high ideal, has little to learn, except by way of
warning, from the conduct of any nation, ancient or
modern. Our country has no cause to blush in the
presence of any other, no cause to envy or to fear any

other. What she requires to fear is the being false to
herself, the preference of the material to the moral,
of riches to righteousness.   Look at the splendour of
her realised ideals,—at her churches, built by pious
forefathers; her universities, her armies, her navies,
her machines, her money, her books.   Her keels are
on every sea; upon her empire the sun never sets.
Out of every age she has gathered an inheritance, out
of every zone she has collected the rarest produce,
diamonds and kindred stones, silver and gold, pearls
and ivory, silks and lace, pictures and sculpture,—all
that the miner, the diver, the hunter can procure, or
art polish or create.   All the old wonders of the world
are eclipsed in the triumphs of her engineering and of
her science; all the great cities of all past time shrink
into comparative insignificance beside London, which
is the epitome of our industrial era, the Rome of to-
day,—a Rome not based entirely or mainly upon conquest, but upon the utility of honest, intelligent work,
and the hard-earned supremacy of a bold, enterprising,
self-seeking, yet self-denying, moral religious race,—a
race not to be created or led to greatness by the gods
of Epicurus, or by those of tropical indolent regions
who promise to reward their worshippers and devotees
by eternal sleep.   .

   All that money can buy our country possesses. But
it has possessions that money cannot buy.   One of
these is the race, compounded by destiny out of Druids
and Romans, Celts and Saxons, husbandmen and soldiers, monks and pirates, and purified into homogeneity

and vigour by those inexorable cruel laws that pro-
vide for the survival of the fittest.　And then there is
the literature of the race—open, no doubt, to all mankind, but specially open to those who speak the same
language, and have a tendency to think the same or
similar thoughts, incorporated, as it were, by the effort
of successive generations into the very convolutions
of their brains.　The modern Anglo-Saxon man lives
and moves in an atmosphere of ideas impregnated
with the influence of Shakespeare, of Milton, of
Bacon, of Newton, of Swift, Smollett, and Fielding,
of Burns, Wordsworth, Coleridge, and Byron, of Scott,
Thackeray, Carlyle, Emerson, and Tennyson.　What
finite insight can estimate, what tongue can tell, the
value of such an inheritance?　Riches may take to
themselves wings and flee away, but spiritual possessions are perpetual—not for a season merely, but a joy
for ever; the heritage of mortals imprisoned in time,
and all that the triumphant immortal can carry out
of it.

Among the various items of our great national inheritance, I have omitted to mention the British
Constitution—not because I think it void of merit, but
because I think it has been the theme of rather too
much laudation, generally by enthusiastic gentlemen
after dinner, and on other occasions of excitement,
when the personal or political centres of gravity are in
a state of unstable equilibrium.　It is an old edifice,
built in different centuries to suit their own tastes and
convenience, and extremely diverse views of the sphere

and duties of government. The old feudal keep, the loop-holed, six-feet-walled lord of the manor's mansion, the Elizabethan palace, the Cromwellian privy-council room, the Stuarts' Star-chamber, the House of Lords' gilded hall, the House of Commons' debating-room, are all in it; and around it, as yet unattached, lie the tents of the people, who are now the actual, though as yet all but unconscious, masters of the whole. It is an amorphous structure, not a homogeneous whole. Now and again there has been a clamour for repairing it, or destroying dangerous parts of it, called Reform, and occasionally fresh air and sunshine have been let in,—and occasionally rats and smaller vermin have been hunted out and extirpated, in so far as that could be done without too sweeping and radical a demolition. One merit of the old edifice is, that it can bear almost any sort of new improvement without having its stability materially affected. It has been altered often and again at the bidding of expediency, and it is the reflection of that system of legislation which, however originating in the sense of right and wrong, is always controlled by prudent considerations as to whether the right time has come for doing the right thing, or whether discussion and agitation, and their consequent popular or party education, ought not to go on for a while longer, so as to enable the legislative boon to be prized and utilised when it has been obtained.

It is not for me to discuss party politics, which are often matters of tradition, of detail, of discipline, seldom

F

of principle. But as men must be governed, I may be
permitted to point out that there are two, and only two,
grand theories upon which mankind can be governed:
one is the theory of the absolutist or the despot, and the
other is that of the democrat, or the assertion of the
right of all the governed to have a voice in the appointment and direction of their governors. The first of these
political theories is expounded earnestly, even passion-
ately, by Thomas Carlyle. He recognises no right in
any man to interfere with social government, so long as
it is not intolerably bad. He approves of despotism—
the fatherly but absolute government of Frederick the
Great, modified merely by the suggestions of a Tobacco-
Parliament; of Napoleon's "whiff of grape-shot," as the
appropriate doing away with sacred right of insurrec-
tion, at the close of the French Revolution; of Cromwell's instant extinction of mutiny, by himself seiz-
ing a horse-pistol and blowing out the brains of the
spokesman of the mutineers; of applying the beneficent whip to indolent Quashee, sitting up to the nose
in rum and pumpkins, and generally of sweeping sluggards and scoundrels — the devil's regiments of the
line, as he calls them—into the dust-bin, "with some
degree of brevity." The other theory of liberty and
democratic right is expounded by Carlyle's friend and
contemporary, John Stuart Mill, and by a much older
Scotchman than either — I mean George Buchanan,
who, in his 'De Jure Regni apud Scotos,' deduces all the
rights of kings and governors from the people. Between
Buchanan and Mill there have been many advocates of

democracy, among them Tom Paine, who would have
gone to the democratic guillotine along with deniers of
the "rights of man," but for the accident that his cell-
door stood open when the mark of doom was chalked
upon it, and was invisible on the outside next morning,
—intended by the fraternal levellers and homicides to
be his last.

But the time for argument about democracy is past;
for the vanguard of civilised mankind have become
possessed of or by the fixed idea that democracy is, in
the close future, to be a matter of experiment, whether
the result is to be success or failure, or a grey mixture
of both. I for one fully sympathise with Carlyle's
idea that a wise, good despot would govern far better
than a mob of representative gentlemen, of whom the
collective wisdom is likely to be far inferior to that of
the best men in it. But there is a difficulty that we
do not know where to find the wise despot, nor to ap-
point him ruler even if we could get him, nor to save
him from dying, like President Garfield, by the hand
of some foolish or diabolical assassin. And there is
another difficulty: the career of democracy is begun,
and has been going forward faster and faster since the
American and French revolutions, and to check it now
is simply impossible. It is therefore useless to declaim against democracy, and vain to play with it and
offer it sacrifices of·sheaves of rushes, as the old Romans, in their half-sceptical moods, did to their god
Tiber, rolling seaward his yellow irresistible flood. The
only wise practical attitude towards it now is to con-

front it honestly and boldly, to try to correct its evils
and to modify its dangers, by attentive consideration of
the divine laws affecting social order, and of the lessons
which history has to tell of the end of selfish and unbridled democracies ; and with the minimum of pretence
and making of wry faces, to allow Destiny and its inspired, largely unconscious instruments, to work out its
will — instruments that have been working strongly
though silently through most of the Christian centuries,
cutting the chains of slavery, whether forged by tyrant
or priest or king, and setting into clearness the responsibility of the individual man or woman, with its pre-
cious rights and awe-inspiring duties.   Futile is the
struggling for and against, exaggerated the hopes—still
more exaggerated the fears : one thing is certain, that
our democracy will go the way of all past democracies,
unless it has and retains uncorrupted conscience to seek
the right and to do it.   The political basis is doomed
so soon as the moral basis is destroyed.

The growing democracy of our country has in it a
great deal of living virtue.   It is thoroughly in earnest,
and does not look upon life as a matter of play or plunder, and in this respect it has the advantage of those
sections of the aristocracy who do little or nothing
except amuse themselves,—eating, drinking, making
merry, and burning cigars and gunpowder, hardly
ever touching reality except in the hunting - field.
The children of hard work and hunger have some
advantages over these children of total leisure and
the silver spoon, and in the struggle for existence it

.is easy to see who will survive as victors. No class privileges, no skilfully devised schemes of bribery and corruption, will long protect the idle and incapable, or maintain unstormed the huge poor-houses which their friends have scooped out for them in the public professions and institutions of this generous and much forbearing country.

But it is also easy to see that the idle and incapable and dishonest are not all embraced in one class, and that the worst specimens even of these are not to be found among the aristocracy, either of birth or of successful trade. They are to be found among noisy democrats, who have not inherited anything except impudence, lively appetites, and sharp teeth; who are as disposed to be idle as any mere game-preserver or fox-hunter can be; who are restrained by no inborn consideration of honour or gentlemanly self-control, and are governed mainly by those forces which originate in a stomach that yearns to assimilate everything, and in a head that cares to assimilate nothing except what may minister to the nether cavities. Except the criminal class, which they closely overlie, they are the class which most require reformation, and reformation truly of a very thorough sort. To exterminate them is a much more pressing duty for an enlightened democracy than to make war upon the foolish drones among the aristocracy, who do little harm to anybody but themselves, and who are busy killing themselves off as fast as they can; or to make war upon the House of Lords, which, in

this current generation, has in it more wisdom and
a higher average of practical virtue than any democracy hitherto developed on this planet. Its members
may neither toil nor spin, but they work far harder
than many captains of industry and wealth, who
scheme and speculate, and reap the profits of multitudes of poor spinners and toilers, for whom they
care far less, and upon whom they expend much less
paternal kindness, than it is common for even very
indifferent peers to expend upon their vassals. The
feudal relation of peerage and peasantry has long
been dissolved as matter of law, but as matter of
kindly humanity it is as fresh as ever, and well
worthy of the imitation of some who make riches
out of the people, and give them nothing in return
except bare dog's wages—enough to furnish food and
clothes, and such cheap flattery, especially about
election times, as is bestowed upon a dog who has
done what it was bidden, and is distinctly expected
to do the like again. "The honour of a peer" is
still a phrase with a clear credible meaning, much
more trusted than a democtratic atheist's oath. The
peer of this age has, as a rule, drunk of the best of
its culture, and cannot divest himself of its elevating
and restraining influences. Veracity, intellectual habi-
tudes, and dignified self-possession, very distinguishable from the offensive self-assertion and oily slippery
tact of an upstart, are matters of nature and habitual
second nature with him. He may not be very wise.
The talents of distinguished ancestors may have slip-

ped past him in the line of descent; but as circumstances develop the queen bee out of an ordinary germ, so circumstances numerous, varied, complex, combine to help to make a peer a capable legislator, a skilful discriminator between the selfish and the equitable, the right and the wrong in popular noises, and a valuable leader and guide of men, lifted as he is above the temptations of avarice by his hereditary wealth, and by the knowledge, not entirely free from bitterness, of how much and how little mere wealth can do for its owner, or for those to whom he may dispense it as a steward. To covet a peer's position is a much simpler task than to fill it; and to rail at social distinction is much easier than to try by honest strenuous effort to raise one's self in the social scale, or for a man to do his duty thoroughly where he is.

" Liberty, Fraternity, and Equality," is an old but mad cry, for no element of it is attainable in a world of iron necessity, of selfishness which knows little or no brotherhood except for selfish ends, and of inequalities that begin before birth, are increased during life through the daily action of the diverse innate faculties and accidental fortunes of every man, and are practically, though not nominally, abolished only in the grave, in which the arts of the embalmer and the upholsterer are of no avail, except, perhaps, to store up poison for the living. The theorist who would reform the face of the planet by levelling down the hills and up the valleys would produce nothing better than the monotony and barrenness of the desert; and

the political or trades-union theorist who would make
all men equal, is equally astray among, and at war
with, the possibilities of nature, as fixed irreversibly
by the supreme Maker of it and of man.

Democracies in the past have fallen, because they
disregarded the fixed laws of nature—because they,
false to themselves, suicidally ceased to respect the
rights of individuals—because the selfishness of the
mob converted them into tyrannies, regardless of justice and true liberty.   By our ancient established
habits of law and order, by our mixed constitution,
by its checks and counter-checks, we and our fathers
have for generations enjoyed an extent of individual
liberty and free personal development never enjoyed
in the world before by any people.   Freedom has
"broadened slowly down from precedent to precedent," and, generally speaking, every man in this
country is, so long as he does not injure others, free
to act as he pleases—to save his money or to squander
it, to work hard or to go idle, to be sober or drunken,
moral or immoral, to walk or stumble according to his
own lights, to expand himself on all sides according
to his tastes, his faculties, and the dictates of his
moral sense.   I doubt very much if democracy will
continue to permit of so much individual freedom; at
all events, it has never done it hitherto, there being,
in truth, much less toleration in it than in the single
despot.   Frederick the Great, to whom all religions
were pretty much alike, was really the first ruler who
proclaimed religious toleration, or, as he put it in his

ill-spelt French document, that every man was to be "allowed to go to heaven in his own way." On the other hand, the Athenian citizen mob condemned Socrates, and the Jewish mob voted for Barabbas. Neither Athenian nor Jew could so much as tolerate the new light that had come into the world. No mob whatever welcomes new ideas, or has charity for any failings but its own, and sometimes not even for them. There is intolerance in its enthusiasm, and in its impulsive self-satisfied ignorance there is neither inclination nor ability to judge fairly between opposing opinions or theories of life and conduct. I do not think any democracy ever consciously chose the evil in preference to the good. But every democracy has been too dogmatic and sweeping in its choice. Though no man can be too intolerant of evil in himself, he may be too intolerant of evil in others, and shut them out from the wisdom of experience, which, though dearbought, is priceless. Drunkenness, for instance, is a great evil—one of the greatest known to this age. But I venture to think that, though every man should be persuaded to be sober, no man — not absolutely insane—should be compelled to keep sober. Sobriety is good, but freedom is better; and it is not right or expedient to prevent any free man from finding out for himself the evils and discomforts of drunkenness. But for experiment, they would never be accurately discovered. Besides, there really is no virtue in keeping sober when it is impossible to get drunk. The virtue which is to be created by Act of Parliament will, I believe, turn out to be only the old vice well wrapped up in the ample garments of hypocrisy. There has been for the last hundred years a steady advance towards temperance. When "Willie brews a peck o' maut," it is no longer necessary to drink till daybreak; and where are now the ten-tumbler clubs of other days, or rather of other nights? They have been abolished, not by permissive bills and local option, but by individual option, brought about by the progress of education and the growth of knowledge touching the dangers and disgraces of intoxication and its noxious brood.

I believe, however, that democracy, until it comes to profit by experience, will try, and persist in trying, compulsion under such insidious and deceptive nominalism as "option" and "permission," and that it will fail—fail as our old Scotch legislators failed in their enactments against profane swearing, and Sabbath-breaking, and the excessive length and cost of ladies' skirts—fail as our modern Scotch believers and pretenders-to-believe in compulsion have failed in putting down Sunday drinking by closing respectable houses where fair drink and decent company could be obtained, and driving men to drink at home, or in "shebeens" where the drink is bad, and the company, if possible, more poisonous and abominable. Neither vice nor folly can be abolished by force, and it is better for society to allow them to exist openly for purposes of education and warning, or even of amusement, than to suppress them under hypocritical names,

imparting to them the delicious flavour of stolen
waters, and denying to the wise the opportunity of
profiting by the errors of the rash or unwise.

One plain duty—perhaps the plainest duty—of this
country is to educate the people, who are now the
rulers of it,—to educate them by every possible means
in all possible schools, so as to avert or modify the
many evils that spring from ignorance. Unless this
be done, we are entering upon an era in which the
selfishness of the rich and of the poor will be in perpetual collision, the one trying to keep what they have
got, and the other to tax capital, and make it the subject of pillage. Capitalists and landlords have in the
past had a little more than justice; in the future they
may expect a little less. Such an era is already
begun in Ireland. For ages the landlords of Ireland had neglected their duties—had collected rents
merely, and spent them in London, Paris, and Rome;
and recent legislation has, in defiance of economic
principles, given the land to their tenants, and left
them only the right of collecting rents. The game-
preservers of Scotland and England have had a similar but milder lesson. Hares and rabbits were cherished by them with such affection, that now a farmer
and his landlord cannot make them a matter of con-
tract. The landlords are treated as oppressors who
compelled unjust bargains, the farmers as children
who cannot take care of themselves, and the hares as
outlaws, except when the poacher appears. The land
laws will not always, nor indeed long, continue what

they are. They will be altered so as to liberate land from being the monopoly of a few, an expensive and unpurchasable luxury; and it will be well if the changes necessary to bring this about do not sap those foundations of the rights of property which both poor and rich have an interest to maintain. In an age of lawless plunder only the beggar is safe, for the successful thief of one week is the possible quarry of the next.

I am afraid that capital and labour have a long battle in prospect, of which strikes are merely the preliminary skirmishes, affording too often clear indications of the frightful ignorance or immorality of the men who fight for the rights of labour. The rights of capitalists — proprietors as well as of masters — are about to pass through the fire, and the fagots and dry brushwood of unguided and misguided unreason are being piled up for the approaching blaze, which will not turn out to be an entirely delightful bonfire for either side. " Property is theft," said some Frenchman or other, and now we have a wild Californian rampaging about the world demanding that the stolen wealth be restored. He may save himself the trouble. He and such as he will never see a community of property until they arrive at the happy huntingfields, and perhaps not even then. Land which belongs to nobody is only fit for hunting-ground. In order to yield a fair complement of proper fruit, it requires to be carefully and skilfully cultivated from year to year; and according to the old standards of

human virtue, which only Comtist and other visionaries can hope to alter, that will not be done by
any man who has not a secure title for a period of
years — say nineteen years, which in Scotland has
been found a suitable term—or in perpetuity. Lands
which have a new cultivator every year—even run-rig
lands, well known among our forefathers 200 years
ago—were never remarkable for anything but barrenness. After the millennium arrives, the experiment
of dividing the land among the community may perhaps be risked; but never so long as every man trusts
himself, and seeks his own interests in preference to
his neighbour's. Meanwhile, all that society can
wisely seek to secure is, that property be honestly
and laboriously acquired, and that, being so acquired,
its tenure may be absolutely certain. Industry and
thrift are left without motive, when property is insecure and confiscation prevails. Communism such as
the amiable enthusiast Robert Owen projected and
wasted his fortune on, is a system fit only for simpletons and spendthrifts, lunatics and paupers. However
unamiable pure selfishness may be, without its urgent
promptings individuals would cease to do their best
each for himself, which, so long as he does not hurt
his neighbour, is best also for the social aggregate
whole. Bees and ants may be superior to selfish considerations, and fit to be socialists, or even communists;
but, as yet, mere men and women are not, and, so far
as seems safe to prophesy at present, never will be.

At present there is thunder in the air passing over

deer - forests, lands depopulated and laid waste for
sport,—warnings, it may be, of a coming storm to which
all may give heed who have temporarily forgotten that
property has its duties as well as its rights.　But I do
not anticipate any immediate State interference with
deer-forests.　The State has only two possible grounds
for interference : one is the ejection of people from their
old homes, and the other is the rendering of ground
useless for food-producing purposes.　The latter consideration might be of some moment if we had no
steam-navy, and if plenty of food could not be bought
abroad more cheaply than it could be produced in this
deer-forest land.　The real question is, whether it is
better for the country that some American or other
millionaire, with more cash than common - sense,
should pay £10,000 of rent for land that could not
pay half as much if under sheep ; and I say that it is
probably better that a Scotchman should get that larger
rent, than that a few thousand pounds of Highland
mutton, excellent though it be, should be thrown into
the market, upon which, in the way of price, it could
have no appreciable effect.　It is calculated that the
consumption of beef, mutton, and pork in Great Britain is about 93 lb. per annum per head of the population ; and it is further calculated, from the statistics
furnished in Mr Malcolm's very sensible pamphlet,[1] that
if the whole deer-forests in Scotland were put under

[1] The Population, Crofts, Sheep-Walks, and Deer-Forests of the
Highlands and Islands.　By George Malcolm, Factor, Invergarry.
William Blackwood & Sons.　1883.

sheep, they would only yield, in addition to the 93 lb. already enjoyed, 2¼ oz. per head of the population. I can hardly think 2¼ oz. of mutton per annum is a sufficient consideration for any patriot crying aloud against deer-forests and all their tenants and owners.

The other consideration is a strong one in point of sentiment. For the sake of selfish sport to push a people like the Highlanders, fond of their hills and glens, and dear, though homely, almost miserable, firesides, to the sea-shore and into the slums of great towns, is very shocking to many of the finer feelings of human nature. For my part, I do not think I could bring myself to do it, however infatuated about sport, so long as there is a lion or a tiger or a bear to be found in the jungles of Africa or Asia, or even a wild-cat or turkey in America. But neither would I be disposed to stop it by the strong arm of the law, because it is much better to respect the rights of property, to permit a man to do what he likes with his own, than it is for the State to undertake the teaching and control of selfish and unsentimental or even inhuman citizens, who, without heeding others, actually seek their òwn pleasure, and nothing else. State interference in such matters would overwhelm the State with duties, put an end to individual freedom, and stifle individual responsibility and enterprise.

There are many rights which the State cannot adjust—rights that must be left to the conscience of individuals, to the operation and friction of public opinion. For example, the decencies of private life

can never be regulated by law, still less the doctrines
of religion and their results.   If the State, by an organisation of schools and churches, maintains machinery for *teaching* religion and the virtues involved in it,
it does all that the State can do; and if its teaching
be efficient, nothing else should be required—at all
events, nothing further can be attempted without mischief.   Every man must work out his own religion, and
he would do it all the better if not disturbed by the doctrines of cant or the clamours of petty creeds which have
little genuine or distinctive in them except hatred.

There are many things that ought to be, and as a
believer in the divine order of the world and in divine
justice, I conclude that sooner or later they will be.
A man may die before he can reach justice; a nation
never will, if they understand what it is and earnestly
seek after it.   Is there slavery in the world?   It will
last only so long as necessary for the protection and
guidance of the slave: it will end so soon as it becomes clear that slavery is brutal oppression, and lust,
and selfishness.   Is there corruption, bribery, dishonesty, the sacrifice of one class for the pleasure and
aggrandisement of another?   They cannot last for
ever: they will be a curse to the oppressor and the
oppressed, to the corrupter and the corrupted, and if
not ended by reformation, they will end in the destruction of one or both.

I do not try to define the rights of man, or to
enumerate them, but I assert that the tendency of this
age, and of every age that is not retrograde, is to give

to every man his rights, and to every woman too, for
that matter; for when woman is denied her rights,—
when she is a slave or a toy, and not a companion and
equal, be it in Turkey or in Africa or in Mormondom,—
the society which enslaves or debases her imperatively demands amendment or dissolution. We of this
country have still some superstitions about women.
We can trust them to pay taxes, to be jostled in the
rough avenues to a tax-gatherer's office, but cannot
trust them to approach a ballot-box and have any
voice in making laws which they are bound to obey.
We can trust them after long trial as the best of
nurses, but we cannot, many of us, trust them as
educated doctors to look at a pimple, or mix a dose of
poison. We could not allow them to preach, even if
gifted as Miriam, though they have "lectured" most
men since the days of Abraham; and though they
began even earlier to pull the leading-strings of human
affairs, they cannot even now be permitted to do it
openly: they must always be shut into a conjuror's
box or hid behind curtains. Instalments of justice
to women have been coming and will still come, and
proportional instalments of shame will come upon
those men who have so far forgot their mothers and
their sisters as to deny intellect and common-sense to
women, and to seek to block their open responsible
passage to political and social power and usefulness,
upon these and similar false pretences.

But to return to these undefined rights of man.
They are perhaps not all discovered yet, which is a

G

good reason for refusing to define them. Some of them, however, do not require to be discovered, but to be practically recognised. I take it that every child has a right to live, to be fed and clothed, and guarded from the poison of infectious disease, and from every contamination, physical and moral, that may injure its health or usefulness, and make it a source of misery to itself or of danger to the community. The State compels vaccination to prevent the dissemination of smallpox; but smallpox is only one danger. Let it be a symbol and type of others too numerous to specify. One of the most terrible of these is ignorance—the fruitful parent of a large black brood of preventable evils. The State has at last denied to negligent, barely human parents, the liberty to allow their children to grow up as uneducated savages, who may prove—and are not unlikely to prove — nearly as dangerous to society as wild beasts left at large. The liberty of individuals to injure and dwarf their own children, to condemn them to mental blindness, to intellectual impotence, has at last been recalled, and not a day too soon—for an ignorant man is always a source of danger to society, both from what he does and leaves undone. He has no fair chance of knowing good and evil, so as to be able to choose between them; and if he be born with fair or excellent capacities, these remain undeveloped and are lost. No doubt education makes a born predestined rogue in some respects more dangerous, but it saves many a frail will from temptation to rush into roguery. And at all events, it offers the best means of utilising human beings for the State, and saves society from the curse of neglected duty and the cost of punishing crimes, which intellectual and moral training might have avoided. No doubt punishment is a mode of education — to a notable extent nature's own mode; but of all modes of human education, it is the most expensive and the least satisfactory. The cost of educating a person is a trifle compared to the cost of sending him into penal servitude or to thè gallows, and so wasting him, except for very temporary scarecrow purposes. Hitherto society has not sufficiently prized the services of the schoolmaster, and has set rather high a value upon the services of those who deal in his waste material;—upon policemen who detect crime often, and occasionally manufacture evidence; upon public prosecutors, who at times have been known to prefer a verdict of guilty to truth; upon governors of prisons, well-meaning but frequently incapable rectors in seminaries, whose patron goddess is Despair; upon judges who, in more or less splendid wigs and tippets, sit disposing of human life and liberty, and sometimes act as if they thought a poor wretch fit for nothing but an example to frighten and deter others, whether clearly guilty or not. In one teacher of righteousness alone by mode of punishment do I discover no sign of infirmity or partiality, and that is the pestilence which walketh at noon-day—whether as cholera or typhus—striking the poor among the foul air of his hovel, and the rich wherever that air charged with poison can find him, bearing to all

the message that the laws of nature recognise no
break in the brotherhood of man, but involve in
the same condemnation intelligence that has failed
to disseminate itself and ignorance that saw no
danger.

Extraneous personal help and guidance are very
necessary in childhood and early youth. After that,
I think there can hardly be too little of either. For
a free and capable agent, "self-help is God's help";
indeed it is the only God's help, for every man with
any real power can help himself much more effectually than any ten outsiders can help him. Of course
it is possible to help a man to go idle, to reap when
he had not sowed, to obtain wages which he cannot
honestly earn—that is, to be a beggar or a robber.
But all that a capable and honest workman requires
is work and freedom to do it. To demand this for
him may seem a modest postulate, but it is not yet
possible to attain it. The ancient trades' guilds and
their restrictions are gone or going; even the *quasi*
slavery of apprenticeship, too often unjust to struggling and aspiring youth, is also passing away. But
the tyranny of trades-unionism is a living atrocity
by which the working classes debase, obstruct, and
plunder each other. They enact idleness and starvation in the name of "strikes," too often in the blind
endeavour to resist irresistible law. They assume that
all men are equal, and they try to make them so by
reducing the clever and raising the dull to the same
level. No wicked master is more cruel to the working

classes than they are to each other when they enter into combinations, and are led by schemers, sluggards, and stump-orators, as they generally are. Great pity it is that so much real earnestness should be so ignorantly misapplied. If it were really applied to trying to help each man to that position in which all his faculties could have the freest and widest scope, the position in which he could best do the best work of which he is capable—that would certainly be an object worth striving for; because, if attained, it would give to each man exactly what he deserved, and would utilise to society those powers that are allowed to go to waste; while the incompetent nominee of corrupt patronage is bungling work for which he is unfit, and demoralising all who come within the range of his influence.

Wicked masters there may be—there are, I doubt not—men who would grow rich by grinding the faces of the poor, who have no generous consideration for the multitudes by which they amass fortunes; but I do doubt if they be so numerous in proportion as bad servants. The intelligence necessary to keep any business moving will, as a rule, save a master from total indifference to the interests of his servants; for it does not require much intelligence to discover that the master who has no regard for fidelity, no mercy for frail health or old age, will soon fail to obtain or to retain good servants; that unprincipled avarice is rewarded by unprincipled eye-service and sham service. I am afraid that many masters are not very

fully alive to their duties; but I feel confident they
will improve.   Respectable horses are now provided
with respectable houses, and by-and-by accommodation
as good may be found for respectable men.

The nervous and the inquiring ask, " Is this country to retain her possessions and her pre-eminence?
When is Macaulay's New Zealander to come and sit
on the ruins of Westminster Bridge, or of our North
Bridge, and moralise, as Volney did, on the ruins of
empires ? "   To the best of my thinking, the New Zealander will never come.   The elements of civilisation
to which he has devoted himself are rum and whisky,
and they will never bring him to London: they will
send him and his race, and are fast sending them, over
the precipices of existence, like the grunting herd of
the Gadarenes.   And so long as the Anglo-Saxon race
are what they are—and they have uncorrupted stood
the test of good and bad fortune longer than any race
except the Jews, who have been, since the typical
transaction of Jacob and Esau, so skilled in buying
other men's birthrights at a moderate price, that it
would not be easy to corrupt them,—so long as the
race does not fail, I do not see why they should not
keep their position in the forefront, and why this
country should not continue to be their favoured as
it is their proper home—the home in which their
characteristics have been most developed, and from
which they have scattered themselves into all climes.
That America may come some day to be a formidable
rival of this old country is not unlikely—is indeed very

probable, if her hot sun and uninvigorating climate do
not deteriorate and shrivel up the race. She has a vast
area, great navigable rivers, and a fertile soil fit to feed
and clothe the whole human race, even if ten times
multiplied. But at present she is terribly oppressed
by quackery, pretence, and all sorts of vices generated
from the active and uncontrolled fermentations of a
young democracy. Private virtue she has in abundance; of public virtue she has next to none. The
bribery and corruption in every form which saturates
most, if not all, departments of the State, ought to
blacken the face of her to every planet in the solar
system. Her boasted liberty is, I am constrained to
believe, little other than a name. How can there be
freedom in a society where so many loaded revolvers
are moving about, so many sleeves furnished with a
bowie-knife?

British liberty is different from American liberty.
It does not afford the same facilities for administering lynch law, for assassination, for tarring and
feathering, and generally for doing to others what
you would rather decline having done to you. America
is great, she will grow greater, but it will only be after
her fermentation of vice and greed is over: she
will require to desist from cheating and lying, and
boasting and tall talk, and to dethrone her almighty
dollar and kindred idols. Already we can see the
work of reformation begun by her satirists; and we
can discern, in the wild exaggeration of their peculiar
humour, its blistering applicability to a people who are

sharp enough to know the truth, but too sharp or too frail
to practise veracity; who postpone their sense of right
and wrong to the instantly profitable. But in another
generation or two American humour may have shaken
and pricked American conscience out of its sleep.
Much is to be hoped for a people from whom arose
Washington Irving, Nathaniel Hawthorne, Walt Whit-
man, Bryant, Longfellow, Mark Twain, Lowell, and
Emerson. The last was scarcely a conscious satirist,
but he smote the moral infirmities of his countrymen with that keenness and arrowy sarcasm which is
inspired by clear insight and strong moral instincts.
They are very proud of him, as well they may be.
Few writers so beautiful, few thinkers so subtle, have
ever appeared to reform and guide an age much in
want of reformation and guidance. No sunnier idealist
ever threw the charm of a poetic and philosophic
genius over the contradictions of nature and the
shortcomings of human life. When the Americans
have incorporated his teaching into their practice, it
may be possible for some patriotic and truthful American to write of his own country what Emerson wrote
of England, when he pronounced England to be "the
best of actual nations." In the meantime, their boasting ought to be subordinated to their blushes, if they
had the complexion which can reveal a blush.

The dread of America as a rival in trade and
manufactures has not yet taken such a hold of those
unhappy persons who are looking far ahead for possible disasters as the dread of the continent of Europe,

especially Germany and France. Germany, it is said, is soon to equal or surpass us in iron, and France in spinning. The purpose of these assertions generally is to frighten us into technical education, and if they have that effect, the means may be permitted in this instance to justify the end. Whenever the art of Tubal-Cain depends upon the same sort of faculty as is necessary to write a treatise in ten or twenty volumes, I shall believe that Berlin may rival Birmingham, but not till then.

The Germans do not possess the physical nimbleness and energy of the English, and the English are always ready to appropriate all the science that can be turned to instant practical use: it is speculative knowledge that they distrust and leave alone, having really little curiosity or turn for unpractical speculation. But far be it from me to dissuade any one from seeking after knowledge. All I wish to allay is idle fears and also idle hopes. Turn over in your minds the names of celebrated inventors, and consider how few of them had any special education for the special bits of work which destiny had appointed them to do, and how they tried and tried again, not merely without encouragement, but in spite of discouragement, of poverty, of doubts and sneers and dissuasion, and the intervention of wives putting their models into the fire, and all other possible obstructions and temptations. Somehow or other the right tools find their way to the hands that can use them; and we are not yet going to admit that these hands are either French or German.

Then, again, other dire foreboders prophesy that we are not to be ruined by competition, but by the exhaustion of coal. The coal strata in our island, it is calculated, will not last above another 300 years; and when their coals are done, it is predicted the British will be done. What will happen 300 years hence need not vex any of us very much, or disturb our sleep for the present. We will probably sleep sound enough 300 years hence; at all events, those who do not will not require to feel anxious about coal. But really this estimate about the time the coal of Britain will last is nothing better than a rough guess. There are no data for any accurate calculation. And if science moves as fast as it has done last century, other fuel than coal may be discovered before the lapse of three centuries. The mechanical force of the tides, for instance, may be converted into electricity and heat,—and I can readily fancy that there is force enough wasted every day in the ebb and flow of the Firth of Forth to keep half the fires in Scotland burning.

Another still more fearful and wonderful set of prophets are those who prophesy the extinction of the sun. Byron and Campbell treated the subject poetically in their fashion, with all the appropriate figures of speech; but the mathematicians, led by Sir W. Thomson of Glasgow, have been applying to it a different kind of figures, and they have settled to their own satisfaction that the sun cannot go on burning above another 15,000 or 20,000 years. He is to swallow up the planets, as Saturn ate his children. The earth, when its turn comes to drop in, will keep him blazing about a fortnight. But long before it arrives at this funeral pyre, all mankind will have died out, the last of the race being likely to be very different from Campbell's "last man"; according to some—Dr Maudsley for one, the eminent lunatic doctor, who has arrived at the idea, perhaps, with a little assistance from some of his patients—that they will be poor shivering creatures, living in snow huts about the equator after the rest of the planet is shrouded in ice. Great is faith, more especially the faith of infidels! I would believe all the tales of the 'Arabian Nights,' and of all the mythologies of all religions, ten times over, before I could believe that the wisdom which made this world has no better use to make of it at last than to keep a useless sun burning for a fortnight; and I do not in the least care whether the visionary who says so has gone crazed over the mysterious texts of the Apocalypse, or the prophecies of a dying dispensation and conquered race, or over mathematical formulæ and theories of energy. So far as we know of the universe (and it is but little we can know), its permanence is perfectly secured.

Laplace demonstrated the stability of the solar system,—that small twig of the boundless star-forest which we know best,—if it were possible to demonstrate anything regarding an infinitesimally small part when in almost total ignorance regarding the whole, except that the whole is infinite, and therefore unknowable. The philosophic midge born at mid-day sees the sun steadily sinking, sinking; and by half an hour after sunset it has arrived at the conclusion that the universe has gone to darkness and extinction, and that it is no longer a fit home for a philosophic midge. It knows as much about the approaching sunrise as Dr Maudsley and his patients and brother speculators know about what will happen in 20,000 years.

But I must draw to a conclusion. What the age is doing I have suggested rather than stated accurately. You do not require to be told what is going on in the world around you,—to be furnished with the statistics of engineering, spinning, weaving, shipbuilding, painting, preaching, book-making, parliamenteering, newspapering, and other industries. Even of taxation you know perhaps quite enough. For the story of our exports and imports, more wonderful if duly meditated than an Eastern tale, I refer you to the proper blue-books when you are very much at leisure. For the statistics of virtue and vice am I to refer you to the subscription lists of charities and churches, to the records of criminal courts and of Magdalen asylums, to the reports of superintendents of police, of city missionaries, of the Registrar-General? Not at all. There are no adequate statistics of virtue and vice except in the books of the recording angel. The most vital virtue is a secret almost to its possessor; the most dangerous vice works in darkness like typhus and cholera. It permeates all strata of society, but presses the poor, the weak, the credulous, the soft-hearted, the simple, into the mire, as well as the ignorant and the un-fortunate.

And now as to the drift of our age. What are we driving at? What are we driven to? Its physical drift is to mechanics and natural science, its political drift to democracy, its moral drift to a clearer and clearer appreciation of justice and the rights of indi-viduals, to a higher ideal of truth and virtue, more especially of temperance; its religious drift is through burning deserts of scepticism into a deeper, more reverent apprehension of man's relation to his Creator, and of his duties to his fellow-man. I do not detect in it any decisive signs of decrepitude or decay. Lon-don is said to resemble old Rome, and I daresay most of the vices of old Rome are to be found in London. But Rome had no credible religion, little public honour, next to no private virtue,—nothing to elevate its life out of gross animalism and materialism.

Gibbon's 'Decline and Fall' may some day come to read like, and indeed to be, a prophetic book; but that day has not yet dawned—let us hope that it may never dawn. The age of Commodus was very different from the age of Queen Victoria. Where the carcass is, there will the vultures be gathered together. Rome was the biggest carcass of history, and the vultures were visible to the far-seeing eye for centuries. As yet the vultures that may gather for London are beneath the horizon. Notwithstanding of its steady drinking of the wine of abominations, its mixed squalor and splendour, its doubts of every inspiration

that does not spring direct from forces common to
men and maggots, it remains, and must long remain,
not merely the capital of Britain, but the metropolis of
the world, the throne of the all-powerful Anglo-Saxon
race—a race that may require other thrones, but will
relax its hold of the sceptre only at the bidding of
that Almighty power which beckons empires into
being and sweeps them into night.

To my inner ear there rush in whispers the un-
answered, the unanswerable questions, "Is Britain's
mission on the planet near its close or its beginning?
How do the stars shine upon her? What do they
tell of her future? What is her horoscope?" It
boots little whether Mars, the blood-red star-god of
war, or Mercury, the star-god of merchandise, be in
the ascendant. It depends not on the stars but on
her sons and her daughters, nor least on these, since
woman's position is the criterion of civilisation, since
she is the herald of liberty, and her genial influence,
like the summer breath of the sweet south, has thawed
down the barbaric frostwork under which each husband
sat as irresponsible family tyrant, the stay and apology
of despotism on the throne. If the stars have any
influence upon human destiny, it is moral and not
physical, compatible with free will, appreciable only
by the serenely meditative mind. Shining afar in
their vast spaces, they still speak to the heart a
strange, inarticulate language, heard not, but felt as
by the Psalmist and shepherd-kings of old. Are you
weary with the routine of existence? Look up to

them. They haste not, neither do they rest. Endeavour to imitate them while you can, for life is short, and passeth away like the trace of a cloud, and there is neither remedy nor returning. Does your pulse bound with joy? temper it in their solemn calmness. Or your bosom swell with pride? come, learn your insignificance on the planet earth, its insignificance in the general assembly of worlds. What are the tinsel jewels of which thou art so vain, in the presence of the diamonds that burn on the raven locks of night? What the dances that kindle thy raptures to "the whirling dance for ever held in yonder azure deeps"? Look up to them in doubt; they are God's handwriting on the infinite illuminated scroll of the universe, to tell you that you are not fatherless and forsaken. Look up to them in resignation and think lightly of thy sorrows: the light that meets thy eye was begun to travel before thy mortal form was summoned from the dust, and its passage has outlived millions of thy race with their million cares; the light that now leaves yonder distant speck - seeming sun will not reach the place thou standest on, until all that can trouble thee and thine has vanished like a dream. Look up to them in faith and hope; they give silent assurance of permanence under continual change, of harmony evolved from discord, of the superintendence of an all-seeing eye, of the omnipotence of the Father of our spirits and the parent of our aspirations, of a universe wider than our fond desires, of space-girt Islets of the Blest, awaiting, it may be, the heirs of immortality.   Be workful, be dutiful, hopeful, humble, resigned, reverent, faithful unto death, is the solemn, silent lesson of the stars.   Thereby you will serve God; thereby you will deserve and secure for yourselves and your nation a favourable horoscope in the ever-ascendant, ever-prevailing house of the heavens, the house of all-balancing, all-rewarding, all-punishing, immutable, eternal justice.

THE TRUE AND THE FALSE
IN HISTORY

H

THE TRUE AND THE FALSE
IN HISTORY.

————•————

ACCORDING to its original and derivative meaning, the word history signifies inquiry,—an endeavour or series of endeavours to ascertain the truth in
some matter of fact, and so gratify that curiosity which
is natural to man, and causes him to thirst after all
useful, and, it may be, some useless knowledge. In
this wide sense of the term history, probably all men,
and still more probably all women, may be looked
upon as historians; for almost every one, if not every
one, of them is seeking to find out something that he
or she does not know. The metaphysician examines
into the facts of knowing and being, and in trying to
solve the question whether or not this solid-looking
earth is a reality or a vision; and poor is his speculative
faculty if he have not often doubted his own existence
and that of everything besides. He therefore is a historian or inquirer into fact—universal, all-encircling,
all-penetrating fact, reaching deeper than the central

fires, and higher than the Milky Way. An inquirer
into fact also is the chemist, the botanist, the conchol-
ogist, the anatomist, the physiologist, the geologist,
and their departments of science are indeed often
spoken of as natural history. So also is the mathematician; and I rather think that his domain is the
only one out of which falsehood is excluded or can
be effectually expelled. All these that I have named,
and many other votaries of "ologies" and "isms," are
historians in the original sense of the term history.
But it has in a great measure lost that sense, and been
narrowed in its signification, and it now means not so
much inquiry as the results of inquiry, and the results
of inquiry chiefly into the actions and achievements of
individuals and nations; it means individual history,
civil history, human history; chapters of the story of
the struggle for existence, of the battle of human progress against elemental, brutal, and all manner of rival
forces.

We see emanating from the press frequently, perhaps too frequently, the history of some man or
woman; and we are familiar with many histories of
nations and empires, showing how they flourished
during particular epochs, or how they grew up from
an infancy of barbarism: what they did, what arts
they cultivated, what fools or wise men ruled them,
what battles they fought and won or lost, and how
they decayed by internal vices or were destroyed by
external violence. All these histories contain or profess to contain the results of inquiries into facts, actual

occurrences which were seen and felt or inferred, the
facts of individual or social effort, or both. They differ
from fictions or romances in that the actions which
they tell of were real actions, and not imaginations
projected from the mind of some man—Sir Walter
Scott, Schiller, Shakespeare, or any other—and made
to wear the appearance of reality. But they resemble
fictions in this, that they contain a great deal that is
not true, or that may perhaps be untrue; that they are
embellished and supplied with vivid details chiefly
from the workshop of fancy; that they sometimes
contain a sprinkling of wilful falsehood; and that, at
the best, they contain a record of incomplete facts,
partly misunderstood and partly mutilated. The consequence is, that romance occasionally contains far
higher and more genuine truth than history, in respect
that it contains truth that will not be rejected by the
mind, but will bear subjective tests; whereas the
alleged facts of history are often so palpably untrue
as to be rejected by the mind as false, besides being
shown to be so by evidence, and thus fall as rubbish
or worse under both the subjective and objective tests
of truth.

If a credulous and superficial visitor from some other
planet were to alight upon this planet of ours, he
would at first, and during his term of childlike inno-
cence and inexperience, think that nothing was so
abundant in it as truth. Every two-footed creature
with an articulately speaking tongue cries "Here it is"
or "There it is." And he would think that the being

man, whom Plato or some other sage described as
the " hunter of truth," was the most successful of all
hunters. But a little thoughtful observation would
soon lead him to conclude that the loud sounds from
the wide hunting-field of life and time were oftenest
the yelling of the pack after some false deceptive
scent, or the noise of them worrying each other for the
possession of a phantom. The truths they scent they
cannot see, the truths they see they cannot catch,
the truths they catch they cannot keep, at least not
permanently. A magical uncertainty spreads itself
over this hunting-field. In it disappointment fights a
never-ending battle with hope. Success is always so
near as to stimulate endeavour, but it visits the weary
only in dreams.

A truthful record of the exploits of this hunting-field,
or of some small divisions of it, would, one might think,
be possible ; to speak without metaphor, few things seem
so practicable as to write a credible history of an
art or a science, or of a nation, or even of a continent.
But to the individual who sits down to try, experience
will soon carry the conviction that hardly any statement can be accepted as an indubitable fact, that most
statements are but guesses, and that some are palpable
lies. Human life is so short, human observation is so
uncertain, human memory is so bad, human veracity
is so defective, and time and oblivion are so hungry
and insatiable, that the truth is for the most part
buried with those who did or *did not* accurately
observe it, and their monuments are covered with

half-truths or with falsehoods, which the winds and
the rains and the frosts make haste to obliterate.
Whether it may be good for man that the traces of
his predecessors should be swept away so ruthlessly
by elemental besoms, it is needless to inquire. Man
does not think it good. He has a kind of yearning
towards his fathers ; and although he might consider
the most of them to be very troublesome and disagreeable if they were alive, he wishes to have an idea
of what kind of stuff they were made, and how they
comported themselves both individually and socially,
or at the lowest, he wishes to have the benefit of their
experience in stumbling through existence. Moreover,
he does not quite care to go into forgetfulness himself.
He abhors and shrinks back from forgetfulness, and
he expects that what he has done for his predecessors
his successors will do for him. Therefore he raises
such barriers as he can against the inroads of Lethe,
in the form of Druidical and Indian cairns, Nineveh
bricks with arrow - heads on them, Egyptian hiero-
glyphs, and pyramids and decorated mummies, Etruscan
monuments, Hindoo coins and medals, Homeric poems,
painted and sculptured portraits, monkish parchments,
parish registers, the lean family record of the Bible
fly-leaf, and modern printed books.

And he achieves only a partial success. Let him
strive after the truth ever so keenly, his modes of
expressing and perpetuating it are inadequate, and the
silent river and its exhalations, corrupting, annihilating,
press in upon his labours to besprinkle with dimness

and blanks, and to lick them away. Not an idea can
he make sure of perpetuating. The largest pyramid
of Ghizeh, for example, was built to commemorate
some idea; and it is the greatest human effort in that
way, having had expended on it nearly three and a half
million cubic yards of stone. But what was the idea?
It does not tell, and the purpose of it is a puzzle,
though the probability is that it was built to be a
monument for some Egyptian king. But his name is
not to be read on one of its numberless blocks of lime-
stone and of granite; and although it is probable that
his bones were built in amid all these tons of masonry,
his huge sarcophagus has lost its lid and does not contain a pinch of his dust. Herodotus, the Father of
History, says that this largest pyramid was built by
Cheops on the hill where he had made his burial-
vault; that the priests of Memphis told him so 450
years after the days of Cheops; and to this tradition
of the priests of Memphis and the uncertain page of
Herodotus, Cheops owes more than to his pyramid,
which tells no tale for him—only by itself the tale
of anonymous ambition. One hundred thousand men
toiled at it for twenty years, according to the same
authority, and of them there is no memory or tradition, except that Herodotus says he saw on the pyramid an inscription, in Egyptian characters, which was
interpreted to mean that 1600 talents of silver had
been expended in supplying them with radishes,
onions, and garlic—surely a very brief history for
100,000 men, and not much more disappointing than

that of their king. And yet they all had their joys
and fears, their virtues and vices, loves and hatreds,
quarrels and jealousies, pride of engineering and pride
of handicraft, some of them who were notable for skill
among the rest of the 100,000, and promised themselves, as well they might, a considerable lease of
fame. But see how they have all vanished, and left
no trace except their vast pile,—a silent witness of
how much man will attempt, how little he can achieve
in perpetuating his memory or thoughts, and warring
with oblivion.

The causes of the prevalence of falsehood in history
are of a twofold character,—what may be called
causes subjective and causes objective: the one class
of causes being due to the imperfect mind of man,
and, in particular, to its inability to observe and
remember truth exactly, which is intellectual weakness—and also to resist the temptations that obstruct
the telling of the truth when known, which is moral
weakness; and the other class of causes being due to
the materials to which truth is committed—to the loss
and decay of documents, the alteration of ideas and
of language, the meaning dying out of old words, and
the truths and the virtues of one age and country
being the ridicule and the aversion of another country,
and of the same country in another age.

To point out all the imperfections, intellectual and
moral, of the human mind, and all the agencies that
abolish the traces of fact, would not be easy. It would
be almost as difficult as to expose all the lies of

history, which would require a century or two for study, and the recording angel's books for constant reference. In our briefer and busier times than Methuselah's, I shall simply try to suggest some of the reasons why the true and the false are so invariably commingled in the history of individuals and nations, without ceasing to be thankful for that history, such as it is. "Happy the people whose annals are vacant," says one grim sage after another. I say, Not at all,—at least not necessarily. The people who have no annals are more likely to have wanted brains and an alphabet than adventures. Happiness is vocal as well as misery. There is comedy in every life as well as tragedy, and both are translatable into melody when the right Homer arrives, even though he be blind and requires to take his history from hearsay. And who that sees or hears may not be a historian, though imperfect ? Was there not history of a kind in the tones of the old parrot heard by Humboldt screeching on a blasted tree, the language of a tribe, every member of whom had perished ?

A glance at the difficulties of autobiography and of biography will afford a sure starting-point from which to realise the difficulties of writing the history of a nation. At the first blush, and probably at the last maturity of reflection also, one would think that the easiest of all history would be the history of one's own self, and that truth would be attainable more readily in that than in any other field of history. Here if anywhere, every act and the cause of every act is discoverable. Every thought once stood forth in the daylight of consciousness; every deed of consequence is preserved in the transparent amber of memory. But put this problem, so easy by hypothesis, to the test of experiment, and try to tell the truth, the whole truth, and nothing but the truth about yourself to even yourself, and observe how the amber of memory is coloured or discoloured by vanity; how self-esteem argues against fact, and maintains that deeds done entirely or partly from selfishness were done through pure benevolence; how this and the other bold adventure with hand or tongue was due to courage and not to anger or revenge; how the pursuit of knowledge did not proceed from simple incapacity to be at rest; how resolutions not to weary in well-doing were due to conscience and not to fear. You will find it all but impossible to confess the whole truth to yourself, and quite impossible to see yourself as others see you. And to confess the whole truth to others, and then to the public at large, would that be possible, think you, even assuming it to be advisable?

Have you ever read an autobiography, from that of Goethe, the German poet and philosopher of culture, and those wonderful Confessions of Rousseau, the Swiss literary man of genius, half madman, half savage, down to the confessions of tinkers, colliers, boxers, and less proper characters who have been canonised by fanatic mobs before and after death, and been able to come to a conclusion with yourself that the truth was told in these autobiographical confessions? I for

one have never been able to believe them, with any
strong force of conviction, and least of all can I
believe the voluntary confessions of those who plead
guilty to all immoralities (except perhaps murder), and
who are so immodest and irrational as to publish and
be rather proud of performances that the last rags of
shame should have been used to conceal.

There are higher thoughts to be found in the pages
of Rousseau and Goethe than in those of Defoe; but,
upon the whole, I am inclined to think that the autobiography of Robinson Crusoe is just about as true as
most autobiographies, and considerably more decent
and interesting than the large majority. Indeed
Goethe does not profess to tell the truth. He candidly avows his intention of giving it a poetical
colouring. He knew human nature too well to suppose
that if he had professed to tell the truth, any intelligent reader would be found to believe him; and he
knew the art of letters too well to dream that the
naked truth was fit to interest or be understood by
mankind without some drapery of fig-leaves, or the
like pleasant and picturesque vesture drawn from
the ideal.

What does a man or woman live for? Is it for
pleasure, or dress, or vanity, or vengeance, or money?
Is it for culture like Goethe, for good cheer like Horace,
for fame like Hume, for duty like Carlyle, for God
like Spinoza and Fichte, and a vast army of saints
and martyrs that no man can number? Is it to peer
into the secrets of life, to watch from midnight to

midnight the growth of cell-germs, to scan the vestiges
of the evolution of race, to watch the monster Nature
unceasingly sending forth and devouring her children
without purpose, without end, and to prepare stoically
for the common lot of eventually disappearing in earth
and air, and being blown about the pendant world?
Or is it to pray to the almighty Father, and pillow
the throbbing head with child-like faith on the
almighty arm? What is the religious faith? What
is the rule, the ideal of life? Who the idealiser?
Is he a Scotchman under a burning sun, dreaming of
his native land and his cloud-capt hills, and his kins-
men there, and hoping for the hour when he can
return to them, not so poor as when he went forth to
seek a fortune? Is he an Englishman, seeking for
substantial comfort, and sticking to reality everywhere,
telling the truth, and doing endless kindness at home,
or swaggering proudly, sulkily, silently, over the planet
as if he had no equal in it! Is it an Irishman, laughing, lying, squandering, tossing bulls out of his hot
intellectual confusion, in his merry moods the cheeriest,
most comical of light-hearted, ragged, hungry fellows?
Or is it an Irishman turned serious, frantic, maddened
by long ages of oppression, setting himself to "make
history" by slugs and surgical knives,—an Irish patriot
and Catholic Christian, searching for the millennium
through experiments in murder? But whatever his
country, whatever his complexion, be he saint, sage,
or savage, his mental idiosyncrasies will affect his
capacity for seeing the fact as it happens, for telling

the truth about it, for adjusting its perspective, and
for estimating its relations to the ideal as shaped by
mental constitution, education, sex, culture, creed, and
time of life. Individualism is a sheet of glass of
divers possible colours and twists, and the white
light of truth passing through it is discoloured, re-
fracted, diffracted, distorted, thereby rendering the
image very different from the reality. And the play
of imagination,—what magic there is in it! "Airy
nothing" is confounded with the actual, — the real
melts into the mythical, the mountain into the cloud,
the rocks into fire-mist, and past, present, and future
are gathered into one.

Consider also for a moment the effect of age in
changing the point of view from which one looks at
the truth and the ends of life; how the objects of
boyish devotion cease to interest the youth, and are
forgotten in manhood; how the cares and pursuits
of manhood pall upon the dull sensibilities of age.
What a curious book, if attainable, the unreserved diary
of a thoughtful and busy life would be! How astonishing would be the difference between the master-
themes of twenty and forty years, and of forty and
eighty! Revenge, that was dear to the teens and
rather suddenly exacted, is thought twice or thrice
about in the thirties, and is an abhorrence to the
feeble and shrivelled hand of threescore and ten.
The high places of the earth, that looked so dazzling in
the distance, have been peeped into and seen to be
nearly as full of misery and meanness as the low, and

more full of inexcusable vice, spontaneous corruption, and hollow hypocrisy. Money, that used to promise everything, has become an indifference or an insanity, —the insanity of the miser who gathers for others to spend. The flaming ambition of youth sinks to a steady red-heat in manhood, and is covered with white ashes in old age. And Hope, that had been bedecked by the rosy-fingered morn of life, has lost its colour, and stands pale and shadowy in the light of evening, spreading its wings to go forth and meet the dawn of an immortal day.

If from the history of self and its difficulties, arising from personal vanity, defective powers of reflection, imperfect memory, fluctuating notions of the chief good, and the like, we pass to the history of another self, the desire to conceal or colour a truth no doubt decreases or disappears, unless the subject of the history be an ancestor or a dear friend (although it is surprising how very candid most people can be about dear friends), but, on the other hand, the opportunities of knowledge decrease. There is not here a full insight into acts and endeavours and motives. The acts may or may not be visible, but the motives that could explain the acts are to a certainty more or less veiled. No human being, however simple in character, is perfectly intelligible to any other human being; for every character is full of contradictions,—vice counterbalancing virtue, caution holding the reins of courage, cunning earwigging candour, and the most transparent simplicity itself having the effect of an unexpected

disguise. To understand any character so far, it is
necessary that far to enter, as it were, into that character—to melt your soul in sympathy, to pour yourself into it and take the impression of that character
and of its ramifications as if it were a mould. But,
then, who has the requisite amount of sympathy and
the power of fusing it sufficiently? Genius has it
sometimes—at least it is believed to have: genius
like that of Shakespeare and of Sir Walter Scott.
They could construct the effigy of a character, and
not merely the effigy, but could give it life. Their
sympathy could enter most of the twists and turns
of humanity and take their impression. But did they
add nothing to that impression? Did they represent
individual character as they found it? or did they not
compound it out of scattered and it may be discordant
single features, like a piece of mosaic, and idealise it?
Who can tell with them what is the impression of the
real human mould, that is, of the individual character,
and what the coruscations of oddity or beauty that
have burst through that mould and been combed out,
touched and retouched and polished in order to improve upon nature or to compensate for those lineaments of nature which even genius cannot catch, and
which defy all powers of reproduction or of representation?

The men and women known to you and to me have
in them elements of romance—the heroism that can
confront death without trembling, the infirmity that
may fall before accidental and trivial temptation, just

as surely as those known to dramatists and novelists. But think how few of them, how little that is in each or in all of them, you could, without exaggeration or artistic curtailment or supplement, put into a dull novel, or the dullest of plays, or the most prosaic of histories; how few firm lines of strict portraiture you could transfer to paper, how few features you could exaggerate even into bold caricature so as to hit off a class,—and avoid if you can the conclusion that fictional artists do truly *create* their characters out of a hint or two, or out of pure nothing, or as a sunset cloud is formed out of two or three pints of water gathered pretty much at random and decorated with prismatic colours. Fictional artists would probably stick to the truth if they could find it at all, or find it to suit them, or if they were free to use all they had observed. But suppose for a moment that *you* were free, and that all the seals of private confidence were removed, and that total immunity were given for every possible slander, would you undertake to expound correctly and completely the character and private history of your most intimate acquaintance? If you would not, and can thoroughly realise the difficulty of the undertaking, you will to that extent at least have realised the difficulty of writing a true biography, and the necessary imperfection and probable consequent falsity of all historical portraits whatsoever.

There are only two very great biographies in English literature so far as I am aware; the one is Boswell's 'Life of Dr Johnson,' and the other is Carlyle's

I

'Life of John Sterling.' The former is the result of
the observation of a small, acute, open-eyed, snub-
nosed impudent little man, upon a comparatively
great man, to whom he was drawn by some unac-
countable attraction, as if he had been a four-footed
creature of the canine species—a sort of faithful intelligent cocker or the like. He watched Johnson as
no gentleman in this planet was ever before watched
by affectionate eyes—the eyes of jealous wives included. He noted all his peculiarities, his style of
dress and address, his habit of touching posts, and picking up pieces of orange-peel, and drinking twenty
cups of tea at a time, and doing kindness to the low,
and insulting the high. He noted all his strong
speeches, and he put everything into a book, which is
a photograph of the outer man of Dr Johnson, in so
far as it manifested itself to the eager camera eyes of
Bozzy, and could be fixed by such chemicals or other
agencies as existed in his restless devoted brain. That
biography is chiefly a sketch of an outer life. No
doubt it contains details of the outer from which the
inner may be inferred, although the reporter of the
details could not himself have drawn the inferences. It
is a great result of affectionate watchfulness, and is in
the main true; true, because though very capable of
minute observation, Boswell was incapable of idealisation; true, because he was content with Johnson as
he found him, and worshipped the actual man in
preference to any ideal that he could create.

John Sterling, the subject of the other biography,

had hardly any outer life that is not common to literary men, except, perhaps, that though rather heterodox
he was for five months a curate. He was a small man
compared with his biographer, though a great man
compared with Boswell; and Carlyle has divined his
character and described the influences that shaped it
with the power and insight of the highest historical
genius. You read it, and you see the man, John
Sterling, with all his friends, teachers, and other
surroundings, his literary efforts, their purposes, their
fate, and their merits and faults; his dashes from
place to place to keep consumption at bay; his father,
the Captain Whirlwind of the 'Times,' talking all day
and writing leaders at night; his wife's death, and
his own slow but inevitable dying from consumption;
his second last letter, with its wonderful stoical declaration, " I tread the common road into the great darkness without any thought of fear, and with very much
of hope. Certainty indeed I have none:" everything
memorable from his cradle to his last breath.

These two biographies give you materials out of
which you can construct a tolerably complete idea
of the men, Samuel Johnson and John Sterling. But
can you understand the character of Walter Scott
from Lockhart's clever history of his life? Or does
Moore's 'Life of Byron,' the work of a man of genius,
give you the least idea of him if his inimitable letters
were left out? Or does the growling, dyspeptic tyrant
disclosed in Froude's 'Life of Carlyle' present you with
much more than a caricature of the man whose benev-

olence burns so fiercely in 'Sartor Resartus' and the 'Latter-Day Pamphlets'?

The difficulty of executing the biography of one man being demonstrated, the difficulty of writing the history of a number of men is settled as an *a fortiori* inference. Indeed the difficulty is increased in an enormous ratio, not to be fixed by any arithmetical or geometrical formula. So great is it, that the history of nations, for the most part, gives no idea of the units in a State,—of how they live, what they do, what they know, what their faith is, and how it affects their works, whether as robbers dealing in conquest and plunder, or traders growing rich by honest or other means. It deals with political and social convulsions and their large results. It counts up the number of those that have been killed in a battle, if the despatches or the fatigue burying-parties tell the truth; and it insinuates a few reflections about the tears of widows and orphans, and passes on to the next battle-field again to chronicle the victory and number the dead. The king, if he be not a mere puppet, and one or two of his ministers and generals, are all that history can see from its eagle altitude as it soars away over square miles and centuries, looking down through battle-smoke and the mists of everyday life.

The most general, and at the same time the most venial cause of falsehood in history, is the artistic or æsthetic tendency of the human mind. The temptation to fill up the gaps of knowledge by imagination, to improve upon truth, and produce something truer

than truth, or at least more beautiful and interesting, is perfectly irresistible—at least it has seldom if
ever yet been resisted.   Look at a painted portrait, for
example, and see how the artist has improved upon
the original.   The portrait-painter is a kind of his-
toriographer, and one who has a better opportunity of
hitting reality almost than any other; and yet the
artistic instinct, aided perhaps by the vanity of the
subject, is so much stronger than the instinct towards
veracity, that the latter is frequently sacrificed to
æsthetic effect.   How many of our grandmothers are
nearly as beautiful as Venus, and like Helen of Troy,
are for ever young?   How many of our grandfathers
seem wiser than Solomon, and seldom so careworn as
he, or any head of an establishment as large as his
must have been ?   The charitable generation of a thousand years hence will look with amazement upon the
abounding physical dignity and beauty of this age,
and will reach, after due meditation upon portraits on
canvas and ivory, in marble and in bronze, one inference at least, to the effect that the English ladies in the
nineteenth century were gifted with perennial youth !

And if this and the like of this idealisation be done
when the opportunities of knowing the exact fact are
so favourable, need we wonder that in ancient history
the æsthetic faculty has taken full scope for itself, and
in the absence of all means of ascertaining the exact
fact, has produced little else than a tissue of poetic
fables ?   One of the finest specimens of this kind of
tissue is the history of early Rome in its narration of

the doings of gods, priests, and heroes, and in that
tissue no power of divination exercised by Niebuhr or
any other can discover the filaments of historical truth.
Its chief value lies in its poetry as disclosed in Livy's
"pictured page," and its only historical value lies in
the indication it gives of the character and civilisation
of the people who invented the stories and believed in
them.

In modern histories truth and probability are, of
course, not lost sight of so completely as in Herodotus
and Livy, nor even as in Tacitus and Sir Thomas
More. Than Tacitus a more veracious historian never
lived; but yet, in the exercise of the æsthetic faculty,
he thought himself so far entitled to take dramatic
liberties with history, as to put fictitious speeches into
the mouths of his characters as his great Greek and
Roman predecessors had done. Clearly, inventing a
speech for a historical character, and giving it to the
world as his, is nearly as objectionable as fathering
upon him some action that he never performed. The
speeches of Thucydides, and of Livy, and of Tacitus are
admirable, and rank among the highest specimens of
eloquence; but they are not history any more than
Shakespeare's historical plays. We can admire, but
we cannot believe in the eloquence of Hannibal or
Galgacus, until we learn a little more about what was
contained in the shorthand reporter's notes of their
warlike orations. This fashion of causing historical
characters to unfold themselves in long speeches which
they never spoke, is now, I believe, confined to plays and

novels. Voltaire condemned it, though I think that he, as well as Lord Macaulay, was prone to put a neat pithy saying into the mouths of those they wrote about, without caring much whether it had been exactly reported or not. That is probably the only liberty that a great historian in this country would now dare to take for the sake of effect; unless he were a violent political partisan, and then a little strong colouring might be pardoned if it stopped short of palpable lying; the counterbalancing advantage of partisanship being that it produces zeal, and zeal is always interesting and animated.

If to the partisanship of politics that of religion is added, historical confusion becomes trebly confounded, and it is hard to see more than one side of the characters involved in the dust and turmoil. This 30th of January [1] suggests an apt illustration of the effects of politico-religious—or rather religio-political—partisanship. At two o'clock of the afternoon of the 30th of January 1649, Charles Stuart, King of England, laid his neck upon a block in the public street at Whitehall, and there died. Those who tried and executed

---

[1] First delivered on the 30th January in the Town-hall of St Andrews, on the other side of the street from the town church, wherein stands Archbishop Sharpe's marble monument, representing the certain transaction of shooting and stabbing him to death on Magus Muir, which lies three miles to the south, and the not so certain subsequent ceremony of his being crowned by an angel. Portraits still exist which indicate that there was nothing very bad in the old man. His face is that of a prim, diplomatic, slightly vain ecclesiastic, but it is also that of a student, and bears on it no taint of the gross prevailing sensualism of his age. A century later he would have been Moderator of the General Assembly, and died in his bed, esteemed of all.

him were sincere, resolute, honest men, and they condemned him as a traitor to the laws and constitution
of his country.   Others, who did not then wield the
sword of government, but who, eleven years afterwards, came to wield it, and who were most likely not
all insincere and dishonest, believed him to be a martyr to the rights of the Crown and to the doctrines of
the Church of England, and he has for centuries continued among the majority of non-eccentric Englishmen to be considered to be Charles the Martyr of
Blessed Memory.   With others of the Puritanic and
Dissenting orders, he has been considered to be a
tyrant at heart and a deceiver in practice, who made
promises " on the faith of a Christian king," especially
when he intended to break them, and who was a sworn
foe to liberty and truth, and all religion that was not
formal and mechanical, and dependent on liturgies and
the like tools.   Of course the truth lies between these
two extremes, but whether it lies nearest the end that
the poet Milton maintained or at the other, is for each
inquirer to determine for himself with such knowledge
and charity as he may have arrived at.   Hume, as
usual, takes the quiet, good-natured, sceptical, gentlemanly mean, and while admitting the intellectual
weakness of the king, he does not ignore the private
virtues of the man.   Either his view, or that of Milton,
or that of the Church of England may be the correct
one.   It is not for me to say which is correct; it is
enough for my present purpose to say that these conflicting views cannot all be correct—some two of them

must be false, and most probably they are all more or
less false, and also more or less true.

The chief of the slayers of Charles I., and his successor, as ruler of England, was Oliver Cromwell, the
renowned Protector; and regarding his character, likewise, the most extreme opinions are held. To the
Puritans he was the greatest of Christian heroes; to
the Royalists and anti - Puritans he was a lucky
canting hypocrite and knave. Even intellect has
been denied him by those who too readily believe in
the possible success of fraud and deception, and who
forget that these cannot be practised without quite
as much intellect as is necessary to the practice of
honesty. To such a length had the idea reached,
that he was a strange compound of the rogue and
madman, who had risen to the surface as the typical
ruler of a mad generation, that we find Hume, usually so cautious and acute, writing this sentence:
"The collection of all his speeches, letters, sermons
(for he also wrote sermons), would make a great
curiosity, and, with a few exceptions, might justly
pass for one of the most nonsensical books in the
world."

His letters and speeches have been collected and
edited by Thomas Carlyle, and those who have read
that book will be able to note how far from the mark
"the good David" has gone in his prophetic criticism.
Instead of being one of the most nonsensical books in
the world, it is one of the best, and rises up like a
pillar of light in one of the most interesting eras of

the human race, over which lies had heaped themselves into an Egyptian midnight.

. Idolatry of the past is an impediment both to ·
writing and understanding history. Like mist it enlarges and bedims everything. The ancients become demigods; and the men of a generation two or three degrees remote impress with the idea that there " were giants in those days." Much of this is delusion, delusion of a very unconquerable kind; but delusion requiring to be conquered in part, in order to the faintest approach to knowing what the actors in the past really were. It is necessary never to forget that they were only men and women, with flesh and blood, and human passions and weaknesses; that they ate very coarse fare and drank a great deal of very strong drink out of horns and bowls and other vessels, with regard to the shape of which they were sometimes not particular, provided they were filled sufficiently well, and sufficiently often; that they made merry and jested, and laughed and talked, and perhaps swore; that they had fast friendships and furious enmities; that they flirted and fell in love and married, and cooed and quarrelled with their wives and agreed again; that, in short, they conducted themselves sometimes foolishly and sometimes wisely; that they fulfilled their duties at some times, and forgot them at others, as men and women do at this day, and have done since the beginning, and will do to the end.

If you hear of golden ages, do not believe in them. No age is quite devoid of goodness, or chaos would

swallow it up; and no age is free from evil in large
measure, for evil is as essential to humanity as a
shadow in sunlight is to the body of man. The
present age is very much like every other; it is
probably better than any previous age. That was
Macaulay's opinion of it, and he knew more than
most men of what like other ages had been. The
error, in his estimate, arises from the excessive value
he set upon material comfort—good eating and drinking, and dress, and the like. To run about half-fed and
half-naked, and build monasteries or cathedrals, and
fight Cavaliers, was not, in his opinion, so comfortable as
to travel in a first-class railway carriage, and read the
'Times,' and dine at the Reform Club. He was therefore content not to have lived in the days of building
monasteries, nor in those of Cromwell and his ascetic
warriors. Carlyle, on the other hand, was discontented
with the present age; but luckily for him he found
his life and its comforts in the present, and his ideas
in the past. If he had been unfortunate enough to
live in those ages which he idolises so much, he would
to a certainty have been burned alive, or had his historical and philosophical labours abridged in some
way. His love for the past gives him an intelligent
sympathy with it, and helps him to reflect its life in
his vivid pages; and so far this love is valuable and
reliable. But his comparisons of the past and the
present are extravagant and without measure, and are
very unfair to the present. He knew the evils of
the present, due mostly to torpor of the moral sense

and the rampant supremacy of mammon, which
pressed upon his observation and tormented him;
whereas those of the past did not, having died down
into dust and darkness with the nettles of their contemporary manners.

The truth probably lies between the two, but where
it exactly lies cannot be known. Our constitutions
and habits have become adapted to the present, and
are not fitted for the rough unscientific past. In both
there is bravery, and religion, and virtue : to determine in which there is most is very difficult—is, in
fact, impossible. The one mistake to be avoided is in
undervaluing the present, and the other and more common mistake is in overvaluing the past, and looking
back upon it as a temple full of heroes, as a theatre in
which nothing was transacted that was not good, and
beautiful, and chivalrous.

Both mistakes, and especially the latter, have been
fruitful in historical delusion; and hence a vast deal
of national and family vaunting — as, for instance,
about pedigree. Some people in this country, at least
in England, boast a great deal about Norman blood,—
and many a Lady Clara Vere de Vere is very proud of
it. And no doubt, physiologically considered, when
free from morbid poisons, Norman blood is very good
blood. But the Normans themselves, who conquered
England in 1066, were a most discreditable congregation—a horde of robbers, pirates, and murderers, and
were not at all a set of gentlemen which modern aristocratic society would recognise. I expect that Lady

Clara Vere de Vere would object to dance a quadrille with one of these unclean Norman pirates, could he rise from the dead as he lay down at the battle of Hastings, with all his old tastes and accomplishments. I think that Lady Clara, and her uncle and her cousins, would cease to boast of the Normans if they could realise the historical fact regarding these marauders and their performances; and to realise that fact, the Normans themselves, with that robust honesty which was the merit of their sinews and of their steel, offered some assistance when they chose for their emblems—now blazoned on coats of arms, many of them—such animals as the wolf, the fox, the wild-cat, and the goat.

In Scotland, the blood that is most prized by connoisseurs is not Norman blood—although some authorities think the royal Stuarts were of that blood—but Highland blood; and with better reason, for the Highlanders were as brave as the Normans, and had fully as many virtues, and fewer vices, though they did a good deal of business in the line of petty warfare—mainly with a view to the "lifting" of Lowland cattle and other movable property, in those feudal ages when fighting and thieving were the only genteel trades. They cut a grand figure in Scotch history, these fighting, thieving Highlanders—rather too grand perhaps; for national predilection does run irresistibly strong in favour of the heroes of Killiecrankie and the victims of Culloden—a race fit to rank with the bravest of the brave, from the grey dawn of Scottish history to the bloody dawn that lately broke upon the Egyptians at Tel-el-Kebir. But there is another class that, in the estimation of many, occupies even a higher place in Scottish history than the Highlanders; and that is the Covenanters. Those who would agree with them in hardly a single principle of faith or practice, agree in admiring the sturdy death-defying resolution of these men—their fierce hatred of what they believed to be falsehoods and empty shows, all the more detestable that they were asked to accept them as consecrated —and in feeling grateful to them for their noble fighting in the battle against civil and ecclesiastical tyranny. And callous must be the heart that does not melt a little at the sight of the half-effaced Bible and broadsword on the stone that, in some heathery or grassy wilderness, marks the Covenanter's lonely grave, where, afar from weeping eyes, he gathered himself to his last long sleep under the eternal blue.

But although these men struggled and died for religious toleration, which we prize so much, they had little or no idea of it themselves; indeed they were as intolerant as their persecutors. They fought the fight of liberty and gained it; but they knew it not. They would have hated and cursed the liberty they gained for us. How would you like to discuss the doctrines of geology, or the miracles of witchcraft, or the sinfulness of reading sermons or prayers, with these old Covenanters? Don't you think you would run some risk of being treated like Archbishop Sharpe? Some patriotic and benevolent persons, who sympathise with lawlessness and rebellion, approve of their rude behaviour to the Archbishop.   One of these is the genial, vivacious, poetical Professor Blackie.   But what if they could catch him after a Sunday-evening lecture, or indeed any lecture, and cross-examine him a little as to his creed, and the reforms he would propose upon theirs? I warrant he would modify his respect for them, though I hardly think he would survive to publish it.   I have in all sincerity an immense respect and veneration for the Covenanters; but I confess also, when I reflect on their narrow dogmas and intolerant practices, to being glad that, long before I was born, they were all gone where they could neither endure nor inflict persecution. Let us look back upon them, in their semi-transparent prison in the dim past, with that pity which is akin to love; and with wonder and gratitude.   They did their duty nobly, although a little blindly.   Let us try to imitate them in their devotion to the right, according to our brighter lights.   Theirs was the right spirit— and the right spirit, earnestly applied, always helps onward to the right end.   The coming centuries will show that we, too, have been in the dark; let them show that we have helped to diminish the darkness— for diminished it will be, whether we help or not.

" We know that through the ages an unceasing purpose runs,
And the thoughts of men are widened by the process of the suns."

The purpose running through the ages has travelled far beyond the Covenanters and their ideas.   Their Solemn League and Covenant to extirpate " Popery, Prelacy [i.e., Episcopacy], superstition, heresy, schism,"

what has it resulted in? Popery and Prelacy, with
them other names for superstition, have not been over-
thrown; heresy is more flourishing than ever; and now
no one can be hanged or burned for it, persecution for
religious opinion having become for ever impossible
beyond such mild manifestations of it as break out
in violent vituperation in pulpits and Church courts,
and in insidious covert slander against the heterodox.
Toleration in religion has been established, not because
of the Covenanters, but in spite of them; and its limits
are expanding still in spite of fanatics and injudicious
ecclesiastics and ignorant theologians, who are more
zealous for narrow creeds than they ought to be for
mere bottles of sunshine or of moonshine, so long as
the Sun of Truth itself is in the firmament to supply the fresh needs of every fresh generation; and
the God of Truth can never leave Himself without a
witness in the heart of every true man and woman
that breathes the breath of life. Touching "schism,"
that is rending of the Church of Scotland asunder,
which the Covenanters hated almost as much as they
hated Popery, reflect for a little upon the course of
Church history in this country, and see how human
aspirations are mocked, how human, ay, even devout
Churchmen's purposes go to wreck, and become
reversed in course of Providence,—a course which
holds its own along unseen depths, regardless of the
froth and bubbles which men and Churchmen raise
upon its surface. The Covenanters denounced schism,
but see how they originate schismatics. They and

their genuine descendants have rent the Presbyterian
Church of Scotland asunder three times at least, and
now their non-genuine descendants are seeking to
destroy it altogether.   After eight years of controversy, in 1740 the Rev. Ebenezer Erskine of Stirling
and his seven truly evangelical brethren got severed
from the Church, then coldly moderate, and all but
spiritually dead.   Violent settlement of ministers by
dragoons forced out Gillespie of Carnock and the few
fathers of the "Relief Church" about twenty years
later—1750 to 1761—they too being truly part of the
salt of the Church like their seceding predecessors.
And then, in 1843, it was thought the duty of the
professed heirs of these old denouncers of "schism"
to rend the Church in twain; to go off and form the
Free Church, which is so well known to all of us,
and a good deal better known than trusted.   I shall
not be so insincere as to profess any love for it,
though some of the best men and women I have
ever known have belonged to it (as well, let me say
parenthetically, as some of the biggest and most selfish
hypocrites I have ever known), but I feel bound in
candour to say that I cannot help regarding the
Disruption of 1843 as one of the most splendid
examples of self-sacrifice on the large scale, if not
really the most splendid, ever ·seen in this world.
But see how the fine gold is changed; how this
Church, which sprang from love of liberty, sets itself
to persecute free thought, to turn the Confession of
Faith into a strange god or fetish, to deny common

K

justice to its ministers and professors, even to the
extent of refusing them such a trial as is the right
of the meanest criminal, and how it is degenerating
into a mere cunning political tool—a tool, let us hope,
without edge in the hands of the oppressor. Because
the Established Church is freer in religious opinion
than the Free Church, therefore it must be over-
thrown. Because the Free Church can't get State
endowment, therefore no one shall get it. Because
we won't have, you shan't take, in respect that that
would be contrary to "religious equality." Compare
the doctrine of the ancient Covenanter, that Christ
is and must be King of the nations, with the modern
disestablishment doctrine that the nation as such has
nothing to do with Christ, and note well how far we
have travelled, and how time plays with the dogmas,
even of bigots, and how history becomes impossible in
tracing the pedigree of fanaticism, and still more of
Jesuitism, playing the best game it can for this world,
come of the next what may. That the State has nothing to do with the teaching of religion may be very good
political economy ; it is, I admit, sound doctrine in the
mouth of a Positivist or any other kind of atheist ;
but it is bad doctrine according to the Confession of
Faith, and the convictions of its authors, and most
of its logical disciples, and very bad Christianity according to the teaching of the fathers of the Free
Church before 1843, being, in truth, from their point
of view, nothing short of atheism, as indeed it *must*
be from every point of view which is based on fact

and logic, and not either on blind charity or unscrupulous expediency, and the supreme though unrighteous
will of "the sufficient,"—the self-sufficient number who
rule the Free Church.   How will you discriminate the
true and the false in the history of such a Church, how
will you retain your respect for truth if you find that
what was true before 1843 is false now, that what was
truth for Dr Chalmers, has changed its character at the
magical command of the small busy enchanters who now
play and juggle with his old divining-rod ?   The truth,
as I think, is that the originating doctrine of the Free
Church, the doctrine of spiritual independence, was a
delusion, a self-delusion, from the beginning.   Wherever you have a Church and a State existing in the same
territory one or other must be supreme.   It is all very
well to say, "Let the Church be supreme in matters
spiritual ;" but who is to decide what is spiritual and
what is civil ?   Either the State or the Church must,
and whichever does so is *supreme*.   The Church of
Rome had spiritual independence, because it could
pronounce anything to be spiritual ; but no Protestant
Church ever had it, or ever desired to have it, except
the Free Church in its anti-Disruption ignorance.   It
knows better now, but instead of candidly admitting
its error and retracing its steps, it is renouncing its
historical principles, and Dr Chalmers has ceased to
be its guide; it is turning its old enemies into its
allies, and adopting their principles, not with the
view of helping forward any millennium, except such
as may be reached through ballot-boxes and political

intrigue, and a general scramble for the Mammon of
unrighteousness. So much by way of specimen of how
truth fares among saints, at least among Churchmen,
when a certain personage, who prefers faith to works,
is "tirlin' the kirks"; furnishing a hint or two of what
may befall it among those who are not exactly saints,
and not even orthodox Churchmen.

The vanity which manufactures pedigrees and glori-
fies families and races and ecclesiastical factions, also
finds ample scope in recording the history of nations.
For a patriotic historian it is very difficult to prefer
truth to his country—even if he could make sure of
the truth, which he seldom can. Among most of the
peoples of earth there is little or no idea of truth. Is
the duty of telling it known to any Asiatic race or
any African? And except from the German and the
Dane, and perhaps occasionally from the Turk, where do
you expect it in the continent of Europe? Have you
read in Chinese or Japanese history of their dealings
with the "white barbarians" of the West, and how
much of it do you believe? How much will you believe of the Egyptian history of the last two years when
it comes to be written by an Egyptian patriot, imbued
with Eastern notions of fact and fiction and their practical identity? And then the tall talk of America:
is it of the exact stature of truth, or a few cubits
taller? America has produced great histories—some
serious, some comic; but when will it write a great
and true history of its own Civil War and its discreditable causes? The American conscience is gradually

being laughed and stung into existence through the
operation of an exaggerative humour—the humour of
Washington Irving, of the Biglow Papers, and of Mark
Twain—a humour which bespeaks a keen appreciation
of truth, but a very lax practice of veracity. Lying
may thus be scorned into disrepute in the course of
years; but before that consummation arrives, some
other hell than bankruptcy may require to be opened,
some other god set up than the "almighty dollar."
Read Russian histories and French histories of the
Crimean War, and compare them with that of Mr
Kinglake, and note well how small a share of credit
and glory France assigns to Britain, and how Russia
is not quite sure that she was not actually superior
to both, and generally how truth fares among conflicting national interests.   French histories, for the
most part, are a disgrace to that quick-witted, and in
the main honest and veracious, though vainglorious
people. They can hardly yet admit that they were
beaten at Waterloo, and they assert that the British
were actually beaten according to the correct science
of war; that their centre was broken and their wings
turned, and that that was defeat; but that only the
British did not know it, owing to their ignorance of the
proper science of war.   But why should we wonder at
a poor Frenchman, with his love of glory and gild-
ing, without any genuine apostle to enlighten him
except Voltaire, and he only perfectly true when it
was perfectly convenient ? Have we not truth fettered
to Whig and Tory, and Catholic and Protestant, and

Free Church and United Presbyterian, and every shade of crazed, conceited, or perverse Kirk doctrine, or narrow, selfish, political, parochial, or newspaper, or trades-union opinion?

So far, the causes of the prevalence of falsehood in history are in part curable. Increased intelligence, leading to a higher morality, might lead to their amelioration and put a stop to wilful falsehood or the want of candour that will not look at any truth which does not quadrate with some preconceived idea. But there is another cause not so curable, and that is due to the weakness of the human powers of observation. "The eye only sees what it bears with it the power of seeing," and the right eye is seldom looking on at the right time. And then there are events the importance of which is developed only in futurity, and the magnitude of which, when in the germ at their actual occurrence, no human faculty can divine. The events which took place in Judea, from which our era takes its date, were the greatest in history, and they attracted next to no contemporary notice; and three generations after, Tacitus, the wisest man of his time, and indeed one of the wisest men of all time, saw in the Christian religion not the germ of a new civilisation that was to flourish over the ruins of Rome—whose religion and temples he knew —and overshadow the world, but an odious and pernicious superstition,—an *exitiabilis superstitio*—the votaries of which should be destroyed, and the vitality of which alone excited his wonder. And the like has been the fate of meaner things, though of things more useful to mankind than the careers of the greatest conquerors.   Who invented the spade? Who the plough?   Who the art of printing? .Who the mariner's compass?   Who discovered the secret of compounding gunpowder?   His secret has been one of the chief agents in civilisation.   With the smoke of the first cannon-shot, the possibility of barbarism overwhelming civilisation passed away for ever.   But his name is a topic for doubt, as it is easy to see that of the inventor of the electric telegraph will be in a few years—if it be not so already.

To avoid misconception, I may remark that, in throwing out these considerations as to the incredibility of history, I by no means intend to dispute the utility of the study of history.   Few studies, indeed, are so necessary and useful.   The actualities of the past are truly in it like flies in amber and footprints in stone, if we could only decipher them effectually, which, unfortunately, we hardly ever can.   But one end of learning is to help us to ascertain how very little we do and can know, and to obtain some idea of the immensity of our ignorance; and another is to prepare us for the experiences of the busy world, and to warn us against believing too much or too readily.   For both these ends history is useful: but to the very youthful mind it is injurious in that it disenchants life and turns into ditch-water the earth-spanning rainbows of the youthful fancy.   The warnings contained in history are many, the worthy lessons and examples are few.

I could not select the names of kings, queens, and warriors, and say to any young person, "These are examples for your imitation." I rather think that it is not out of history that the loftiest lessons in morality (which alone are worth being engraven on the soul of youth) can be found, but in revelation, and in poetry, and in philosophy, and in thoughtful religious books, and even in novels. In them it is possible to find the ideal, which is far higher and better than the real. Reality generally arrives soon enough, and it almost always arrives as a disappointment, which our knowledge of the past can partially alleviate, but seldom can avert. Faith in a sound principle is better and more safe in an emergency than many facts of past experience, and sound principles are taught by reason and conscience, and the ideal in their schools, and are not readily learned from history, but must be persisted in in spite of our limited or misunderstood experience, simply because we believe that, however wickedness may prosper, divine justice will reach it at last, and that

> "The fire of heaven is not in haste to smite,
>   Nor yet doth slumber."

False details of history are common, and inevitable; false views of history as a whole are nearly as common and inevitable. One is the atheist's notion that history has merely to take note of a series of social phenomena, producing each other and bound together by some occult tie of cause and effect; to watch the

evolving links of a vast chain, of which the one end is
hidden in a past eternity, and the other extends into
an eternity to come,—a series of causes which had no
first cause, a chain which had no creator.   Not a little
there is in history to counteract this notion.   The
innocent and the guilty perish together : the children
suffer for their fathers' sins ; the people for the madness of their rulers.   The tower of Siloam seldom,
if ever, falls at the right time and the right place.
But the tolerated existence of what appears to us
to be evil in the world need not blind us to the
certain existence of good, to the love and wisdom
revealed in nature, to the constant revelation of
a supreme mind in the mind of man, and to the
flat impossibility of believing in a dead mindless
universe.

Whatever theory may be true, the atheist's theory
must be false ; and no amount of barking to cell-
germs and the cinders of the moon will ever make it
believable by any meditative man in his meditative
moods—moods in which the inner mental light com-
mingles with the light of stars, and the common puts
on its miraculous vesture and becomes transfigured
into the divine.

Another delusion is that of the fatalist, who refuses
to recognise human free-will as one of the independent
forces of nature, to whom the heavens are as brass and
the earth as iron, and man an atom of the hot desert
of life, drifted hither and thither by winds of circumstances.   The fatalist, if he can be troubled to move,

lays his ear to some orifice of the long-drawn, faintly-
sounding aisles of history, and hears therein only the
sullen and muffled crash of the feet of destiny tram-
pling through generations and eras and worlds.   The
God of the fatalist is not a father but a despot.
Yet, withal, he is a king; and that cannot be said of
the divinity whom mobs of zealots in all ages have
professed to worship, and wearied with imprecations
against others and prayers for themselves,—a being
narrow-minded and capricious, whose purposes alter
day by day, to whose overruling wisdom the bloody
crusades of old, and the bloodless crusades and clamours
and petty persecutions of modern times, offer no insult,
and whose providence is always the better of human
assistance and advice.   If we were not so familiar
with this impiety, and the creatures who for the most
part unconsciously practise it, we should be mightily
amazed, and wonder how it could find a place in beings
to whom the light of reason has been vouchsafed.
Those infected by it have acted history, and read it as
if the entire system of nature existed for them and
other insects like them.

But it is not as they fancy, or perhaps as any man,
be he prophet or poet, can fancy.   The system of
nature must be looked at and imagined as a vast *self*-
consistent whole, though not always visibly so,—a
system not fully intelligible to the finite mind, to any
mind that cannot see it and grasp it in all its relations,
but so far intelligible as to render it impossible to believe that it exists for any purposes and to any effects

that are not, if rightly and adequately comprehended, supremely good and wise and just.

It will not do to omit God from this universe, as the atheist does; to listen with him to the storm of existence as a storm which no one guides, and not wonder why it should have ever been a storm at all, still less to avert conviction that if so it must soon (and cannot too soon) rave itself out into annihilation. It will not do to deny the presence of free-will among men, when we realise it in every moment of wakeful consciousness, when we see it in the flint arrow-heads of early races, that have gone with the mammoth and left no other history; in the stone-circles of the Druids or their fathers; in the winged bulls of Assyria; in the collapsed mounds of every battle-field; in the fitful breath of the steam Samson that snorts and pants and toils over the civilised earth; in the turbid streams of life that split and disperse at the corner of every street.

It will not do to suppose that all who do not think as we think in our narrow, darkened caste, or creed, or coterie, are orphans and aliens to the divine father-hood; or that the presence on the earth of all who differ from us is due to some oversight of Providence, and that to watch their extermination is one of the leading objects of history. It will be wiser to believe that all things work together for good, that difference makes the world larger, that contradictions are an inseparable condition of finite knowledge and human life; that the attitude of charity is the proper attitude of man to his brother man, as humble unfaltering trust is his proper attitude to the Parent of all who has created nothing in vain.

Without exultation, yet not without hope, may we look back upon the past and forward into the future. Mists and thick darkness are behind us and before. Of the past we know little, of the future positively nothing, except that the Power who protected and guided our fathers will protect and guide us. We follow them in the busy path of life, and can see that it has always been strewed with some thorns and watered with not a few tears, though there were daisies among the grass and roses by the wayside : the old, old path, which the vulture's eye hath not seen nor the lion's whelp trodden, from mystery to mystery, from grey dawn to midnight and the stars. Sad it may be to contemplate the infinite journeyings of mankind from grave to grave, almost insupportably sad, if it were believable that this is all, and that the result is nothing for eternity and nothing for time except the manifold cohesion for threescore and ten or fewer years of a little dust. If this were all, who could realise it and continue to live ? Would not the heart grow cold as it felt itself drifting, hurrying, rushing, powerless in the grasp of the Niagara of Fate, to the precipice and the abyss ? Would not reason, ere it reeled and plunged into the last eclipse, protest to time and to eternity against the cruel tyrant power that sent it here in mockery to interrogate nature in vain, to torment itself and die, without a ray of hope

to relieve the blackness of utter despair; to see in the
flowery, smiling loveliness of the world only a mask to
conceal the horrid reality of the universal charnel-
house? And does not every highest element in man,
every monition of the divine, every ray from heaven
that penetrates his soul—love of justice, hatred of
wrong, kindly, self-forgetting, self-denying affection
—revolt against a Creator who is a mere reservoir of
blind force, against a God who merely dreams the
huge dream of existence, for millions of years, from
monad to man, from type to type, from race to race,
from generation to generation, and back again to everlasting sleep and extinguished suns?

Notwithstanding of the clouds and darkness that
hang thick around our mortal lot, we feel driven to
recognise humanity in its long march of progress to
be an enduring miracle of miracles, more truly sublime than the sweep of dead planets in their courses,
testifying to a Great First Cause, to a Fatherhood
adequate to create with their wisdom and their virtues
all "the heirs of all the ages in the foremost files
of time," and are unable to escape the necessity of
looking upon the long procession of generations, of
every tribe and colour, emerging age after age and day
after day from the almighty Hand as a God-created,
God-ordained host of workers and of warriors, sent here
to work His work, and that only; to execute diverse
labours; to engage in battles that they dimly understand, the ultimate results of which may be—most
probably are—hidden from the intelligence of the

mortal and the finite—the near command and the ready reward for which lie in the doing of whatever duty conscience directs—the ultimate reward for which, like the ultimate result, waits behind the veil, invisible in detail even to the eye of faith, but sure as the foundations of a universe that rests upon Omnipotence and All-seeing Justice.

SIR ISAAC NEWTON

SIR ISAAC NEWTON.

———◆———

THE name of Newton has found its way into the seventh heaven of fame, into high transcendental regions above the clouds, or among the clouds. His life and work are largely enveloped in the mythical, owing to the mystification of years, the total ignorance of the mass of mankind in regard to what he did, and the not inconsiderable ignorance of many of his most eloquent and earnest eulogists. The most unmeasured of these, and not the least ignorant, are the atheistic Comte and the Christian Brewster. The latter in much stilted rhetoric seems to pronounce him to be the "chief benefactor of mankind," the "prince of his race"; and the former styles him "the legislator of the heavens," identifying, in his half-cracked irrational way, the man who but yesterday has been able to decipher the law with the God who from eternity had ordained it. Both of these eulogists have a great popular reputation as mathematicians,—a reputation far above their actual attainments; and having them-

L

selves the benefit of extravagant over-praise, it is quite
right they should give it. Neither had conquered for
himself more than the simplest elements of mathematics. Of course neither could have done what
Newton did; and that they were probably capable of
apprehending, though Comte was so vain, owing to
innate conceit and mental disease, as to be barely
capable of admitting it; but it is, to say the least,
doubtful if either was quite capable of following the
steps in Newton's mathematical demonstrations, and
correctly understanding what he actually did. That
both were ignorant of the higher mathematics is manifest from their blunders, and from their boyish exultation over the mere elements of the science; and if
their eulogy have such a questionable foundation, what
can be expected of the host of preachers, lecturers, and
talkers at large who set the fame of Newton, where
Horace expected his head to go when he came to be
ranked among lyric poets?

But notwithstanding of ignorance, and extravagance,
and baseless eulogy, Newton did have a human life,
though it is difficult to discover it under the mass of
more or less irrelevant matter with which Sir David
Brewster and others have overlaid it. Sir David has
written and re-written the 'Life of Newton,'[1] and has
produced a really great though not faultless work, now

[1] Memoirs of the Life, Writings, and Discoveries of Sir Isaac
Newton. By Sir David Brewster, K.H., A.M., D.C.L., &c., &c.
In two volumes. (Edinburgh: Constable & Co. 1855.) [2d ed.
1861. The references are to the 1855 edition.]

contained in two respectable-looking volumes which
do their publishers much credit, and their author not a
little, for he has industriously collected and honestly
set forth a vast quantity of material, the bulk of it
dealing with Newton's life and labours, or at least with
the subjects (generally the outside of them) upon which
he worked. That it is a work of finished literary skill
or method, or of general scientific accuracy, cannot, we
fear, be said with truth by any competent critic. It is
a string of disquisitions, many of them loosely knotted
together, upon Newton's biography no doubt, but also
upon optics, telescopes, the flagrant sins of omission
in modern governments in their neglect of science,
the position of various sciences at Newton's era, their
altered position since, and a great deal about science
in general—fit enough for a place in some loose history
of physics, but just as pertinent to a life of Pythagoras,
or Archimedes, or Herschel, or Arago, as to a life of
Newton. All or nearly all that Brewster has written
about physical science is interesting, for he had an
immense knowledge of experimental physics, gathered
out of reading and untiring personal experiments;
and what with internal conviction, what with ill
temper, he was thoroughly in earnest, and generally
threw a red-hot zeal into his subject—a zeal born with
him, and cultivated rather by his ecclesiastical than by
his scientific training, which lent a fascination to his
inaccurate, affected, stilted style; but when he ventures
above the experimental field into the theoretical, which,
knowing his weakness, he never does when he can help

it, he requires to be read with caution, because he is
not at home there, being, in truth, whatever ignorant
Philistines may suppose and assert to the contrary, not
a mathematician at all, at least not more of a mathematician than many a well-educated schoolboy gifted
with a fair mathematical faculty, which was really
not one of Brewster's many superior natural gifts,
the reasoning faculty in him being distinctly inferior
to his powers of observation and of memory, which
powers, with his literary energy, constitute his true
title to fame.   The human element in Newton's character is a good deal lost sight of in Brewster's bulky
work.   This is due to two reasons: first, Brewster's
genuine devotion to science as almost the one thing
worth writing about or living for; and second, his foregone axiomatic conclusion that Newton was far above
all human infirmities, except a hasty temper, which
those who know Sir David and his own very pretty
explosions of rage in Church courts, colleges, and
literary circles, can readily conceive he thought no
infirmity at all—on the contrary, rather *the* meritorious
fountain of righteous indignation.   Feeling though we do
a good deal of respect both for Newton and his enthusiastic biographer, we do not feel quite able or willing
to accord to either the superhuman attribute of perfection.   We rather incline to believe that to be frail is
to be human, and that the curiosity of mankind about
perfection is very soon satisfied.   But apart from all
theory, we prefer to look at Newton as he is, and to tell
his story as a man, and not as a prism or a telescope.

It is not a very long or stirring story, embracing merely the common beginning and ending,—boyhood with its sports, sweetmeats, and scientific toys; youth with its dreams of study and of love; manhood with its poverty, its wrestling with the unknown, its dipping into poetry, and prophecy, and alchemy, its diving into chill fluxionary depths, its soaring to ask the sun for the secret of his light, and the planets for the bond that held them together; old age with its recognition of victory, late but sure, wealth and honour with their compensations, the jealousy of rivals, the envy and cavils of the mean, coveted seat in the House of Commons, but along with it the doom to sit silent and listen to the talk of the shallow, incapable alike of honest invention and of doubt; a long life of toilsome meditation, fuller of success than almost any meditative life, but full also of disappointment, and hostility, and affliction. All that is memorable in it shrinks into a few facts, and crystallises round a few dates.

Isaac Newton was born at the manor - house of Woolsthorpe, in Lincolnshire, on the 25th December 1642, ten months after the death of Galileo. His father, Robert Newton, died a few months after his marriage to Hannah Ayscough, before the birth of his son. In the estimation of gossips, who affect to trace genius almost exclusively in eldest sons, youngest sons, and posthumous sons, the probability of attaining eminence must have been strongly in favour of the young mathematician, for he had all these three desirable accidents of birth. Physiologically consid-

ered, there was another accident of birth not so much
in his favour: he had been ushered into the world
prematurely, and, according to his own account,—derived from his mother,—was so small that he might
have been put into a quart-mug, and was not reckoned likely to live. Rather similar was the weak and
precarious condition in infancy of Voltaire and James
Watt of the steam-engine; and yet these three princes
of science—two of them at construction, the other at
destruction—outlived eighty, notwithstanding severe
and incessant bodily and mental labour.

" Man is immortal till his work is done,"

and can hardly die till he believes it finished.

When Newton was three years old, his mother, still
a young woman, married again; and, fortunately for
the growth of his mind, he was taken charge of by her
mother, for there is no nurse so efficient to develop
both the good and the evil of a child's nature as a
kind grand-dame or aunt. Mischief is mildly re-
proved, and every indication of cleverness is a subject
for excessive wonder and praise. The old lady re-
sided with her charge in his paternal mansion-house,
and in due time he was sent like other boys to a
village school near by to learn reading, writing, and
arithmetic. As he had been left pretty much to the
freedom of his own will, he was a poor scholar; nor
did he improve greatly after he was put to the public
school of Grantham, which happened when he was
about twelve, until a boy that stood above him in the

class had managed to excite his anger and emulation by presenting him with a painful kick on the stomach. Fairly enraged for the first time out of Woolsthorpe, he fought this aggressor in the churchyard, triumphantly rubbed his nose against the wall, and prosecuted his revenge by preparing his lessons so as to get above him in the class, and eventually to the top of the class. This incident is noticeable as an index of his future public career: in his maturer years he continued to treat his rivals in a kindred spirit, and surpassed them not unfrequently under the influence of kindred stimuli. No motive less powerful could overcome his modesty, or timidity, or indifference. However, he was far from insensible to applause and the claims of kindness. At Grantham he was boarded in the house of Mr Clarke, an apothecary, and had living under the same roof a few young friends who could admire his water-clock, dials, kites, and windmills; in particular and by preference a beautiful and talented Miss Storey, for whom he had the gallantry to make little tables, cupboards, and other playthings. He was a mechanician by this time, and, we have reason to believe, a lover. He was a "sober, silent, thinking lad," reading in Mr Clarke's garret, or working at the construction of modern machines, avoiding play except when he could induce his compeers to "play philosophically." Genius was in him; it had already taken its bias, and he was nursing it in solitude. It had shown itself in mechanical imitations, and as infallibly happens with its first-born

throbbings when there is love in a young heart, they
took the form of poetry. But his verses were only
the transient coruscations of molten metal cooling in
its mould. From the mass of cold solid reason which
he gave to the world, it were hard to divine that he
had ever believed himself a poet, if we had not his
own testimony, and were not sure that every original
thinker is more or less so, especially in youth; and
mathematicians do not evade this general law. At
first every thought comes up as a vague fancy; if it be
beautiful it satisfies the poet, but the reasoner rejects
it unless it be capable of being proved to be true. To
reason too much is dangerous for the poet; to believe
without reason is fatal to the philosopher. Newton
was born to be a reasoner, to appreciate truth and not
beauty; and his poetic fancies soon died out, or existed
only to supply him with theories for the tests of
experiment, or logic, or figures. No authentic specimen of his verses is preserved; but if we can draw
any inference from the unimaginative style of his
prose, it is that he had acquired the bare art of trans-
posing words to rhyme, as he afterwards acquired the
art of reducing algebraic formulæ to convenient forms.

Youthful dreams continued to haunt him after he
left Grantham, and had gone home to his paternal
farm. His mother had returned to it on her second
widowhood with two girls and a boy, and with matronly
discretion resolved to make Isaac a farmer and grazier.
The small property, worth about £30 per annum, had
given bread to his grandfather and father, and his

mother had in her own right another estate worth £50 per annum. He was now fifteen, and sober dulness will settle that the widow had decided wisely. But the dreamer was unfit for the business. Much to the distress of his kind parent, and the scandal of an industrious neighbourhood, he let the sheep and cattle eat the corn while he sat musing, or superintended toy water-wheels of his own manufacture; and, when sent to market to sell the corn, deputed that duty to a servant, and betook himself to Mr Clarke's garret to reading and other enjoyments, or sat under a hedge by the wayside, book in hand, until the servant's return. His mother having, doubtless, some of the philosophic talent which she had transmitted to her son, saw that the experiment of making him an agriculturist had failed, and through good advice or a conviction of the futility of fighting against nature, determined to do her endeavour to send him to Cambridge, though it would be a great tax upon her limited means. He went back to Grantham to prepare; and in 1661, in his nineteenth year, was written in the records of that university for the first time the name of Isaac Newton, the modest name of a modest youth, but destined in after-ages to be often written in Granta's august halls, and to be there honoured with the highest order of scientific canonisation. No one then augured his future eminence (save perhaps Miss Storey, with the prophetic hopes of her sex), least of all himself; he had turned to study because he had not the humble qualities requisite for cultivating the little farm of his forefathers. Providence had work for him to do, and it had arranged to drive him to that work. It had given him a spark of the spirit of the wild zebra that will not endure the dull unchosen yoke; it had made him averse to hand-labour, and too poor to be idle. Some occupation he must find, and it can only be that of a scholar. And as a scholar he has to continue long poor, for his tongue was not agile enough for the Church, and science has little to give her votaries but fame. Had he been rich, or successful in finding a comfortable livelihood while young or willing to plough, he would have married Miss Storey, and conjugal felicity would have prevented the meditations requisite for fluxions and the binomial theorem. Had he been so poor as not to be able to enter college, he would have secured the pity and contempt of all his acquaintance as an idler always scheming and starving; he would have died and made no sign.

Young Isaac matriculated at Trinity College—one of the sixteen colleges that at that time were united to make up the University of Cambridge—as a sizar, a student of the poorest class, who received free commons and other emoluments in return for "certain menial services," which have since been allowed to fall into desuetude as degrading to a young man struggling to raise himself. Whether he was well prepared to enter the university is nowhere recorded,—we should suspect not. He had not the method of application requisite for respectable preparation. Whether these sixteen colleges threw any inspiration into his soul is

a dubious question. One man belonging to them at
least was useful to him. Two years after he began to
eat his "free commons" there, the Lucasian professorship of mathematics was instituted, and Dr Barrow received the appointment. Gifted with versatile powers
for philosophy and eloquence, and widely read in
classical learning, he was well fitted to adorn a mathematical chair by his intimate knowledge of the ancient
geometry, and his mastery over concise and elegant
original methods. His sermons have not the concise-
ness of his geometrical investigations; but for native
force of intellect, and as masses of collected thought,
they are surpassed by none in the English language.
Their fault is the diffuseness and prolixity incident to
one who strives to exhaust a subject in all its intricate relations, and has the acuteness to detect them.
Though an able theologian and preacher, he neglected
the duties of the toilet to such a singular extent as
to frighten the polite London ladies out of the church
when he entered the pulpit; and this negligence in
dress was one of many traits of the erudite and indifferent bachelor mathematician. From a professor
so devoted to science, so vigorous in mind, so simple
in his habits, and kind in his disposition, an impulse
is given to study to thoughtful pupils which is silently
irresistible. Intellectual enthusiasm, like every other
enthusiasm, is contagious. That of Barrow infected
Newton, naturally predisposed, when he attended his
lectures on mathematics and optics. His views on
the latter were mere guesses, far from truth; but in

geometry, in addition to other discoveries, he had improved the indivisibles of Cavalieri into a method of tangents, which was within one step of the differential calculus. To tell how much Newton owed to him is impossible, but it was more than he owed to all Cambridge besides. He persevered in the habit of musing and reading, which he had acquired under the hedges and in the apothecary's garret, and he found out his own problems before he found out their solutions, which is a tedious manner of learning adapted to train a genius rather than a Senior Wrangler. At the fair of Stourbridge, near Cambridge, he had bought a work on astrology, and finding himself unable to understand a diagram of the heavens in it, he *began* to study Euclid; but, finding the propositions in Euclid self-evident (as too many of them are), he threw it aside as a trifling book; and in 1664, when Dr Barrow examined him as a candidate for a scholarship, he found that he had not mastered the demonstrations, particularly some about the equality of parallelograms on the same base and equal bases—and no wonder, for they are an ingenious insult to common-sense. Luckily for the unstinted development of his mind, he had not to write and rewrite these elements of geometry thirty or forty times, like the poor lads who now aspire to scholarships, and gain them only by turning themselves into problem-grinding machines. In this easy, desultory, learn-for-love style, Newton read the geometry of Descartes—the father of algebraic analysis, Wallis's 'Arithmetic of

Infinites,' and ventured upon colours and acoustics. When he came to a stubborn difficulty, he re-read what he knew; and this expedient, like stepping backwards a few paces for a race to leap a fence, carried him over it in a satisfactory way—fully as much so as modern *coaching*. Throughout life he studied without external coercion, and external coercion could not make him study or do anything else. It has been customary for those convenient moralists, who are never at a loss, to hold up Isaac Newton idling away his time and neglecting his mother's business as an ·example of laudable diligence; and to talk of him as a model student, which he never was—if a student be estimated by the knowledge he acquires, by the resolution with which he masters a prescribed course, and by the college prizes he manages to gain. We do not hear of Isaac's prizes, because he never in all likelihood deserved any. He was not constituted to fetter his attentions to a prescribed subject, and "get it up" for an examination. He would not have gained an appointment to the civil service of India, and very properly, for he would have made a sorry civil servant. His example to students of ordinary abilities, desirous of immediate success, is useless, or a warning. With them it is prudent to cultivate their little visible field well, and not to allow their thoughts to wander over waste wildernesses, where they cannot take root. To keep within ascertained limits is the policy of little or ordinary souls; to break them down is the privilege of great souls. If Newton's example be worth anything,

it is only to the few who are possessed with a ruling
passion, and who have resolved to gratify it at all
hazards, since in his success they have ground of hope.
Before resolution, patience, and ability, every obstacle
goes down. His experience involves a cautionary re-
proof, moreover, for parents, and tutors, and professors,
who would force learning upon reluctant natures.
There is no surer means of choking ability. A way-
ward and negligent Chatterton, or Byron, or Scott, or
Newton cannot be educated by an extraneous teacher.
Genius is endogenous: it grows like the palm, from
within. It gathers materials from without—not what
it is offered indiscriminately, but what it can assimilate; and growth that is not spontaneous is mischievous. Could Newton have drudged to become a
Senior Wrangler, we should have never seen his name
out of the Cambridge calendar.

Prying into all he saw, musing over all he knew,
curious about conditions and causes, credulous of all
that was not proved to be false, crediting nothing
which was not proved to be true, allowing his fancy to
wander at its own sweet will, and fabricate innumer-
able theories, he had, before he was twenty-five, lighted
upon the germ of his three great discoveries—of the
non-homogeneity of light, of gravitation, and of fluxions; and had elaborated the first, while the other two
were still unplanted acorns, in which vast forests lay
hid. To calculate had become as natural to him as
to breathe. The ten digits found a place in all his
amusements from boyhood upwards, directly or by

implication. On the day of the great storm, when
Cromwell lay dying, Newton, then a lad, idle and
experimenting, was leaping in the wind, against it and
with it, to determine its force. When at college he
sometimes spent a little money upon what ordinary
youths would have judiciously called "sundries" in an
account, if they kept one; not so with Isaac. In a
note-book, beside investigations on series and geometry,
every sixpence of his pleasure expenses—" *Otiose et frus-
tra expensa,*" as he calls them—for China ale, cherries,
custards, cheese, and all other luxuries, is faithfully
recorded. What he spent at a tavern, what he lost at
cards, what he lent to friends, what he gave for prisms
and putty, what he gave for oranges to his sister, is
registered there as significant evidence of his cipher-
ing propensity, of his excellent manners (for a fast
youth keeps no note of expenses), of his social enjoyments, of his ideas of dainties, of his benevolence and
brotherly affection. From this moral thermometer we
infer that his goodness of heart was genuine, but not
of that high order which forgets itself; that his generosity was not free from meanness, for it kept accounts;
and that his love could be weighed or measured, for it
had no wings. Poor Miss Storey had the sad fate to
realise this. Calculation turned his passion for her in
a purely Platonic direction, which, to his honour and
her pecuniary advantage, it never forsook. At the
age of eighty-two, and after being twice married, on
due interrogation, this lady "confessed" that Newton
had been in love with her, but that both being poor,

and he the fellow of a college sworn to celibacy, their marriage would have been imprudent. She *confessed*, indeed, as if it had been a great sin; whereas the sin lay at the door of an unnatural system prolific of broken vows, and broken hearts, and broken laws, both human and divine, poisonous to the peace of many besides Miss Storey. Newton himself does not seem to have suffered much by the breaking up of "love's young dream." But then he had an acquaintance with the principles of dynamics, and could calmly estimate the force of his love and the force of circumstances, and fix the resultant in the proper direction; he could give up marriage with as little regret as any other insoluble problem. That is the grand moral advantage of mathematics.

Less than half a century after Newton's amatory calculation, there fell out in this country the more famous love-affair of Dean Swift with his Stella and Vanessa. Unfortunately for the gentleman, he was not versed in the mathematics, and could not marry his first beloved for poverty, nor give her up though poor. He resolved to wait for better days, and while he waited another lady arose and declared a fierce passion for him. He had firmness to decline her love when it was offered, but had not the hardness of nature requisite to cut the acquaintance of the fond woman who had rashly and unasked given him her heart. For this softness and ignorance of the mathematics Dean Swift was rendered miserable, and at last mad; and his memory has been an object of hooting and denunciation to beings who had not one tithe of his virtues, and who reckon every spring of human conduct as despicable as their own.

How strong the arithmetical affections of Newton were we have seen, also how they affected his social attitudes, and we now turn for a moment to observe how they affected his position at Cambridge. He gained a scholarship, despite his ignorance of Euclid, which helped to maintain him until he was elected to a small starvation fellowship. But his wants were few. He had been able to purchase materials for a reflecting telescope, which he made with his own hands, after a plan differing from that devised by Gregory, who was the first inventor. The Royal Society had heard of this performance, and, for the asking, got a description of the instrument from Newton himself, and finally the instrument altogether. In the belief that he was the inventor, the Royal Society chose him as one of its members, and to justify their choice he communicated to them his discovery of the composition of white light of differently coloured and differently refrangible rays, made years before and promulgated in his professorial lectures at Cambridge. For by this time, on the retirement of Dr Barrow in 1669, his mathematical merits had raised him to the honourable poverty of the Lucasian chair. Poverty certainly it was, for his income, together with his fellowship and patrimonial estate, did not afford him the means of paying a shilling a-week as his contribution to the Royal Society, so that he had it dispensed with rather

M

than that he should retire. England did not at that
era pamper her sons of genius even so much as now—
though she does not yet content Sir David Brewster,
nor any one who is a respecter of genius over Norman
blood; but then she gave Dryden to choose between
cleanness of teeth and Popery, and having laughed with
the inimitable Butler, gratefully starved him to death.
The geniuses of our age may thank their stars that
Government is not the only nor the best channel of
public rewards. Through busy years Newton worked
on, expecting no reward beyond the pleasure of working, which is the truest of all; or perhaps, when he
kept his laboratory fire on for six weeks at a time
experimenting upon metals, the delusive never-to-
be-obtained reward — in the search for which fortunes, and lives, and reputations were wasted—the
famous and fabulous philosopher's stone. For mere
amusement, as the story goes, when the great plague
of 1665 had put to flight the philosophers of Cambridge, and he had taken refuge at his birthplace, he
tried the gravitation problem on a hint from a falling
apple in his mother's garden. He hit upon the happy
thought of treating the moon as an apple, and trying
to elicit according to what law it falls towards the
earth; and though his calculation failed at the time
for want of accurate data, it succeeded many years
afterwards, when the communications of Hooke to the
Royal Society had recalled his attention to the subject.
Sir David Brewster treats twice of this apple story in
terms so careless as to give a thoroughly inaccurate

idea of the law of gravitation. Without pointing out his slips, which any tyro in natural philosophy will at once detect, we may here state that law, as it ranks the highest of Newton's discoveries, though the proof of it only is due to him. It may be thus briefly enunciated: Matter attracts matter with a force directly proportional to the mass, and inversely proportional to the square of the distance. Thus compact is the kernel of the ' Principia '; for to prove this proposition, and collateral and preparatory propositions, and to develop its consequences or corollaries, is the object of that great work.

About the year 1665, also, Newton had amused himself working at problems according to a method which was subsequently named the method of fluxions, and led to a long ill-natured controversy about priority of invention between Continental and English mathematicians, after Leibnitz had published a universal method which swallowed up that of Newton. Dr Barrow had seen Newton's problems and their solutions, and through him they had been circulated among a few friends; but Newton himself either thought them of no consequence, or he wanted to turn them into his own private instrument, and enjoy the delight of astonishing the uninitiated by his wonderful results. If ever he chuckled over his hidden treasure in this ungenerous, unphilosophical spirit, he had cause to mourn afterwards, for Nemesis transferred his hoard to the franker Leibnitz, and left him in possession of unavailing regrets.

After his fame was noised abroad, and Englishmen
had grown proud of him, Newton began to expect
some reward in the shape of a Government appointment, through the intervention of Locke the metaphysician, and Pepys of the 'Diary.' Vain expec-
tation! Though they did their best, hope deferred
made his heart sick. He distrusted his friends, and
in the latter part of 1693, his reason was so far shaken
that he wrote insane letters to these two, and alarmed
both as to the state of his mind. The disorder was
but temporary, yet it weakened his intellect for the
rest of his life. At last fortune favoured him at the
hands of a genius whom fortune had largely favoured,
Charles Montague, afterwards Lord Halifax, who, when
fresh from Cambridge, was Matthew Prior's coadjutor
in the composition of the "Town and Country Mouse,"
and had thereby recommended himself to the capricious patronage of King William. On being elevated
to be Chancellor of the Exchequer, Montague did not
forget his old college friendship, but proved it, by
having Newton appointed Warden of the Mint, with
moderate work and £500 or £600 per annum. This
was in 1695, and four years later, owing to the same
kind influence, he was appointed Master of the Mint,
with an income of £1200 to £1500, which he enjoyed
till his death. He in this way attained, what he seems
to have long desired, an abundance of money; and he
distributed it liberally among his poor relations, to his
youthful love now married and in difficulties, and to
all who had any claims upon his hearty but slightly

swaggering munificence,—such, for example, as the celebrated Cheselden, to whom he offered a handful of uncounted guineas by way of fee. He left a considerable fortune to the descendants of his mother by her second husband; Woolsthorpe passed to the nearest relation of his father, who squandered it, and falling one night when drunk, killed himself with the stalk of his tobacco-pipe. In his last years, Newton was afflicted with gout and gravel, the arch-tormentors of the sedentary, and he died on the 20th March 1727, in the eighty-fifth year of his age. Towards the end of his life he had been amply honoured: he had been a silent member of Parliament for Cambridge, he had been for twenty-five years President of the Royal Society, he had been knighted by Queen Anne, he had been deified by the English natural philosophers of the age of Bolingbroke, and at its close Thomson spun a long blank-verse eulogium on him. Pope perpetrated the well-known couplet:—

> "Nature and Nature's laws lay hid in night;
> God said, 'Let Newton be!' and all was light."

Medals were struck at the Tower in his honour; Cambridge set up, at her own expense, a white marble statue of him; and his relations, out of the fortune he had left them, erected to his memory a splendid monument with an inscription almost fit to make the cold stone blush. Of these panegyrics, that on the Tower medal, applied by Virgil to the poet, is the truest— "*Felix cognoscere causas.*"

We get some glimpses of his cloister life at Cambridge from Humphrey Newton (who acted as his amanuensis during the preparation of the first edition of the 'Principia' for the press), and other observant gossips; and we can distinguish pretty clearly the form into which his ruling passion had moulded the modest, meditative, and abstracted mathematician, and the habits and manners it had made for him. His meat and drink were to try to detect the occult principles of nature. For six weeks, at spring and fall of the leaf, his laboratory fire was never out, and he watched by it anxiously while his hair assumed the colour of quicksilver. He walked incessantly through his room musing in peripatetic mood, but never took out-door exercise. If he stepped out into his neat garden for a turn or two, on some thought striking him he wheeled about, "like another Archimedes, with an εὑρηκα," rushed up-stairs, and committed it to paper without wasting the seconds by sitting down. If he entertained a party of friends in his rooms, and had occasion to go to his study for a bottle of wine, he ran great risk of forgetting to come back. On public days, when he had to dine at the hall, he was apt to appear in the guise of a pure mathematician, with stockings untied, shoes down at the heels, hair uncombed,—doubtless to the entertainment, and perhaps horror, of the noble nothings who study gastronomy at sumptuous academical tables. Like all men who have shown themselves capable of intense and protracted thought, he partook of wine sparingly, and only at meals. He often forgot

to eat his food, and when reminded of his neglect, used
to swallow a hurried morsel or two standing. "He
kept neither dog nor cat in his chamber, which made
well for ye old woman his bedmaker, she faring much
ye better for it; for in a morning she has found sometimes both dinner and supper scarcely tasted of, which
ye old woman has very pleasantly and mumpingly gone
away with."[1] He seldom sat by the fire, except in
severe frost; never slept in the day-time; he stood
when he took his meals alone, and seemed to grudge
the time he gave to eating and sleeping. Honest
Humphrey, during the five years of his engagement,
saw him laugh only once, and that, if Dr Stukeley's
account be correct, at an infinitesimally small matter,
being neither more nor less than the simplicity of a
friend who had borrowed "Euclid" from him; and
on being interrogated as to how he liked that author,
asked (maybe he was a Scotchman) what benefit in
life the study would be to him? "Upon which Sir
Isaac was very merry." He had a better taste for
apples than jokes, and liked a few of them roasted
for supper. Down to this point his juvenile luxurious
tastes had dwindled, save that he used orange-peel
water to moisten his bread at breakfast as a substitute
for tea, which had been for years, only in trial quan-
tities, introduced into our country. He had not

[1] Brewster's Life, vol. ii. p. 95. This statement of Humphrey
has been held by Sir David to disprove the existence of the dog
Diamond, and his fire-raising among Newton's papers. But Diamond
might have been Newton's companion either before or after Humphrey's five years—from 1683 to 1689.

leisure for formal private prayers, nor to attend chapel morning and evening; but he frequently went to St Mary's Church on Sunday forenoon. His daily life was at this period an earnest, inarticulate—partly answered—prayer for clearer insight into the book of nature, which is one of the books of God.

Among men he was not immediately successful, with all his learning, industry, and intellect. It is conceivable how his eccentricities were laughed at by the wags of Cambridge, how his labours and discourses were sneered at by the envious, how his expositions were slighted as abstruse and unintelligible by those who were jealous of their effect. As a professor, he was far from popular. Like Sir John Leslie and all great scholars, he was not understood; he lectured to a small audience as incapable as the walls, or had no audience at all. Every new truth must burn its way through cold neglect and indifference, if not fanatical opposition. Most units of the human race desire to know nothing that does not conduce directly to the comfort or feeding of the body. Of the learned even, the minds of the majority cease growth almost as soon as their bones; and these care for no doctrines which threaten to displace those that they have acquired with difficulty, and on which they depend, it may be, for bread. Genius alone retains perfect assimilative powers; it alone has the resolution and the vigour to pull down the old house when the foundations are shown to be on sand, and build another on those rocks of truth which the progress of science lays bare. But genius is rare; and the honesty which can acknowledge the full merit of contemporary scientific discovery is still rarer. Appalling evidence of this is not wanting in the martyr-roll of philosophy: in the compulsory recantation of Galileo,—in the threatened ruin of Jenner, the discoverer of vaccination, and of Harvey, the discoverer of the circulation of the blood. Newton was several scores of years too late for the fires of Smithfield; but he had to "lecture to the walls," to endure neglect, and other small but galling persecutions, which ought not to be allowed to be forgotten. One fact is sure,—and it illustrates the respect in which a living prophet is held in his own country and university,—not before the Newtonian philosophy had become famous all over Europe had a sufficient number of tutors died out to allow it to displace the Cartesian at Cambridge.

At that time the authority of Descartes was dominant in nearly all science. Upon doubt he had based a system of metaphysics, which he had applied, somewhat loosely in many cases, successfully in others, to the properties both of matter and of mind. He had discovered that powerful instrument of analysis the application of algebra to geometry, without which fluxions would have been as impossible as in the day of Archimedes; he had brought optical investigation under the power of mathematics; but with an unwarrantable licence of fancy, he had accounted for the revolutions of the planets by the hypothesis that they were swept round in the vortices of an ether that filled all space like water in a whirlpool. Gravitation superseded these metaphysical vortices, but in every other instance Newton built upon the labours of Descartes, and did not pull them down. Had Descartes been blessed with a strong healthy body, had not arms and pleasure engrossed much of his brief life, had he been willing to be burned for the good of science and the Church, he might have prosecuted his studies with a vigour that would have left Newton nothing to do. His genius was equal to the highest efforts of human thought. But accidents fell across his path, and physical discovery depends somewhat on accident.

Never was any genius more fortunate than Newton, as Laplace has remarked, clearly not without a wish that he himself had been the lucky individual, and a conviction that he would have done just as well. He came, the rightly endowed man, at the right time. Two thousand years had been laying up substantial materials for him to put in order. For him Pythagoras had devised geometry, and Euclid had written it; for him Archimedes, Pappus, Napier of Merchiston, Cavalieri, Barrow, Roberval, Fermat had elaborated operations in infinitesimals; for him Tycho Brahe watched by night, Kepler [1] performed his enormous

---

[1] Before all astronomers, I think, Kepler deserves the title of "Legislator of the Heavens," if any human being can deserve such a title. Besides his three "laws," he certainly did as much in the discovery of gravitation as Newton did; some think more. That law is explicitly stated in various parts of his writings. What Kepler achieved in his wretched circumstances, casting nativities,

numerical calculations and established his three laws
of the planetary motions, Copernicus discovered the
revolution of the planets round the sun, and Galileo
completed and enforced that discovery; for him Hooke
experimented upon optics and the attraction of the
earth; and Bacon, Bouillaud, Sir Christopher Wren,
Hooke, and Halley plainly proposed and helped to
solve the gravitation problem. The ship which they
freighted so richly, he managed to bring to the shore,
and served himself heir to the cargo. These and many
others had laboured, and by generalisation or completion he entered upon their labours. As he has
himself honestly confessed, if he saw far it was because
he was borne upon the shoulders of giants. But he
had eyes which could look long and steadily, and
distinguish between mist and solid land, and therein
is his merit. Were scientific discovery protected by
patent, so that it could not be made the basis of improvement, were Newton's own dogma accepted that
"second inventors have no rights," his niche in the
temple of fame would vanish, stone by stone, and

writing almanacs for bread, and hardly obtaining it, is to me more
wonderful and truly great than what Newton achieved in his quiet
Fellow's rooms, with starvation, bailiffs, and other troublesome
intruders securely bolted out by the bars of two doors. Named in
the order of time, these mighty wrestlers with the unknown were
Copernicus, Tycho Brahe, Kepler, Galileo, Huygens, Hooke—
contemporary of Newton—and Halley his junior. Destiny sheltered Newton better than any of them, and there is no sufficient
reason to assert that among them all he had not been endowed with
the strongest intellect. He at least solved the most difficult scientific
problems which Destiny, or, in other words, the growth of discovery,
had matured for *that* age.

grain by grain, until *colour* only was left and the outline of a shadow. No great man whatever was so deeply indebted to his predecessors. Such a want of originality was essential not to his mind, but to the nature of his subject. In poetry, the field is illimitable; and beyond using the same language and culling the same flowers, no two travellers need resemble or accept the assistance of each other; but in physical inquiry it is necessary to keep the beaten tracks, for progress is the traveller's object; and Methuselah himself would hardly have had time to make the observations and experiments, to establish the mathematical principles and invent the methods absolutely essential to the speculations and success of Newton. It was his good fortune to complete the work of others, and receive nearly all the honour; it is the misfortune of his successors in scientific pursuits, that physical theories can be completed only once.

He did not, however, escape one necessary consequence of his good fortune—namely, controversy sifting the originality of his discoveries. His discovery of the nature of the composition of white light stands uncontested; his gravitation theory has been shown to belong, except the mathematical proof, to Hooke, Kepler, and Halley; and his fluxions have been claimed as part of the calculus by Leibnitz. The fluxionary dispute embroiled the mathematicians of England and the Continent, and brought out failings in the character of Leibnitz as well as Newton. Nor is it very satisfactorily settled. Of course, Sir D. Brewster takes the side of Newton, and animadverts severely upon some apparent dishonesty of Leibnitz, but he has the candour to admit that Leibnitz was the independent inventor of his calculus, though some years posterior to Newton. Out of an immense collection of facts, letters, authorities, slanders, we come to the conclusion that the chief honour of inventing the new calculus is due to Leibnitz. By the fluxionary method Newton had worked out some curious and difficult problems, and he mentions that in a letter to Leibnitz, several years before his invention; but unwisely, and unluckily for himself, he concealed the method. Leibnitz was less secretive. When he had discovered his differential calculus, he communicated it at once to Newton, who found that its method included that which he had discovered many years before, and had left in an imperfect state, and unpublished, except to a few friends. In a scholium to his 'Principia,' Newton acknowledged the independent invention of Leibnitz; but after charges of plagiarism began to pass, through their friends or otherwise, Newton had the meanness to expunge this scholium in next edition. Throughout, the conduct of Leibnitz disclosed nothing more mean than that, and it may be doubted if as much be proved satisfactorily against him, though there is reason to suspect that he was capable of descending to the "infinitely little" as well as of speculating upon it. His ostensible conduct was frank, confident, indifferent, and apparently incautious, not indicative of one who was oppressed with the consciousness of a bad cause.

He appealed to Newton to testify in his favour, which a plagiarist would scarcely have mustered the impudence to do. Newton preferred to fight behind shelter, but then he was a nervous, timid man. He secured the decision of his friends of the Royal Society in his favour, and prepared for them, *sub rosa*, the materials of 'Commercium Epistolicum,' in which, to be sure, the controversy is settled in his favour. Posterity is not to accept the verdict of a handful of mathematicians, to which they were guided by an interested party, in the absence of the other party, who was, besides, an alien in more senses than one. We believe that, independent of Leibnitz, and before him, Newton had solved some dozen isolated fluxionary problems, as had Fermat, Barrow, and others; but we do not believe that his method was at all general, still less complete; that, in fact, it could not be called an available workable system, until several years after Leibnitz's had been published, and that even then it was much inferior to his, and not so universal. The calculus depends upon a metaphysical principle, the doctrine of the infinitely small; it is the monads of the Leibnitzian philosophical system applied to quantity,—and who should be so original there as Leibnitz himself? The truth is, Newton had not that wide comprehensive mind requisite to create a system: his was the *intense narrow mind of a special problem worker*. Therefore he interpreted the spectrum; therefore he demonstrated the gravitation theory; therefore he solved the problems proposed by Bernouilli, at the instance of Leibnitz, "to feel the pulse of the English analyst." Therefore he worked *special* problems in fluxions; therefore it is likely he neither did invent, nor could have invented, a complete infinitesimal calculus. Leibnitz was intimately acquainted with every branch of knowledge, and he threw light upon most,—law, history, philology, geology, mathematics, metaphysics. His power was only surpassed by his versatility. *Nihil tetigit quod non ornavit.* He was an unwearied successful system-builder; in that walk Newton cannot be compared to him. Newton did not aim specially at system. His genius was characterised by intensity rather than breadth; and though he could be both broad and strong, he inclined to be strong rather than broad. One of his admiring intimate friends says of him, "He never asked a question, but answered one with great readiness," which is not the characteristic of a genius who feels it to be his mission to gather up the scattered fragments of truth into a complete whole. Newton devised solutions for hard isolated problems; Leibnitz devised systems, and the calculus among the rest. But, on the other hand, it is not to be concealed that he had a special affection for systems devised by himself; that he never admitted the truth of Newton's theory of the universe; and that he manifested far greater inclination to despise the 'Principia' than to read it: indeed it is all but certain that he never did read it. Neither ought it to be concealed that his contemporary Voltaire found in him material chiefly for satire, while he declared Newton to be "the greatest genius that ever, existed."

Controversies, and this fluxionary controversy in particular, embittered the twilight hours of the long-protracted evening of Newton's life. With all his honours, knighthood, presidency of the Royal Society, mastership of the Mint with its wealth, and scientific fame, he was as jealous of rivalry as a young lady of forty-five. When he laid aside timidity to defend his own rights, he manifested more zeal than discretion; when he shrank from self-defence he primed and loaded the carbines of desperadoes like Keill. He could not calmly, like Bacon, leave his name and fame to other ages and countries, and his anxiety defeated itself. It stained his moral nature. He showed no generosity to opponents, only a brave resolution to conquer. Perhaps this was due to his timidity, to the recoil from that caution which made him advise a young gentleman about to travel on the Continent, to endure any insult rather than be provoked to fight; for the animals that run fastest from pursuers are often most furious when brought to bay. Perhaps it was due to the defect of his classical education, that he did not imitate Homer's heroes more in paying chivalrous compliments to his rivals. The melancholy truth must be told, that Newton, a sincere Christian, a prince of science, had no forgiveness for his enemies, whom his rashness made for him; had little of the dignity almost universally associated with true greatness. Like some vain Eastern potentate, he delighted to receive the adulation of flatterers, and could not brook the semblance of independence among those about him. Hooke, Leibnitz, Flamsteed, Abbe Conti, were all quarrelled with without sufficient cause, and treated like his first rival, the little boy in the church-yard. The mental disease which seized Newton is the best apology why the wisdom and decorum of age did not restrain the quick temper and boisterous passions of boyhood. During his studious years, it is said, his usual deportment was mild and gentle.

It is natural and amiable to forget the faults of great men; they are never remembered in epitaphs: but it is to be regretted that Sir David Brewster has, with the best intentions, set himself to hide or palliate New-ton's failings; to admit their existence grudgingly under absolute compulsion, or not at all; to attack with undue severity his opponents wherever it is practicable; and to maintain the improbable notion that all his friends were of stainless reputation. This is hero-worship bap-tised into blind superstition. Nothing less sweeping will satisfy Sir David than the dictum that Leibnitz, by hinting that the Newtonian doctrine tended to atheism, has "cast a blot upon his name which all his talents as a philosopher will never be able to efface." Will Laplace or Comte, or any positivist, say that his criticism was unfair? Who of his many admirers has heard of it? Cannot the partial bio-grapher infer from facts not beyond *his* reach, that even the faults of the famous are forgotten? Flam-steed, the Astronomer-Royal, had been of important

N

service to Newton; but they had quarrelled, as was natural with two individuals so highly choleric. Newton took his revenge by leaving out Flamsteed's name in the second edition of the 'Principia' in most places, which Sir David admits was hardly justifiable. Once when they met, Flamsteed complained that he had been robbed of the fruit of his labours. Newton, on comprehending this insinuation, "grew outrageous," and, says Flamsteed, "called me many hard names— puppy was the *most innocent* of them." The acute rather than accurate biographer moralises, "How simple-minded must he have been, in whose vocabulary of vituperation the epithet given to Flamsteed was the *most prominent!*" Halley, one of Newton's friends, and editor of the 'Principia,' was generally understood to be sceptical in his religious opinions. This Sir David cannot believe, because Newton would not have kept company with him had such been his views; as if even a shrewd man of the world can always discover the views of those about him—as if no avowed sceptic had ever kept company with individuals just as pious as Newton.

Next there is the character of a lady to vindicate: a Miss Catherine Barton, the favourite niece of Newton, his housekeeper, the friend of Swift, beautiful and witty, but reputed to be the mistress or private wife of Lord Halifax, Newton's patron. This nobleman, by will, left to her his jewels, £3000, and an annuity of £200 for life, "as a small token of the great love and affection he had long had for her." He was a widower,

and might have married her. Mr de Morgan thinks
he had done so, but did not care to avow the marriage
publicly, owing to her humble extraction. Sir David
denies that there is any proof of this marriage, or of
Miss Barton having even spent a night in the house
of Halifax; and insists that she was a woman of the
strictest virtue, one of the toasts of the day, admired
vastly both by bachelors and married men—and that
the bequest of Halifax was made through pure Platonic
affection. The evidence does not preponderate either
way, and it certainly does not destroy whatever pre-
sumption there may be in favour of a witty lady
of that age. Voltaire visited England not above two
or three years after Newton's death, and he had a
strong liking for scandal, which he took every means
of indulging not manifestly at variance with truth.
But he had as much respect for Newton as he could
feel for any human being, and if there was any man
whose memory he was not likely to traduce it was
the author of the 'Principia.' Yet a solitary human
defect does not receive the entire brunt of this sneer.
" I believed in my youth that Newton had made his
fortune by his extraordinary merit. I imagined that
the court and city of London had promoted him, as
it were by acclamation, to be Grand Master of the
Mint. Not so. Isaac Newton had a very lovely
niece who happened to please the Lord High Treas-
urer Halifax. The calculus and gravitation would
have been of no service to him without his handsome niece." At the time Newton was first ap-

pointed to the Mint, Miss Barton was scarcely seventeen, and it is improbable that Montague had then seen her. But this inaccuracy does not strip the treasured morsel of London gossip of all significance. Clearly Voltaire did not invent the story; in some shape or other it was part of the floating scandal during his English exile, and probably had gathered itself round the undisputed nucleus of fact in obedience to the promptings of a sarcastic, uncharitable generation, much given to coarse unbridled talk. Both Halifax and Miss Barton were friends of Swift: in his familiar letters to Stella he makes mention of them both, but never together, nor yet of any connection between them. Sometimes he dined with Miss Barton at her lodgings, and he frankly informs Stella that he loves her better than anybody in London, and he was too proud to say this of any man's mistress. Sometimes with the frankness and licence of the times, and of the wits of every time, they talked over queer stories. Miss Barton, in comical fashion, tells Swift of a humorist who had left legacies to as many individuals of each sex as were necessary to carry his coffin to the grave, provided that each took a declaration of having preserved chastity inviolate; and somehow his coffin had been allowed to stand without bearers. The story is suggestive. Two classes of people only would speak of it: either the perfectly virtuous, who feel that " to the pure all things are pure;" or the utterly vicious, who have thrown off every restraint of modesty and reputation.

The secretly vile and outwardly respectable do not expose their frailty in jocular talk. Probably Miss Barton proposed that Swift and herself should serve themselves heirs to the legacies; and really it would be difficult to fix upon two of their contemporaries better entitled to this peculiar bequest. On watching the balance of probability, it is as likely that Halifax left his fortune under the influence of Platonic affection as not, since rakes forget their victims. Much weight must be allowed to the friendship of Swift, whose virtue is beyond suspicion; beauty, intellect, and virtue almost invariably go together, and Miss Barton had beauty and intellect. She married afterwards, and became the mother of an only daughter, who became the mother of the Portsmouth family.

There is another matter of controversy touching Newton himself: was he ever insane? "Yes," says M. Biot,[1] one of his French admirers, and writes a long life of him to prove it. "No," says Sir David Brewster, extremely indignant at the idea of a philosopher becoming insane, and adduces documentary evidence, arguments, and assertions. Our readers will find the facts and pleadings at length in their books. We think it clearly proved, from Newton's own letters to Locke and Pepys, that about the year 1693 he was liable to fits of temporary alienation of reason. He fancied that Locke had "endeavoured to embroil him with women;" and that must have been an insane delusion. He wrote to Pepys intimating his resolution

[1] Biog. Universelle, tom. xxx.

to withdraw acquaintance from him and the rest of his friends, and stated that he had not slept well for a twelvemonth nor enjoyed his "former consistency of mind." To Locke also he states, as an apology for having indulged suspicion against him, that by sleeping at the fire he had contracted a distemper which was "epidemical" during the summer of 1693, and which at the time he wrote the delirious letter had allowed him not more than an hour's sleep a night for a fortnight, and for five days together not a wink. Sleeplessness is a frequent forerunner and concomitant of insanity. In some asylums there are patients who have not slept for years, and the sleep of a lunatic is generally perturbed and shallow. Newton's own admission that he no longer enjoyed his former consistency of mind, the incoherence of some of his letters, the dread of embroilment with women, the desire to shun his friends, the inability to sleep, are strong proofs that at times his mind was clouded. Whatever the cause of these fits of temporary insanity might be, whether sleeping by the fire, or disappointment with his want of success at alchemy, or in the endeavour to obtain a Government appointment, or melancholy superinduced by excessive study, or vexation caused by the destruction of his papers at which the dog Diamond is said to have officiated, or the thousand unseen influences that act upon a sensitive, irritable nature, there was no want of a sufficient cause, and there is no denying the certainty of its lamentable effect. During the intervals of health, Newton worked at mathematics and theology with considerable vigour; upon which Sir David rests the assertion that his mind was never in a state of derangement, never afflicted with any disorder, but was always fitted for the highest intellectual efforts. We do not think this assertion adds either to Newton's fame or the credit of his biography. Sir David has two horns of a dilemma to choose between, equally too sharp for him. Either Newton's mind was visited by these ailments, and permanently weakened by them, so as to be unfit for making further discoveries, *for he made no more;* or he was a mere favourite of fortune, and not the genius which he is reputed to be. Either his intellect was enfeebled, or it was never strong. No averment can be more palpably absurd than that of the biographer—namely, that for the last forty years of his life Newton retained the highest genius ever given to man, and made no use of it, after he had learned how to use it; that he buried his ten talents as soon as he had counted them and knew the value of them. Charity will allow his misfortune to acquit him of a waste of time and ability so criminal. Sir David, in explanation, says: "The ambition of fame is a youthful passion, which is softened if not subdued by age. Success diminishes its ardour, and early pre-eminence often extinguishes it. Before the middle period of his life, Newton was invested with all the insignia of immortality, &c." [1] Therefore it seems he had no motive for working. What gospel yet preached

[1] Vol. ii. p. 155.

has told any man, low or high, that he is to strive merely for fame—that he need not care to do his utmost to leave the world wiser and better than he found it? But Newton did try to the last; he attempted the lunar theory and found it too hard for him, and that it kept him awake whole nights, so he gave it up and took to chronology and theology. His chronology is not unworthy of him; it is ingenious but unsatisfactory. His views on prophecy are sensible, when the impracticable enigmatic nature of the subject is considered. Voltaire hinted that his commentary on the Apocalypse was written with the intention to console the human race for his individual superiority. None of these later works would entitle his name to be remembered. And seeing that the physical and mathematical sciences have made vast advances since his time of activity, are we to suppose that the fruitless latter half of his life was due to wasted or to prostrated powers; or that what he left undone in science could not be done without higher powers than his, which have been found in famous men who have come after him? Or is it not also possible that he fully completed his life-work, and that he finished it early? The history of science shows that each discoverer has had generally prepared for him, by the growth of discovery, his appointed task. He executes it, and departs, and leaves the successively maturing fruits of the tree of knowledge to be plucked by others.

Sir Isaac Newton was at one period a great man, all agree,—a few insist that he was the greatest; the students of nothing but physical science and positivism do with general acclaim. Says Comte—"The heavens of old were said to declare the glory of God, now they declare the glory of Newton and Laplace." There is a slight difference, positive enough, we humbly whisper, between making and seeing what is made. Sir David Brewster delights to call Newton the "high priest of science." Well, then, where were his litany, his hymns, his sphere-music? Is it the duty of a high priest to measure the length of a pew or two, to calculate the solidity of the altar, and surround it with mathematical symbols? Sir David styles him the "chief benefactor of his species." If his species be not mere mathematicians, but mankind in general, we tarry not to prove that the nameless boor who first made a spade or yoked a plough (overlooking James Watt with his industrious engine) ranks above him as a human benefactor. What though the world carries its inhabitants through space according to a certain force of attraction? What though white light be composed of seven colours, or seventy times seven? Astronomy, it is true, has lent the radiance and the glow of other suns to the burning, brilliant eloquence of Chalmers—has given man to know the littleness of his mother earth in the universe, and of himself on it —and has opened space to the seraph wings of poetry, and permitted it to revel in the glories of immensity. But, with its code of iron inflexible laws, it has prompted the atheist in his folly to dispense with the unseen, self-concealing Lawgiver, and has furnished no

means of negativing the assertion that space is a vast
Sahara of unpeopled stars, cinders, fire, and mud—of
spheres dedicated to desolation, created to no purpose;
and by implication, that the Creator is not wise, or that
He does not exist. Sir David sets Newton above the
heroes of battles and the conquerors of kingdoms.
But there is no point of comparison. Unlike Horace
and Demosthenes, Newton would not have run away
without his shield, for he was too timid ever to have
lifted one, or any other instrument of war. His is
not the fame of the patriot; the blood of patriotism
responds to forces which were beyond his ken, or even
his powers of calculation. The name of Tell is pronounced in Switzerland, that of Napoleon in France,
that of Wallace in Scotland, with far nobler and deeper
emotions than any Englishman can feel on pronounc-
ing the name of Newton. To the majority of the inhabitants of Britain it suggests no definite idea of
any kind.

Few men of extensive and liberal acquirements
venture to pronounce dogmatically who the greatest
of men has been. He may waver between Shakespeare
and Goethe; his tastes may incline him to give the
pre-eminence to Homer, or Plato, or Dante, or Milton,
or Bacon; but Newton will hardly occur to him until
he has gone somewhat down the scale. The cultivation of physical science will never secure the highest
honours of human intellect, because it does not call
forth the highest powers of human intellect. Patience
and good eyes are the requisites of that sort of busi-

ness; accident one condition of success. The patient,
good eyes may watch for ever in vain, if good fortune
be awanting: the lucky purchase of a toy prism, the
lucky twitching of a dead frog's leg, may open up the
paths to fame. If the observant scientific individual
notice some law or appearance of nature hitherto un-
noticed, and show it to the curious, his work is done—
further than the exhibition of as much pride and the
reception of as much praise as if he had made a new
world instead of seeing only a little bit of the old
one. Towards patience and good eyes, with the micro-
scopic and telescopic aids, we entertain the highest
respect; but we recognise the same excellent faculties
in herons watching eels, and owls watching mice, even
in more than human perfection; so we hardly can
suppose them to be the highest faculties in man. In
mathematical study also, patience must predominate
over intellect, and keep strong analytic reason waiting
for some combination of symbols which will evolve
the desiderated result. We grant that the reason
requisite for original mathematical investigation may
be—generally is—of the highest order; but it is
not necessarily so. By repeated efforts almost any
strong, determined, logical mind will solve problems
which have made their first discoverers famous.
Higher than the mathematical reason is the metaphysical. To Descartes and Leibnitz, both eminent
in metaphysics, and disciplined into intellectual Milos
by metaphysical puzzles, mathematics were an agreeable relaxation of effort—mere child's-play. By way

of recreation they solved problems at which Newton
would have toiled by day and lain sleepless by night.
It is disputable if his additions to mathematical science
are more considerable than theirs; if they are, it is
another verification of the fable of the hare and the
tortoise. And who will venture to hold Newton above
Archimedes? Are the problems solved by Newton *the
most difficult* in exact science? If so, on due allowance being made for the happy fortune that cast
them in his way, Newton's superiority may be pro-
visionally admitted, until more difficult problems arise
and are grappled with successfully; if not—which is
the alternative to which we incline, from the comparative facility with which these can be solved now
by a student from the bare data—we cannot but conjecture that Newton has been overestimated, apart
from the intellectual merit of his discoveries, and
owing to their luckily wide application. It is thus
an open question whether Newton be the first of
mathematicians. Yet, again, it is scarcely an open
question whether they hold the loftiest walk of
genius. Labour and logical faculty will make a respectable mathematician: labour alone will not make
a poet or metaphysician. Newton had the good sense
to perceive this in his own case. He abandoned
poetry in despair; and it might have been as prudent
for him to have left metaphysics to John Locke. If
rarity be the essential of honour and value, then is
the poetical genius the highest of all; for it is the
rarest of all—inborn, unquenchable by circumstances,

not to be reared in hothouses by the lavish expenditure of fuel and labour. What would Newton have been had he been allotted the evil days of Milton—had he been destined to plough with Burns? The path to poetic fame is open to all, is the most inviting of all, is entered upon by all, but leads to renown only the truly deserving. The path to scientific fame is virtually closed by university gates against the many; the few that enter upon it have tried the poetic in vain, and their ultimate success does not cover their failure, much less entitle them to rank with those who have attained eminence in a career from which they have turned back, and which is open to all the world.

Of one opinion only do we almost approve in the estimate of Newton's character, and it is his own. He reckoned himself a common man, with uncommon patience. Modesty here, if it influenced him, kept him singularly close to the truth. His mind emitted few of these flashes of intuitive power peculiar to genius. In conversation he was uncommonly dull, if he was not altogether silent. He was an impassive, unsympathetic, uninteresting, undesirable companion. None of his sayings are household words, except that modest one in which he compared himself to a youth picking up a pretty shell or two by the great unknown ocean. In his appearance there was nothing remarkable. When young his eye had some brightness, which it lost as he grew old; his hair turned grey at thirty, while he toiled day and night at attempts to trans-

mute metals. Fancy a short, thick-set, slightly cor-
pulent man with white hair, perfect teeth, overhanging beetle brows, a wedge-like retreating forehead;
deep-set, slow, penetrating eyes; firm, irascible mouth;
abstracted, meditative air, tinged with melancholy; a
tendency to avoid society, to shrink from the annoy-
ance of self-defence, and to fly from timid modesty
into uncontrollable, abusive, indiscreet anger,—and you
have a tolerable idea of Newton's personality. Fancy
a mind of narrow, iron powers, keen faculties of observation, moderate imagination, acute analytic reason,
decided mathematical bias, slight inclination to credulity and superstition, balanced by inordinate curiosity
and extreme patient persistence in the quest of truth;
also strong general tendency to persistence in friendship, in hatred,[1] in alchemy, in problem-solving, in
pretty-shell seeking, in quarrelling about the rights of
possession after the pretty shells were found, in every
line of action,—and you have a not inadequate idea of
Newton's internal personality, if the entire known deeds
of a life can give any adequate idea of a mind, any satisfactory insight into the "mystery of a person." He
was as sincere a Christian as his calculating nature
would allow; in religion, as elsewhere, his overmaster-
ing, all-engrossing intellectual bias intruded: he was

---

[1] Newton broke an intimate acquaintanceship with Vigeni because
he told him a loose story about a nun; he would never again see a
promising young mathematician who, on the first interview, had refused to take money from him; he was chary about forgiving Bernouilli; he did not forgive Leibnitz after his death, but persisted in
attacks upon his fame. However, he was equally true to his friends.

an Arian; he had a mathematical limitation to assign
to the orthodox doctrine of the Trinity; he could not
understand how Father and Son should be coeval, how
Three could exist united in a coequal, coeternal One.
All honour to his candour and sincerity! Had he not
been a true inquirer and a true believer, he would
have conformed to the fashionable political faith;
he would have taken orders, and enjoyed the wealth
and gouty idleness of a bishop. All honour to the
patient persistence which enabled him to unfold the
laws of nature and of number, which hollowed out
steps for him in the precipitous and slippery path
to fame, and is his legacy of exemplary, continuous
effort to mankind! But let us not honour him, the
genius of calm serene reason and iron accuracy,
with the inaccurate empty titles of "prince of his
race," "almost superhuman genius," and the like—the
hollow, sonorous, sentence-balancing epithets of rhetorical extravagance. He did an arduous work which
many men have had sufficient talent to do—singularly few the opportunity,—from the doing of which
the impatient crowd would be glad to escape to the
mines of Siberia. The lesson of his life is that of
the restless, persistent rill, cutting a channel through
the obdurate granite. Great was he, but not "The
Greatest."[1]

[1] Like Voltaire, Hume is of an opinion very different from this.
Hume (Essays, vol. iv. p. 555) places Newton and Galileo "at the top
of mankind." But Newton, Hume, and Voltaire had little in common.
They were not much more capable of appreciating his mathematics
than he was of appreciating such scepticism as theirs. They had a

If natural philosophers and mathematicians can agree, they are entitled to enthrone him as the prince of their order; but it is part of our creed that no jury of wise men or wise women would pronounce him the prince of the human race. They will rather extend the sceptre to Plato of the broad shoulders and the broad brow, the victor of the Olympic games, the thinker of all thought, the discoverer of boundless realms of speculation, which the ages will people apace with practical ideas; or to Shakespeare, with his manly beauty and his universally sympathetic and creative mind; or to Goethe, the cultured and complete, with the mien and figure of Apollo, majestic pile of forehead, overhanging eyes through which a serene and melancholy spirit looked in silent lightnings. They will rather postpone their decision from day to day and wait for wisdom; their difficulties will increase with their waiting, and they will reverently leave the highest prize of humanity to the award of Omniscience.

tendency to exalt the material and underrate the transcendental, even as manifested in Shakespeare and Milton.

BURNS

AND

THE PEASANTRY OF SCOTLAND

BURNS

AND

THE PEASANTRY OF SCOTLAND.

———————•———————

[THERE are Burns Clubs in various parts of the world, wherever the natives of Scotland collect in clubbable numbers. They afford Scotchmen an opportunity of meeting together, of knowing and helping each other, and generally of keeping alive national sentiment and feelings of national brotherhood. There are several of these clubs at home also which are not without their uses, social as well as convivial. But whether at home or abroad, there is one festival in the year kept by them all—it is the celebration of the day of Burns's birth, which happened on the 25th January 1759, and is a kind of festival of hero-worship, not of a serious character, but not, except by sour-browed bigots, to be reckoned heathenish or profane. No doubt it is marked conspicuously by what some starched persons, in white neckcloths, of the order aforesaid, have denounced as "the idolatry of genius," whatever that may be, and no inconsiderable glorification of everything Scotch, from haggis and cocky-leeky to the peasantry and literature of Scotland. The two speeches that follow were delivered each at an annual dinner of the Edinburgh Burns Club—that on "The Memory of Burns," on the 25th of January 1870, and the other two years thereafter,

when my old college friend, the Rev. Dr Wallace, proposed the
toast of the evening with a vigour of intellect and liberality of
creed worthy of one of the living teachers of a people " who
sing by turns the Psalms of David and the songs of Burns."
These speeches are reprinted from the 'Scotsman,' two or three
slight slips being corrected.]

BURNS.

THE committee that manage the toast department
have laid upon me a burden which I would have
preferred to have seen laid upon broader shoulders,
and borne aloft with more strength and dignity than
I can bear it. They have done so with a kindness
and a friendly confidence which adds to its weight
and aggravates the dread of failure, for it is not so
unpleasant to gratify the malignity of enemies as to
disappoint the expectations of friends. I felt honoured,
though astonished, by their request—honoured beyond
my hopes or deserts—and I shrunk from accepting
their flattering invitation. But it came a second time
in a form which had about it some of the aspects of
the inevitable, and I reluctantly undertook what I
now falter to do. Do it, however, I must, after some
fashion or other. That I realise most distinctly, and
I bow to necessity as resignedly as any philosopher
that ever denied the freedom of the human will.
Hardly even John Calvin, I believe, could have gathered himself up to discharge the duty of burning a
heretic or of marrying a widow with such unflinching
resolution as I have exercised in collecting my wits

and repressing my natural modesty to enable me to propose this toast.

The theme of it is not new to you; it is not new to any civilised creature out of China or Japan. Scores of orators all round the globe will dilate on it to-night. Hundreds of orators have expatiated on it in time past; and probably thousands will do so in time to come. You have heard it year after year illustrated from all, or nearly all, points of view, and such light shed upon it as can be shed by all styles of eloquence, ranging through lofty prose poetry, splendid rhetoric, patriotic declamation, rollicking humour, enthusiastic eulogy, justified by recitation of the fitting quotations, and that calm incisive criticism which grows by the practice of logical disputation, and which bears on its face the hard bright glitter, and on its edge the sharpness, of steel. And you have read Carlyle's philosophical essay, which contains, according to my judgment, the truest and justest estimate of Burns yet written, or ever likely to be written—an estimate arrived at by a deep-seeing, sincere man, who is, in many rare and high qualities of mind, not second even to Burns. You have read Professor Wilson's glowing, warm-hearted panegyric, and sweeping, tempestuous, fiery abolition of adversaries; you have read Jeffrey's sharp, clear, superficial lucubrations, and have probably seen therein the smart, trig, dapper little tomtit (a most admirable creature for slaying wasps and blue-bottles, and suchlike, and worthy of all praise in that department), finding fault with the clumsiness, the indecency,

the vulgarity of the eagle; you have read Alexander
Smith's graceful, polished poetical tribute, which is
full of quiet appreciation, and fuller of sympathy than
at first sight appears; you have read the Rev. Hately
Waddell's gushing eulogies, which are wild, headlong,
and irrepressible, as if written by the grateful spirit
of Bruar Falls; you have read Lockhart's admirable
life of Burns, and Dr Currie's, and Dr Robert Chambers's interesting accumulations of facts and of gossip:
you have read Gilbert Burns's unaffected, touching
story; you have read Burns's own letters—which to
my mind pretty clearly disclose their author—and
you have read and re-read his poems, and have had
them haunting your memories from your early days,
and have extracted from them probably more intellectual and ethereal pleasure than you have extracted
from any other work of human genius.

What, then, can I tell you about Burns that you do
not already know, and say of him and his performances that you have not already heard? Nothing, I
fear, or next to nothing. But we are here to-night
not for the sake of acquiring knowledge, but of keeping it. We drink not to the memory of the mean and
contemptible, of

"Souls ignoble born to be forgot;"

but we drink to the memory of that nobility holding
its "patent direct from Almighty God," which we
wish to be held in everlasting remembrance. We do
so out of patriotism, out of gratitude, out of veneration

for poetic genius, which is one of the best gifts Heaven has given to man. Burns has made our country classic among all civilised lands, and in the centuries to come it will be remembered as Greece and Rome will be remembered, because of him and Walter Scott. Burns has benefited us all as individuals, not inwardly merely, but outwardly, for his thoughts have been among the most potent forces in striking down tyranny of all kinds, and in letting the oppressed go free. He truly has been one of the unacknowledged legislators of the world, and has led, and will lead, British Parliaments and American Senates by ways that they know not, and to goals that they dream not of. Let us clearly recognise, then, the nature and extent of the achievements of this man, what he was, what he did, and in the face of what enormous difficulties and obstructions he did it. He was born poor; the front wall of his native cottage fell in shortly after his birth and exposed him to that old winter storm, the forerunner and emblem of many storms that beat upon him through life, and still howl occasionally over his grave when the lunacy of fanaticism is not wholly engrossed by revivalling, or reviling the Pope, or railing at Sunday trains, or persecuting some misguided brother who has carried Protestantism to the audacious pitch of thinking for himself and disbelieving that the final view of God's ways to man was settled at Westminster 231 years ago.

Though born a peasant, and in spite of poverty and tempests without and within, and, indeed, partly because of the latter, he burst upward through the superincumbent strata of society, and reached a position that kings might envy—that hardly any king has ever obtained. He truly is one of the "dead but sceptred sovereigns who still rule our spirits from their urns." His writings, his hasty thoughts dashed down on paper, in the intervals of severe toil, have affected the thoughts and cheered the hearts of more men and women than those of any modern singer or thinker—than those of any man, so far as I can calculate, that the world ever saw. Unfortunate he has been called, and lamentations have been poured forth over his miseries. He poured forth not a few of them himself, and probably, in the spirit of Job, cursed the day when a man-child was born,—that day which we are now celebrating as an auspicious day to mankind. Dean Swift did the like before him, and Byron after him. They all thought in their gloomy moods, and most poets have at times thought, that life was and is a bad bargain, and would have concurred in Byron's bitter verse—

> "Count o'er the joys thy years have seen,
> Count o'er thy hours from anguish free,
> And know whatever thou hast been,
> 'Tis something better not to be."

Man in general, and poetic man in particular, is not easy to satisfy—all the realities of existence fall so far short of the idealities. But not deserving anything at all, he certainly obtains at least as much as he deserves, and I, for my part, am quite unable to join in the notion that Burns was unfortunate: on the contrary, I think that in his life, and the results of it, he was specially fortunate; and I cannot doubt that, if he could enter into a compact with Fate to live over again, he would not desire another course of life than that to which he was appointed from the beginning. I think he was fortunate in his father— sagacious, severe, irascible, religious—the high priest of "The Cottar's Saturday Night"; that he was fortunate in his mother, so kindly, shrewd, and affectionate; and that he was fortunate in being born among the only race on the face of the earth, or that has ever been on it, that could have afforded materials for his poetry, and encouraged and cheered him on in the production of it,—the industrious, humorous, superstitious, virtuous, inquiring, speculating, truth-loving, God-fearing, Lowland Scotch. He could not have transmuted the experiences of the poor into poetry if he had not shared them. He could not have found the themes for his serious poetry, nor for his satires, except among the descendants of the Covenanters— their true descendants being among the best of men, and their false being among the worst; for it required a giant effort of hypocrisy to counterfeit the faith of those who cherished it not as a code of barren dogmas, but as a possession secured to them by their forefathers' blood, as a creed to be resolutely lived by, and, if need were, died for. I think he was fortunate in his patrons, at least as fortunate as any man of genius ever was, or is likely ever to be. They were

not all like the patron figured in Dr Johnson's gruff
letter to Lord Chesterfield, written four years before
Burns saw the light,—that patron who sees a man
struggling for life in the water, and when he has
reached ground encumbers him with help. They did
not help him much; they could not if they would. But
they helped him as far as his proud spirit would
permit, and in so far as help is good for any true,
brave man who is cast by destiny, not upon a bed
of down, but upon the rocks, and whose life problem
is to

> "Breast the blows of circumstance
> And grapple with his evil star."

To eat and drink and wear fine clothes, and be for
ever merry and at ease, would be truly unfortunate
for any man, and totally fatal to the growth of a great
man, who can be perfected only by suffering,—

> "For life is not an idle ore,
>   But iron dug from central gloom,
>   And heated hot with burning fears,
>   And dipt in baths of hissing tears,
>   And battered with the bolts of doom,
>   To shape and use."

I think, then, that it was better that Burns was not
encumbered with too much help. And if he was fortunate in his patrons, I think he was, if possible, still
more fortunate in his uncharitable detractors, who
have been in the mass an odious band of cold-blooded,
blear-eyed, half-blind bigots. If any of them was, or
is, pure enough to throw a stone at Burns, it was

mainly because he was, or is, personally so disagreeable as to be exempt from most human temptations. Of course, Burns's chief good fortune lay in his vast and·rare mental endowments, his clear insight into men and things, his large sympathy, his scathing wit, his joyous, tumultuous humour. The like of them had not been given to any man of his century, and in their peculiar combination to no man of any century.

Truth was dear to him, and the real lay open to him as it lies open only to the eye of a lover. He could see into the "open secret" of the universe when atheism was worshipping its oracles of reason and staggering blindly about Europe preaching its mad gospel of despair. His sympathy ranged over all living things from the soul of the hero of Bannockburn to the crimson-tipped daisy. His poetry poured itself over all human misery, and had a half-genuine, half-comic drop to spare, even for the "verra deil." His humour and his wit scorched into cinders whole hecatombs of hypocrites and knaves, and his name is one at which Holy Willies of all degrees, and homicidal Dr Hornbooks, both with and without degrees, ought to tremble. I do not quote verses for illustration of his mental qualities, not because I do not know Burns's poems, for I once could repeat the larger, and can still repeat a large, part of them, but because the apt illustrations will recur to your memories as well as to mine. It has been thought that Burns's sympathy had an unfortunate bias, that it ranged too widely, and that it led him into company that he

ought to have shunned; and it is not for me to say
that it did not.   But I do say that it was one of the
essential forces of his nature, and that he bore all the
sorrow of it, and that mankind has reaped the best of
the fruits.   Even Carlyle gently hints that he was a
little too convivial and indiscriminate in his company.
But Carlyle is delighted with "The Jolly Beggars";
and I ask, How could Burns have written that poem if
he had not been somewhat indiscriminate in his company?   Would it have been half so real if he had
looked across the street through Poosie Nancy's window with an opera-glass?   Think you, is it possible
to explore the bowels of the earth and preserve white
hands and spotless linen?   The unsurpassed merit of
Burns's poetry is that he saw with his own eyes, and
saw not from afar or from genteel altitudes; that he
heard with his own ears; and that he felt in his own
wild pulsations the riot to which he has given vocal
embodiment.

Burns was, in my humble but deliberate judgment,
not unfortunate in his life, and very far from unfortunate in the results of it.   And as to his early death
—unfortunate though it was for mankind if his work
was not done—we know not; it is not given to the
living to know.   Whom the gods love die early, was
thought of old; and to-day we see no deeper into the
darkness that environs life and seals the portals of
death, than did the youngest children of speculation
in the world's dawn.   To go away from wife and
children, and friends, and the fields that are familiar,

may be, must be hard; but I can conceive it possible
that, to the traveller who has arrived at the untroubled
country from which there is no return, his regret may
be, not that he has reached it so soon, but that he has
reached it so late. Sufficient, however, it 'is here and
now, to feel assured that a man has fought his life-
battle bravely and well. Burns did so, and he conquered. Though he fell before noon, he fell as heroes
fall. We commemorate not his birth, not his death,
but his victory; not his victory merely, but his invincibility, the victory of the ethereal over the earthly;
the invincibility of the divinity that burns in men of
genius, and is a pillar of fire to illuminate the path of
generations through the untravelled depths of time.

THE PEASANTRY OF SCOTLAND.

This toast is not inappropriate to a festival in
celebration of the genius of Burns, the greatest of
Scottish peasants, and one of the greatest of the sons of
men. Wherever Burns is understood and honoured,
the peasantry of Scotland are honoured also, for he
was a real representative of the Scottish peasantry in
all their peculiarities, intellectual and moral. The
mind-moulding forces which had been at work for
ages among them culminated in him. He was their
poet, their preacher, their prophet: he threw the light
and glory of his genius over them; but they supported
him by their sympathy, by their well-diffused intelli-

gence. They rendered his intellectual existence possible. But for those long peasant heads of Ayrshire, who confronted him in the flesh, who could tell him much, and listen to all he had to tell, he would in all probability have gone to keep silence with the "mute, inglorious Miltons" who have found no audience of human souls to whom they could speak the secrets they had brought with them from heaven. If Burns lifted the Scottish peasantry out of the primeval darkness of a people unsung, they combined, by their history and their native faculties, to give him the power to do it; and they remained above the darkness, because they had not a little about them better worth looking at in peaceful, moral, industrious times than any other people as yet planted by Providence on this planet. I declare my conviction that no race on the face of the earth, or that ever flourished on it, could have produced Burns except the Lowland Scotch, which, however, is not so much a race as a mixture of races, descendants of Druids, and Romans, and Danes, of ancient vagrant Celts from Ireland, of ancient Welshmen of Strathclyde, and of ancient Britons of Northumbria, linking us in remote cousinhood to the natives of Yorkshire and Cumberland, and helping us to understand Chaucer's language better than ordinary modern Englishmen can do. For many of the qualities which distinguish us from our ancient English relatives we have been indebted to John Knox and John Calvin, and the Solemn League and Covenant; and for the hereditary prudence and unrelaxing industry of our race we

have been indebted to those favourite topics for satirists
—our reluctant soil and our severe climate. That soil
would yield little to the sluggard, and that climate
would not permit him to live. Long centuries before
poor-laws were invented, cold and hunger weeded out
the weak, the ineffectual, and the imprudent. Ireland
is a beautiful island, set like an emerald in the sea,
very pretty for half-sincere poets and orators to cele-
brate; but I am rather afraid that in the ancient centuries the climate of Ireland must have been too mild,
otherwise in these current days hereditary imprudence
would not be so prevalent there.

The virtues and vices of the Scottish peasantry are
well known to you. They are all reflected in the
poetry and life of Burns; and I am inclined to believe
that in temperance, tolerance, charity, and some other
virtues, there has been a little advance since the days
of Burns, though I am afraid I must admit that the
ideal of "The Cottar's Saturday Night" has become
rare. I wish I could believe that Scottish prudence
and thrift were as stanch as Burns knew them to be,
when there were no savings-banks, no banks at all
accessible, except an old stocking-leg hidden under
the thatch, or some similar receptacle. I wish that I
could feel sure that the Scottish peasantry all prized
as he prized, and his contemporaries prized, "the glorious privilege of being independent," and that there
was no truth in the common assertion that many of
them now look upon the parochial board as a mere
mutual benefit society, instead of a refuge only a little

less objectionable than the grave. To those who accuse
the Scottish peasantry of these days, of drunkenness,
and lecture them thereanent, I wish every success in
the abolition of that vice; but, at the same time, I do
not believe that those now living are nearly so drunken
as their fathers and grandfathers were, or that if the
Excise officers were now to allow Willie to brew a peck
of maut, he would set himself to drink so much of the
juice of it at once as was done by the companion of
Rab and Allan.

There is another vice of the Scottish peasantry—
though I doubt if it be entirely confined to them—of
which we hear a good deal at every publication of
the Registrar-General's reports. If you have not already guessed what it is, I give the further hint of
saying that Burns spoke of it as his " ae wee faut."
One would feel half driven to think sometimes that
in this " ae wee faut " Scotland was the worst country
on the face of the earth. But that, I, for one, don't
in the least believe; and I beg to say this for Scotland—that she is the only country that has dared to
look the truth in the face, and to publish accurate and
complete statistics. No other country has done this.
In no country except Scotland does there exist the
machinery for doing it. In Scotland every birth must
be correctly registered under pains and penalties, but
this is not so either in England or Ireland. At the
census of 1861 there were, if I recollect aright, 20,000
children in England under ten years of age—children
who had come into the world somehow between 1851

and 1861—whose births had not been registered at all. A few of them were no doubt born in India and Australia; but there is just as little doubt that the vast majority of them were children about whose births it was thought the less said and written the better. Not one of these mysterious births would have escaped registration in Scotland. I say, therefore, that Scotland alone can be bold enough to look at the facts, and that is, I venture to think, more likely to lead to reformation than simply ignoring them : and I say further —and let those who can read riddles reflect upon it— that the grossest immorality of Edinburgh, of London, of Paris, of all cities and countries, eludes all statistics; while that which puts Banffshire and Wigtownshire in the pillory is, in comparison, scarcely immorality at all, but is rather a frail and slightly deficient kind of virtue.

I, for my part, wish Scotland to grow better and better as the years go by, but I shall be fairly well content if Scotland, even in Banffshire, do not grow any worse. I can anticipate brighter years for the Scottish peasantry. It is easy to see that the weight of manual labour will cease to lie so heavy on the sons of toil as it has done, and will leave them time for that calm reflection which is essential to reading and mental improvement. Out of the leisure which machinery will secure in the coming years we can anticipate that many men of intellect will emerge from among the peasantry of Scotland—men of letters, men of science, engineers, artists, explorers of the secrets

P

of nature, perpetuators of the beautiful, leaders, bene-
factors of mankind—in this restless, inquiring, industrial age; but from among them we need never expect
to see another Burns. There are plants said to flower
once only in a century, and the Scottish peasantry is
the austere but not unfruitful forest that has bloomed
out once only in all its glory in the genius of Burns.

Other buds and blossoms it has put forth at intervals. There was the Ettrick Shepherd, whose imagination could follow Bonnie Kilmeny into fairyland.
There was Tannahill, who could pour poetry upon the
craw-flower's early bell. There was Allan Cunning-
ham and Telford the engineer—both of them masons
and both of them poets, the one latterly publishing the
creations of his imagination in massive stone and
iron. There was Hugh Miller, also a poet, with his
gifts of utterance, bursting into splendid poetic prose.
There was Alexander Smith—known to most of us,
too soon called away, who had eyes for the glories of
sun and sea such as have been given to few. There
was the author of the " Cameronian's Dream," and the
author of " Jeanie Morrison "; and there is the author
of the " Rover of Loch Ryan," a veteran octogenarian,
still writing vigorous Scotch verses on the other side
of the Atlantic; and there is the author of that soothing, delightful enforcement of one of the duties prescribed by the Tenth Commandment—" Ilka blade o'
grass keps its ain drap o' dew." [1] Long may this vener-

---

[1] This last was James Ballantine, long the energetic secretary of
the Club, and one of its most active members. Other songs of his

able plant put forth such flowers. The world does not require another Burns; but it requires new singers to lighten its new-born cares, and new seers to look into and cut through the heart of its new-born problems. Long may the Scottish peasantry produce such singers and such seers, and may it never cease to be worthy of being the stock whence Burns sprung.

are well known and widely popular; but he is perhaps better known in another branch of æsthetics than song-writing—to wit, that of stained glass, many of the churches in Scotland having been decorated in these days of innovation by the firm of which he was the head. He was a self-taught and a self-made man, entirely genuine, and full of rough fun and homely shrewdness and sense. He was a native of Edinburgh, being born in the West Port on 11th June 1808. He died at Warrender Lodge, in the suburbs, 18th December 1877, in a very different home from that in which he spent his youth.

Hew Ainslie, the author of the "Rover of Loch Ryan," was a native of Ayrshire, being born there in 1792. He produced during a course of sixty years a good deal of miscellaneous verse, a considerable part of it first appearing in a volume of his published in 1822, entitled 'A Pilgrimage to the Land of Burns.' Previously he had been a clerk in the Register House, Edinburgh. That book contained his farewell to his native country, which he left immediately on its publication. He emigrated to America, and there pushed his fortune, not without success, as farmer, brewer, and engineer. He died on 11th March 1878, at Louisville, Kentucky, aged eighty-six.

W. Motherwell, the author of "Jeanie Morrison," had a far more ethereal spirit, but a much briefer career, the life being crushed out of him in huge, overwhelming, materialistic Glasgow, at the age of thirty-eight, finally, on 1st November 1835.

The "Cameronian's Dream" was the production of James Hislop, a shepherd lad born in the parish of Kirkconnel, near Sanquhar. He was befriended by Jeffrey, who helped him to the appointment of schoolmaster on board a man-of-war. He died through a fever caught by sleeping one night on the island of St Jago, at the age of twenty-nine, an "inheritor of unfulfilled renown" but for this beautiful poem, the local inspiration for which was drawn from Airsmoss, where his sheep and his fancies wandered together.

REALISM, IDEALISM, AND POSITIVISM

REALISM, IDEALISM, AND POSITIVISM.

———◆———

THE external world, if it be known, is known either directly or in representation. An act of perception involves three distinguishable elements: *first,* the external world or part of it, or *object; second,* the *mind* itself, *ego* or subject; and *third,* the relation between the two, be it antithesis, contrast, image, idea, or whatever it may be called. According to the theory before Berkeley, the image or idea or impression was accepted as evidence of the existence of external things. But Berkeley saw that mind could be certain of nothing beyond itself, and that the *idea* in it could never be accepted as proof of something unknown beyond it. He therefore denied that there was any distinction between the idea and the thing supposed to be represented by it. He maintained their identity. He himself contended that he denied the existence of the idea, and maintained the existence of things in themselves; but he has, in spite of his own contention, been supposed to assert the existence of the internal idea *alone*—to be an *idealist*—and to deny the existence of matter, while all he did deny was, that there was sufficient or any evidence of the unknown substratum or noumenon which was supposed to produce the appearances of the properties or sensible qualities of matter. When Dr Johnson refuted him by kicking a stone, he refuted what had never been affirmed by Berkeley, nor by any other sane man; and that is the kind of refutation, only duller in its manner, which is furnished by Dr Reid's maundering about disbelieving his senses, and "stepping into dirty kennels," which proves nothing except that he was incapable of understanding Berkeley. What Berkeley did assert his belief in, was the "evidence of sense"; what he did deny was the intangible, hypothetical, external cause of sense postulated by the philosophy of his day—a sort of parent of phantoms which Dr Reid continued to believe in, just like Berkeley's predecessors, but, unlike them, incapable of being taught and warned, *even* by the scepticism of Hume, for of that teaching they had not the benefit.

Sir William Hamilton had in him powers of apprehension and of reasoning of a very different order. He could see that Berkeley and Hume were not to be answered by the jests of the ignorant or the "grins" of coxcombs. He could see, further, that Berkeley was right in holding that the outer world is directly perceived, and that to admit any intermediate relation or idea is to let slip reality, the reality of consciousness, and to substitute an *inference* in an arena where reason is helpless. Perception is in his view the arch that spans and brings together subject and object—the outer and the inner world. They are both there together, so revealed in the consciousness of the instant, set over against each other antithetically and in contrast, but as real as anything revealed in consciousness can be, as certain as every revelation of consciousness must be. Sir William is a *realist*, or *natural realist*. Ferrier, on the other hand, while agreeing with both Hamilton and Berkeley as to the veracity of consciousness, and the contents of perception as disclosed in consciousness, holds that object and subject though distinguishable are inseparable,—that matter without mind is unthinkable and unknowable. He therefore gives such predominance to mind as essential in perception, as *the* constant essential, that he falls to be classed with idealists—that is, with those who refuse to place matter on a co-ordinate footing with mind. What Comte may have been I cannot venture to conjecture. He ought to have been a materialist, as every atheist is logically bound to be. But John Stuart Mill, the most subtle and acute of his partial disciples, was an idealist, an admirer of Ferrier's system, and liberal in its praise; and yet by his destructive logical analysis he resolves existence into a " permanent possibility of sensation." Thus much may be of use by way of introduction to the three papers that follow. The battle of the Scottish Philosophy has raged round perception, and it is well to ascertain where the standard stood in this hard-fought field, though the

flag that waved from it may have been a mere rag, of
value only as a symbol.

SIR WILLIAM HAMILTON.

Since Sir William Hamilton's death—which happened on 6th May 1856 — his name has grown to
be more .widely famous than it was in his lifetime.
The attacks of Mr John Stuart Mill and other opponents, not less than the eulogies of friends and disciples,
have helped to prolong and extend human interest in
the life and labours of the great Professor of Logic and
Metaphysics in the University of Edinburgh.   Known
first to a few acquaintances as a devourer of old books
and master of Greek, Latin, and medieval lore; next,
and still only to a few, as a critic of philosophers and
destroyer of pseudo - philosophies in the 'Edinburgh
Review'; then to his students as a most resolute,
stimulating, severely intellectual, climber of the highest icy Alpine peaks of speculation, and guide thereon ;
a man who loved and sought after truth as if he had
loved truth ever, and her only ; a teacher who believed
his favourite dogma, " On earth there is nothing great
but man : in man there is nothing great but mind ; "
and latterly as a theologian, who fully and deliberately
accepted " faith as the evidence of things not seen,"
and who maintained, notwithstanding St Paul's de-
clarations to the men of Athens, that " the last and
highest consecration of all true religion must be an

altar to the unknown and unknowable God,"—he has left a name which will abide as long as Scottish philosophy is of any interest to mankind, and which will probably provoke inquiry as to what manner of man he was for several centuries to come. To gratify human curiosity about him is the object of a Memoir[1] which has been carefully put together by his old pupil, Professor Veitch, of Glasgow, out of materials furnished by his family and many friends; conspicuous among whom are Mr Thomas Carlyle, Mr George Moir, and the Rev. Dr Cairns of Berwick; and it is our present object to gratify to some extent (and it may be to incite to a larger extent) curiosity about him, and about this faithful and elaborate biography of him, the reading of which we should desire to encourage rather than supersede.

The subject of this biography, who was named in his youth William Stirling Hamilton, was born in No. 1 of the Professors' Quadrangle of the College of Glasgow, on 8th March 1788, and was the son of William Hamilton, Professor of Anatomy and Botany, and of Elizabeth Stirling his wife, the daughter of a Glasgow merchant, who claimed descent from the Stirlings of Cadder. His grandfather, Dr Thomas Hamilton, occupied the same Chair before his father, and was a partner in practice of Dr John Moore, the author of 'Zeluco,' and father of Sir John Moore. His father died at the early age of thirty-two, leaving

[1] Memoir of Sir William Hamilton. By Professor Veitch. William Blackwood & Sons.

him and his younger brother Thomas, who afterwards wrote 'Cyril Thornton,' to the care of their accomplished mother, from whom, in great measure, William inherited his good looks—particularly his fine dark eyes—as also his more remarkable mental endowments. Humour was one of the gifts of his father's family; but that one descended chiefly upon his brother, and was exercised by him with known results. Other inheritances of a more material, if less valuable kind, had once belonged to that family in the shape of an estate at Airdrie and the estate of Preston; but they had passed away before it became Hamilton's father's turn to possess them, and the outward resources of the family had then been contracted to skill in the medical profession and the Glasgow Chair of Anatomy. There was, however, an unsaleable item of inheritance of which tradition kept record, and that was the baronetcy of Preston and Fingalton, which had been in abeyance for a hundred years. The boy William, when he grew to be a man, hunted out the truth of that tradition; and proved himself, after he became an advocate, to be in fact the heir-male of Sir Robert Hamilton of Preston, who led the Covenanters at Drumclog and Bothwell Bridge, and as such entitled to the designation of "Sir William Hamilton, Bart."

Twenty-five years before Hamilton's birth, Dr Reid had succeeded Adam Smith in the Chair of Moral Philosophy in the University of Glasgow; and when Hamilton was tottering about the "smoky" college square there as an infant, Dr Reid was tottering about

it also as an old worn-out professor, who taught by an
assistant, and whose day's work in the world was done
—done, at least, as well as *he* could do it, and that was
not very well, as it was the fate of the child in after-
years to experience. Glasgow was not, in 1788, so like
its modern self as it is like modern St Andrews. It
had then a sort of simple academic life about it, and
merry Anderston and Hodge-Podge Clubs, at which
it was possible to be comfortable with hen-broth and
whisky, and happy in free and jocular conversation.
The reign of smoke and mammon, of which Watt and
Adam Smith were the prophets, had not begun to
begin. How the little boy William grew up, how
he played with his dogs, and toddled down to the
Molendinar with his nurse—who may have done court-
ship on its banks in its clear transparent days before
it began to look like a tributary of Styx—and whether
Dr Reid ever patted his head and gave him sweeties
or not, are all left to conjecture. It is, however, told
that he went to a public school in Glasgow; that he
entered the Latin class of a Mr James Gibson, and
remained with him for four years; that he then entered the Latin and Greek classes at the University;
that he was not in these earliest teens specially distinguished for intellect, but was rather more remarkable for gymnastics and mischief; that he lived in the
manse of Mid-Calder, and learned to swim and leap
and study there, under Dr Sommers's kindly and intelligent care; that he did open up mentally so far as to
attain the highest place in the Logic and Moral classes

at Glasgow University; that he chose, or had chosen for
him, medicine as his profession, and spent the winter of
1806 at the College of Edinburgh in studying, or trying
to study, medicine (we believe in actual study, for he
had a keen relish for physiology and anatomy, and
knew them well—at least he knew more about them
than most doctors do), and also in buying old books
and in reading them in his wild, confused, insatiable
way; and that in May 1807 (encouraged thereto by
ambition or his mother, or both, and assisted by a
Glasgow Snell Exhibition) he went to Balliol College,
Oxford, and so drifted away from medicine for ever,
except as a sceptical denouncer of the science and
practice thereof as dangerous to mankind.—(See 'Discussions,' second edition, p. 256.)

His life at Oxford seems to have been the happy
life of an ardent, high-aspiring, solitary student. He
had several friends there, who have helped to cast
some light upon these industrious days and nights.
Lockhart, who followed two years after from Glasgow, was one of them. In 'Reginald Dalton' he
has recorded some of his Oxford observations, and in
particular has sketched Mr Powell, Hamilton's only
and very temporary tutor, under the name of Daniel
Barton—a strange recluse, who never appeared in
hall, or in chapel, or in academical dress, and held
no counsel with any human being, beyond giving a
few lessons to Hamilton. Hamilton and Lockhart
were fast friends, and they continued friends for many
years, until some untold quarrel in Edinburgh dis-

severed their friendly relations, respect evidently
remaining on both sides, not unmixed with regret.
Neither ever told the cause of separation. Hamilton
would not speak of it at all; and Lockhart, though he
often began to tell, never finished the narration. From
our knowledge of the two men, we have no hesitation
in concluding that the fault was probably Lockhart's,
and due not to malice against his friend, but to some
necessity of his position as the scorpion of 'Blackwood,'
"who delighteth to sting the faces of men;" and that
his act was trivial in itself, but assumed an exaggerated
importance from Hamilton's extremely delicate sense
of honour. To the best of our judgment, Lockhart
had not a bad heart. That at least was the opinion
of the late John Ramsay M'Culloch, who was at one
time persistently abused by the 'Blackwood' wits, and
pre-eminently by Lockhart, and who became quite
reconciled to Lockhart in the latter years of his life,
and used to speak of him with more kindness than
could have been believed possible to exist between
two literary foes, who had both proved so much
capacity for hatred. A similar opinion was entertained by John Sterling, another acute observer of
human character, as can be read in Carlyle's life of
him. Professor Veitch mentions a tradition to the
effect that Hamilton, as Lockhart's friend, was present
at the concoction of "the Chaldee MS.," and contributed a verse. We do not think there is the least
truth in this tradition, and we decline to believe it
unless Hamilton himself actually said it. When Pro-

fessor Ferrier edited the 'Noctes Ambrosianæ,' he had
before him the original MS. of that celebrated contribution to "Old Ebony," and it was plain to him that
the original conception of it belonged to Hogg, and
that he was the author of the greater part of the early
half of it; but that the latter parts of it were written
by Wilson and Lockhart. Hamilton is almost the
only Whig that is spoken of in it with respect. Him
it happily describes as "the great black eagle of the
desert, whose cry is as the sound of an unknown
tongue, and whose dwelling is in the tombs of the
wise men." But it is incredible that an honourable
gentleman like Hamilton was present at the concoction
of a satire which ridiculed and exposed even the personal infirmities of all his political allies, and many
of his literary associates.

Other two of Hamilton's Oxford friends, Mr Christie
and Mr Traill, both barristers, have furnished reminiscences of him. Both write delicately and gracefully,
and express an admiration which has a fine lingering
glow of youth and college friendship about it, and is
manifestly sincere. From Mr Traill's paper we pick
a glimpse of

HAMILTON AT HIS STUDIES.

"At the period of my entrance at Balliol, Hamilton was
in the second year of his residence. His habits of study
were then confirmed, though somewhat irregular. His
manner of reading was characteristic. He had his table,

chairs, and generally his floor, strewed with books; and you might find him in the midst of this confusion studying with his foot on a chair, poising one great folio on his knee, with another open in his hand. His mode of 'tearing out the entrails' of a book, as he termed it, was remarkable. A perusal of the preface, table of contents, and index, and a glance at those parts which were new to him (which were few), were all that was necessary. It was by this facility in acquiring knowledge, and his great faculty in retaining it, that he was able, in the short period of his undergraduateship, to become the most learned Aristotelian in Oxford. In addition to the usual Oxford course of the ethics, rhetoric, and poetics, and the politics and economics, he had studied the analytical, physical, and metaphysical treatises, and the history of animals, and had consulted all the principal commentators. His reputation as an Aristotelian collected a large audience in the schools at his examination. Few of them were capable of estimating the amount of his learning; and to judge from their style of examination, the examining masters themselves seemed to feel his superiority. Still his examination, in the Oxford sense of the word, was not a brilliant one. Though a sound and even learned scholar, his was not the kind of scholarship that told in an Oxford examination. His early education in Scotland had not been fashioned after the model of an English public school. He wrote Latin prose with ease and correctness, but he was not in the practice of verse-writing—not that he was without a thorough knowledge of metres and of the niceties of the languages. Taken altogether, his examination, both for scholarship and science, has never been surpassed. His reading was not confined to the ordinary college course; it embraced also the learning of the period of the Reformation, and of the fourteenth and fifteenth

Q

centuries. His attention was at this period turned to medicine as a profession, and the early writers on this branch of science formed part of his study. We may well be surprised when we consider this amount of labour, and remember that it was the spontaneous and unassisted effort of his own mind."

These Oxford studies and distinctions seem to have lifted him above contentment with the choice of medicine as his profession in life, and to have led him in his difficulty to select in preference the profession of advocate. The exchange was one that could be well justified to reason. He had in rarely exampled perfection all the highest intellectual and moral qualities that ought to combine to make a great lawyer and "high priest of justice." For industry no Scotch advocate of this century could surpass him; and for strength of memory and power of distinction, and of exact expression, he had probably no equal. But, alas! it is not exact memory that is always useful at the Scottish or any other bar; sometimes judicious forgetfulness is more necessary. It is not always exact logic that will serve the purpose. The ideal advocate and the real advocate, at least the really successful advocate, are very different characters. Success is more often due to weakness than to strength, and to those low qualities that serve as a substitute for strength among animals and men. The truth is, the practice of the Scottish bar can teach a great man much that he will not readily learn elsewhere; but it will seldom if ever support

him. It had little or no bread to give to Sir Walter
Scott, or John Wilson, or Lockhart. The conditions
surrounding it are such that it will never yield its
highest remuneration and honours to a truly great
man till the end of time. He is unfitted by nature
to convince commonplace men on the bench; and
unluckily the majority of Judges are and always
will be—very rare instances excepted—little above
commonplace. Nor can a great scholar or a great
thinker ever secure the confidence of the vulgar, who
are often lower than commonplace. The common
litigant, the common W.S. or S.S.C., is incapable of
understanding true merit which is a grade or two
higher than his own, and to his mind genius is nearly
as dangerous as absolute lunacy. Therefore it is that,
though Sir W. Hamilton chose his profession of law
on solid grounds of theoretical reason, he failed in the
practical result. He had more real intellect than any
Scotch Judge of his day, and yet he solicited (having
written a characteristically candid and manly letter to
" My dear Rutherfurd," then Lord Advocate, begging
him, who among holders of his high office was certainly more capable to listen and understand than
most) in vain for an Inner House clerkship—such as
was held by Walter Scott, and for which some knowledge of law and penmanship, but next to no special
faculty, is required beyond the faculty of keeping
awake, and not snoring or otherwise making a noise.

He passed to the bar in 1813, and did in the course
of years obtain a moderate practice. There are always

a fair sprinkling of the members of the College of
Justice capable of appreciating to some not altogether
inadequate extent a man like him. He had the good
fortune, moreover, to pass in the days of written
pleadings, before learning and exact argument were
superseded by deluges of confident talk and gusts of
wind. He had friends in Jeffrey, in Cockburn, and
in Cranstoun, all distinctly smaller men, but all men
of very high intellect (Cockburn's humour, indeed, rose
to genius), and all men capable of estimating the intellectual strength and vast erudition of Hamilton, for
they were all gifted with metaphysical subtlety and
logical powers of no common order, though they were
more capable of doing dexterous common work than
he was. They and others loyally helped him to the
Professorship of Civil History in 1821, to the Crown
appointment of Solicitor of Teinds in 1832, and to the
Chair of Logic in July 1836. For appointing him to
the Chair of Logic, however, be all honour paid to the
Edinburgh Town Council of that day, and especially
to Mr Adam Black, who stamped upon the lying
religious cavils of the minority with the force of a
giant. Eighteen of that old Town Council, which is
now remembered for little except that vote, supported
Sir William, and fourteen supported Isaac Taylor, the
author of 'The Natural History of Enthusiasm,' a
book of nebulous eloquence, which might and should
have helped its author, had he been otherwise eligible,
to some handsome church preferment, but which ought
never to have been referred to as other than indicating

disqualification for a Chair of Logic, seeing that it is a
book which could never have proceeded from a logical
mind, or from one capable of reaching or even going
direct to the centres of belief.

A few other dates fall to be filled into the years
between his call to the bar and his election to the
Logic Chair. In 1816, in consequence pretty much
of his own investigations in the Register House and
elsewhere, he was adjudged heir-male of Sir R. Hamilton of Preston, who had died in 1701. In 1820, he
was a candidate for the Edinburgh Chair of Moral
Philosophy, but was defeated by the Tory influence
of the brilliant and poetic John Wilson—perhaps in
the end to the advantage of both; for Wilson certainly
helped Hamilton to the Logic Chair, and there he, at
least, was the right man in the right place. On
January 13, 1821, he accompanied Cranstoun to a
Lanark county meeting with Whiggish intentions,
which were carried out against the Ministry of the
day; and he contributed a report of the proceedings
to the 'Scotsman'—so far as we know his first and
his last newspaper report. In January 1827, there
occurred the death of his mother, who had lived with
him in Edinburgh for ten or eleven years, and who
was a woman well worthy to be the mother and the
trusted friend of such a son. Her death left him
miserable and desolate, and he continued in a measure
homeless until 31st March 1829, when he married
Miss Marshall, his cousin, and once more escaped
from loneliness, and found in his wife a helpmeet

such as few men and far fewer philosophers have
ever found—a constant companion—a steady check
upon idle speculations and aimless roving through
the infinite—a monitor who did not allow him to
forget in discursive reading that a lecture or an
article must be written by an hour or a day—and
an amanuensis who wrote out for the printer all his
compositions that have ever seen the light. Up to the
time of his marriage he had not printed anything, and
does not appear to have written anything except entries
in commonplace-books and letters; but that event con-
curring with Mr Macvey Napier's appointment to the
editorship of the ' Edinburgh Review,' and the persua-
sions of the new editor, probably seconded by those of
Lady Hamilton, induced him to execute for the number
published in October 1829 his demolition of Cousin's
doctrine of the Infinite-Absolute in an article in which
lofty thought and severe dignified philosophic eloquence
reach the highest level he ever attained. This was
succeeded, exactly a year after, by his celebrated article
on the Philosophy of Perception—an article which,
both in language and in thought, occupies a lower level
than the former, but which, according to Professor
Ferrier, a capable and impartial judge, contains a
greater amount of condensed philosophic learning
than is to be found in the same number of pages in
the English language. Articles on Logic, Idealism,
the *Epistolæ Obscurorum Virorum*, Mathematics, Classical Learning, and University Patronage, followed
before the Logic professorship arrived—all well-known

articles either in the 'Review' or in his volume of
'Discussions,' into which the 'Review' articles are
collected. That on Patronage had spoken of the
Edinburgh Town Council with a freedom of contempt
which it required some magnanimity to forgive, and
which has since borne fruits which one magnanimous
act, one conscientious and satisfactory appointment,
could not avert. For dragging Sir William into print,
and, in effect, creating him Professor of Logic, and
giving his thoughts and learning to the world, not a
little credit is due to Macvey Napier. His letters,
published in this volume, show that he was a man of
parts and insight, who knew what could be got out of
a contributor, and who could also scold a little when
he had to deal with an unpunctual contributor who,
like Sir William, wrote too long articles, and sent
them in too late.

Sir William's literary and philosophic life, as it presented itself during his unemployed or half-employed
advocate years to literary and philosophic eyes, can be
best told by quoting in part a letter of reminiscences
by Thomas Carlyle, written obviously for publication
in this book, in which, after erroneously placing his
residence in Gabriel's Road, where he never lived, and
puzzling about when and how he first heard of him,
dating it about 1820, he goes on to depict graphically
(except as to small-pox, which is another mistake of
memory or of eyesight, rare if not unexampled in so
accurate an observer and narrator)—

"It was years after this—perhaps four or five—before

I had the honour of any personal acquaintance with Sir
William; his figure on the street had become familiar, but
I forget, too, when this was first pointed out to me; and
cannot recollect even when I first came to speech with him,
which must have been by accident and his own voluntary
favour, on some slight occasion, probably at the Advocates'
Library, which was my principal or almost sole literary
resource (lasting thanks to *it*, alone of Scottish institutions!) in those obstructed, neglectful, and grimly forbid-
ding years.   Perhaps it was in 1824 or 1825.   I recollect
right well the bright, affable manners of Sir William,
radiant with frank kindliness, honest humanity, and intelligence ready to help; and how completely prepossessing
they were.   A fine, firm figure of middle height; one of
the finest cheerfully serious human faces, of square, solid,
and yet rather *aquiline* type, a little marked with small-
pox—marked, not deformed, but rather the reverse (like a
rock rough-hewn, not spoiled by polishing); and a pair of
the beautifullest kindly beaming hazel eyes, well open, and
every now and then with a lambency of smiling fire in
them, which I always remember as if with trust and gratitude.   Our conversation did not amount to much in those
times; mainly about German books, philosophies, and
persons, it is like; and my usual place of abode was in
the country then.   Letter to him, or from, I do not recollect there was ever any, though there might well enough
have been, had either of us been prone that way.

"In the end of 1826, I came to live in Edinburgh under
circumstances new and ever memorable to me: from then
till the spring of 1828—and, still more, once again in
1832-33, when I had brought my little household to
Edinburgh for the winter—must have been the chief
times of personal intercourse between us.   I recollect
hearing much more of him, in 1826 and onward, than

formerly : to what depths he had gone in study and philosophy ; of his simple, independent, meditative habits,
ruggedly athletic modes of exercise, fondness for his big
dog, &c. &c.: everybody seemed to speak of him with
favour, those of his immediate acquaintance uniformly
with affectionate respect.

"I did not witness, much less share in, any of his swim-
ming or other athletic prowesses. I have once or twice
been on long walks with him in the Edinburgh environs,
oftenest with some other companion, or, perhaps, even two,
whom he had found vigorous and worthy : pleasant walks
and abundantly enlivened with speech from Sir William.
He was willing to talk of any humanly interesting subject ;
and threw out sound observations upon any topic started :
if left to his own choice, he circled and gravitated, naturally
into subjects that were his own, and were habitually
occupying him — of which I can still remember animal
magnetism and the German revival of it, not yet known
of in England, was one that frequently turned up. Mesmer
and his 'four Academicians,' he assured us, had *not* been
the finale of that matter ; that it was a matter tending
into realities far deeper and more intricate than had been
supposed ; of which, for the rest, he did not seem to augur
much good, but rather folly and mischief. Craniology,
too, he had been examining ; but freely allowed us to
reckon that an extremely ignorant story. On German
bibliography and authors, especially of the learned kind—
Erasmus, Ruhnken, Ulrich von Hutten—he could descant
copiously, and liked to be inquired of. On Kant, Reid,
and the metaphysicians, German and other, though there
was such abundance to have said, he did not often speak ;
but politely abstained rather, when not expressly called on.

"He was finely social and human in these walks or
interviews. Honest frankness, friendly veracity, cour-

ageous trust in humanity and in you, were charmingly
visible. His talk was forcible, copious, discursive, careless, rather than otherwise; and, on abstruse topics, I
observed, was apt to become embroiled and revelly, much less
perspicuous and elucidative than with a little deliberation
he could have made it. 'The fact is,' he would often say:
and then plunging into new circuitous depths and distinctions, again on a new grand, 'The fact is,' and still again
—till what the essential 'fact' might be was not a little
obscure to you. He evidently had not been engaged in
speaking these things, but only in thinking them, for his
own behoof, not yours. By lucid questioning you could
get lucidity from him on any topic. Nowhere did he give
you the least notion of his not understanding the thing
himself; but it lay like an unwinnowed threshing-floor,
the corn-grains, the natural chaff, and somewhat even of
the straw, still unseparated there. This sometimes would
befall, not only when the meaning itself was delicate or
abstruse, but also if several were listening, and he doubted
whether they could understand. On solid realistic points
he was abundantly luminous; promptitude, solid sense,
free-flowing intelligibility always the characteristics. The
tones of his voice were themselves attractive, physiognomic
of the man : a strong, carelessly melodious tenor voice, the
sound of it betokening seriousness and cheerfulness; occasionally something of slightly remonstrative was in the
undertones, indicating, well in the background, possibilities
of virtuous wrath and fire; seldom anything of laughter, of
levity never anything: thoroughly a serious, cheerful, sincere,
and kindly voice, with looks corresponding. In dialogue, face
to face with one he trusted, his speech, both voice and words,
was still more engaging; lucid, free, persuasive, with a bell-
like harmony, and from time to time, in the bright eyes, a
beaming smile, which was the crown and seal of all to you."

Writing lectures, when it required to be set about in earnest, was not an easy task for Sir William. He went to the country to prepare for the winter session, but he came back with a great deal of fresh learning in his mind and next to nothing written down for lectures. He thought of postponing the commencement of his course, but was advised against that; and, necessity compelling, he delivered his introductory— and a noble introductory it is—and for the rest of the winter, and next winter, delivered on three days a-week lectures written out by himself roughly in the course of the night before, and copied by Lady Hamilton, or dictated to her, the process being rarely finished before five in the morning, and sometimes only a few minutes before the class hour, which was one o'clock. On the other days, he conducted class examinations, getting from the better and bolder students *vivâ voce* reports of the substance of the lectures, or of their very words; or oral abstracts of readings in books bearing on the subject-matter of the lectures— a method of examination which worked well with him, but would probably break down into stealing help from notes and note-books in a less commanding presence than his. How great, how popular, how much esteemed a professor he was, all the world knows. If any vulgar fractions of the world are still ignorant and desire to be enlightened, there are intelligent and enthusiastic testimonies in this book from the Rev. Dr Cairns of Berwick, from Professor Baynes of St Andrews, and from Professor Veitch himself (who is not the least competent of the three), that will help to dispel their ignorance in so far as it can be dispelled by description, which it never, indeed, can effectually be. Fortunate beyond expression or comparison were the students who looked on and listened to him and his contemporary, Professor Wilson. They saw two of the finest, strongest men, both physically and intellectually, that had ever lived in Scotland or on this planet. They heard eloquent discourse on the grandest topics of human thought, spoken in tones that kindled into life the noblest youthful aspirations, and illuminated with glances that split the rocks surrounding the everyday prosaic world.

In 1844 Sir William was struck by paralysis, which completely disabled his right side, and affected the muscles of the tongue and throat so severely that he required to be fed with the stomach - pump. His mind, however, was left intact, and the day after his seizure he was irrepressibly ready to communicate his physiological meditations on, and views of, his own case, and its peculiarities, to his medical attendant, Dr Douglas Maclagan, with a frankness and acuteness not lost on that auditor. He recovered steadily, though slowly, but he never afterwards regained the use of his right limbs. His class was taught for him during the winter of 1844-45 by Mr J. F. Ferrier, afterwards the celebrated Professor of Moral Philosophy in St Andrews, who had grown to be one of Sir William's most intimate friends—a frequent companion in long walks, an enthusiastic explorer in

speculative fields, and a steady contradicter in regard
to Berkeley the Absolute and Dr Reid, for which latter
entity he had a hearty contempt, but was, nevertheless, so warmly attached to his disciple that he walked
under Hamilton's window on the street during the
night of his paralytic stroke when life was in suspense, silently watching the movements in the house
in his anxiety, yet refraining from making his presence known. After his tedious recovery, Hamilton
buckled to his edition of Reid, which he had been
annotating at for years, and it was published in 1846,
as far as the middle of a sentence a little past the
middle of Note D. The 'Discussions,' upon the
Appendix to which he bestowed great labour, were
published in 1852, and reached a second edition in
1853. In that year, at the request of Miss Stewart's
trustees, he undertook to edit a collected edition of
Dugald Stewart's works; and looking over the proof-
sheets of it with Miss Petre, who was governess in the
family, was the last of his regular literary tasks. The
autumn of 1855 he spent at Auchtertool, in Fifeshire,
and there he wrote some fragments on Scottish philosophy, which were intended for the Memoir of
Stewart, and which are printed at the end of his
Metaphysical Lectures. He left his Edinburgh home
no more until next May, when he was summoned to
his long home in that undiscovered country towards
which his thoughts in life had often strayed.

To Sir William's reputation as a philosopher this
volume does not add much of moment. Indeed it

does not alter his philosophical character materially
from that to be gathered from his works previously
published.   Some of the processes of growth, however,
are shown or suggested in the records of methodical
industry expended upon his commonplace-books, large
and small, and by hints of the irregular, impetuous,
irresistible style in which his "demon of energy" tore
out the hearts of books and the available or memorable contents of libraries.   His Covenanting ancestor
could not have pursued Claverhouse at Drumclog with
more eagerness than he pursued forgotten opinions
and controversies of much older date than Drumclog.
In his actions, the cold stately indifference of a philosopher did not appear.   He wrote philosophy, but he
lived the life of flesh and blood, and blood so hot, too,
that mankind may well take an interest in him.   So
much we could guess from his writings; but now
learn distinctly from this book, which does set his
character as a man in a pleasant and lovable kind of
light, and helps a stranger to understand how all who
came near him, whether students, or women, or children, were spellbound and fascinated by him.   Haughty
he seemed to strangers, haughty to some extent he
must have been, but not so much so as to prevent him
from making elaborate kites for boys and flying them;
or from vaulting over garden-walls and leaping five-
bar gates in the region of Oxford; or from haunting
old-book shops, and auctions, and mending old books;
or from talking frankly, candidly, and unreservedly to
all intelligent listeners of every age and sex.   In the

matter of affection, he certainly was not by any means
demonstrative.   Indeed he seems to have been so conscious of sincerity in his affection, and so well satisfied
that he could not be doubted or misunderstood by his
mother and others dear to him, that he makes no pro-
testations or professions whatever.   His letters to his
mother show nothing so clearly as that he trusted her
fully, and was ready to accept of gentle reproofs for
extravagance in old-book buying or the like, and of
maternal blessings, with equal composure and freedom
from fear.   Hypocrisy in all its manifestations was
obviously far from him, as indeed was every other
moral infirmity so far as we can see, except a rather
headlong indignation, which, however, broke out more
in his writing than in his living speech and conduct,
and with greater vehemence, perhaps, after his illness
than before.   His capacities for hatred must have
been great, and would in all probability have given
more overt proof of their existence had they not been
restrained by a lofty philosophical contempt for everything likely to provoke either indignation or hatred.
Of other strong emotions he gives no conspicuous sign.
We infer some other emotions must have been with
him often too deep for either words or tears.   Certain
it is, he could not have secured so much love from
others if he had been devoid of it himself—if he had
not given as much as he received; for the man who
does not buy it with the false coin of the busybody,
or the hypocrite from the easily deceived, must pay
for it with that untold gold which true instinct alone

can recognise and reciprocate, and value as it ought to be valued.

What Sir William was as a thinker can and must be learned from his writings, more especially from the 'Discussions.' The next conglomeration of his thought in importance, though not in method and still less in articulate expression, is his edition of Reid with its Titanic appendices; and the next are his class lectures on Metaphysics and Logic, published in four volumes, and their valuable but amorphous appendices. What he was as a fierce devourer of books may be very clearly inferred also from these very chaotic materials. He had sought to compass and conquer all speculative knowledge; but death came while the spoils lay in disorder on his desk, or in his large commonplace-books, or in his enormous appendices, which are little other than store-houses or lumber-rooms, only a little swept and garnished. Others to come may appropriate and utilise, none can fail to moralise a little upon his ambitious and irregular, and almost of necessity incompleted labours.

These mixed masses and fragments of speculation, collected and original, or at least turned to original purposes and lit by new lights, are full of instruction and thought, and the stimulus to thinking. They are quarries out of which metaphysical systems may be built, if the fit builders were born. But they suggest a thought which is not in them. Why should this great man have left so much work half begun or half done? We can see that far smaller men have

worked out to the end of their hopes and powers
systems of philosophy; and we have seen the *pros* and
cons about insoluble problems duly set forth on eight
days' notice, and the infinite supposed to be set in
order and packed into a few pages of foolscap in a
month, by the weakest, shallowest of mortals, under
the angelic guidance of vanity and dulness. But the
mind of this mighty thinker is working incessantly
during a moderately long life over the wide domain of
accumulated human knowledge and meditation, and he
cannot come to a conclusion. Not he, indeed!—and
his life is a verification of his philosophy, which says
that "We can never escape from ignorance. The pursuit of knowledge is but a course between two ignor-
ances, as human life is itself only a wayfaring from
grave to grave. . . . Science is a drop: nescience is
the ocean in which that drop is whelmed." So he
believed, taught by experience, and by Socrates,
Seneca, St Chrysostom, Tertullian, St Augustin, and
a hundred sages, who had each come to believe for
himself that

"All that we know, is nothing can be known,"—

a creed which, however sublime and however capable
of teaching religious humility, is not the best for helping to do the utmost possible while life lasts. We
point to these fragments and to this creed, which
makes life itself a fragment, not on purpose to lament
the want of work achieved by Sir W. Hamilton—for
he did the work of a hundred remarkable men—but to
call attention to the connection between a man's creed

R

and his performance, the one here being the reflection
of the other. Probably we may at times have lamented that Sir William Hamilton had not more resolute faith in himself, and that he did not build up
his own philosophical thoughts into a self-contained
edifice instead of piling such ponderous props about the
turf shieling of Dr Reid and the elegant garden-house
of Dugald Stewart. On the other hand, we can see
that in this annotative tendency of his there lies the
compensation that but for it he would not have wandered as he did over all human speculation, and become, as it were, the annotator and arranger of the
philosophy of the world. Had he written the history
of philosophy, what a magazine of learning it would
have been ! With what clearness principles and doctrines would have been expounded, with what crushing force errors would have been exposed ! It would
have been a monument of erudition and acumen such
as these islands never saw, and are not likely ever to
see ; for they have waited several hundred years now,
and have only received from the destinies one Sir
William Hamilton.

What we have obtained, however, we shall be
thankful for, and the historian of philosophy who
will not be greatly indebted to his labours, will not
do his own work well. Taken altogether, his ' Discussions,' Notes to Reid, &c., and lectures, constitute a
mass of materials, critical, historical, and speculative,
such as no British philosopher ever accumulated. For
him they vindicate the foremost place among British

philosophers for learning; for acuteness and lucidity of style he is only surpassed, if surpassed, by Berkeley, and Hume, and Ferrier; and for candour, sincerity, and red-hot logical power, burning fiercely through philosophical dogmatism, conceit, stupidity, and error, he is unsurpassed. His sentences roll together like molten lava, and in our country we must look for such intensity of expression and of conviction in other regions than those of philosophy, which are generally cold, calm, and obscure.

His writing and thinking are to be found at their best in the 'Discussions,' which are the literary produce of some ten years of his prime. Originally published in the 'Edinburgh Review' they were twice republished in his lifetime (of course with a colossal appendix, containing enough to furnish out several volumes for an author less set upon the terse and the essential), and they have been extensively bought, and read, and admired, and plagiarised. They fill a volume of 710 pages, and they contain the essence of an Alexandrian library. No book in the English language, or probably in any language, of the same dimensions, contains so much condensed thought and condensed learning; and hardly any philosophic utterances—except, perhaps, Fichte's 'Vocation of Man,' and an occasional optimistic inspiration of Emerson—can so effectually lift the mind into the clear dry ether of intellect and of uncreated light.

As a philosopher he takes up a modest position. He reckons man's faculties finite, and therefore unable to grasp, to *comprehend*, the infinite, for the less cannot contain the greater. In consequence, he has a deadly feud with the ontology of Cousin, and Schelling, and Hegel. To his mind the transcendentalists of Germany have been ploughing, sowing, and harrowing acres of cloud-land for a harvest of dreams. All our knowledge he declares relative—the consummation of knowledge, a "learned ignorance." We are conscious only in and through limitation, therefore we cannot comprehend the infinite; we cannot establish the science—the *nescience*—of man on an identity with the omniscience of God.

He turns from the ambitious philosophers who would penetrate the mysteries of being and compass the unconditioned, to consort with the unambitious philosophers of "common sense," in whom alone he sees refuge from scepticism. His own consciousness shall be his philosophical Bible. In his discussion on the theories of perception, he classifies them according to the belief they contain in the veracity of conscious- ness. And "if that veracity be admitted uncondition- ally; if the intuitive knowledge of mind and matter, and the consequent reality of their antithesis, be taken as truths, to be explained if possible," but, explained or not, to be held paramount to all doubt,—the doctrine is established which he calls "natural realism," and believes true in preference to all the others. He be- lieves the twofold testimony of consciousness; that mind is, and that matter is—mind with its thoughts, matter with its properties; and does not, with the idealist, hold that mind is conscious of itself alone and nothing external,—nor with the materialist, that mind is blank and non-existent without matter—is, in fact, nothing but matter. Thus he establishes, on the evidence of consciousness—which is the basis of all evidence—the independent existence of mind and of an external world, evading the consequences of Berkeley, who sublimated the latter, and of Hume, who threw doubt upon the existence of both.

Modest as a philosopher, Sir William is not so modest as a logician. Logic is the laws of *human* thinking, and as they are within man's intellectual reach, it, as a science, will bear probing and sifting to the bottom. And certainly Sir William does probe and sift the doctrines of logicians with vigour—sometimes with vengeance. Poor Archbishop Whately becomes very small in his hands, and so does Augustus de Morgan. Better had the divine stuck to sermons, and the mathematician to the calculus. In fine, he discovers all logicians since Aristotle to be in error, and, strange to tell (only for once, however), Aristotle himself, in maintaining the doctrine that "the predicate in affirmative propositions can only be quantified as a particular." To remedy this defect—"to place the keystone in the Aristotelic arch"—he has devised what he calls "the thorough-going quantification of the predicate"— which, however, is too technical for description here. Many a great man—Carlyle, for instance—values logic at less than nothing: all such, and hundreds beside, will excuse the boldness which does not scruple

to believe Sir William Hamilton to be the greatest
logician that ever lived.

With our educational institutions his feud is nearly
as extensive as with our writers on logic. And it may
be reasonably supposed that a man who has himself
learned so much could give excellent counsel on this
matter of education, yearly growing in urgent importance; yet, singularly enough, what he has written on
this subject has been comparatively little attended to.
Though he was the first, in the pages of the 'Edinburgh
Review,' to call attention to the advances making in
Germany and France, and to give an alarm-note that
Britain was falling rearward in what was once a
national boast; and though he has anticipated nearly
all that has been since written on this vexed question,
he is seldom quoted with acknowledgment—seldom referred to as an authority; albeit it would be difficult
to name one more competent. Perhaps the true reason
is, that his statements are rather more plain than
pleasant for English vanity, and the changes proposed
too sweeping to be carried out conveniently for a century or two. He humours no caprice, tears the veil
from all rottenness and pretence, and would drive
rather than flatter his countrymen to the ways in
which they ought to go. With a bludgeon of blunt
honesty, he causes ignorant British conceit to stick to
its throne, instead of tilting it off adroitly with the sly,
thin wedge of a politician, who knows the inexpediency
of running in the teeth of prejudice, or knocking it
directly on the head.

In the two great English universities he discovers much to blame and little to praise. He elaborates a masterly argument to prove that mathematical studies are pernicious to the mind, and in support of his view quotes numerous high authorities, among whom Pascal, Goethe, Voltaire, Berkeley, Gibbon, Lichtenberg, and D'Alembert, rise conspicuous for their decisiveness, if not for their competence. Strengthened in his own convictions by their testimonies, he denounces mathematical Cambridge as a "slaughter-house of intellect" —often of body also; and points in sad triumph to its wrangler lists, averring that for one named there who is of mentionable service to society, there are ten illiterate incapables who are a burden to themselves. When Dr Whewell essays to defend his university— as is meet for "its most eminent member"—and states that high wranglers sometimes become great English lawyers, Sir William wheels round quickly, and gives him to understand that mathematics have disordered his own logical powers; that to infer the excellence of mathematical training from a man's success in law is to confound cause with antecedent, consequent with effect, to be guilty of the logical sophism, "*Post hoc, ergo propter hoc*"—which a person of Dr Whewell's parts should have discovered, had not mathematics blunted the fineness of his mental perceptions. Mathematics, Sir William believes, test the "bottom" of a student, his dogged workfulness, which is essential to success in law, exactly as hanging a terrier puppy up by the ear tests whether it be "of the right sort"; but

the mathematics do not make the lawyer any further
than the pain makes the hardy, tenacious dog. As a
manifest improvement for Cambridge, he proposed
many years ago the establishment of three triposes
of co-ordinate and independent honours; one for
philosophy, another for mathematics and physics, and
a third for classics, philology, and history. Since then,
three shams have been set up, not much for any good
purpose.   There is a classical tripos which requires
the absurd preliminary of a mathematical degree, and
a moral science tripos which gives no distinction or reward, and a physical science tripos which hardly deserves any. Often and again he denounces the present
system of things in both Cambridge and Oxford as
founded on perjury, and tolerated by neglect. From
his love for classics and for his *Alma Mater*, Oxford,
he had hopes of her reform, and thought her the university best, as also most susceptible of reform; but in
recent years he is forced " to contemplate nothing but
our universities one and all declining into popular
seminaries for a cultivation of the superficial, the
amusing, the palpable, the materially useful." Upon
all corruptions he is bitter, not forgetting that piece
of *vulgar* academic snobbism which makes "to pay
more, to learn less" the criterion of a—"gentleman!"
The poorly endowed universities of Scotland he speaks
of not without a kind of pity, and feels with all thinking men, that while the professions called learned (in
irony?) are so illiterate, no aid can come to them:
none, so long as roaring lungs are the grand essential

for the Church; none, so long as the examiners in medicine are more eager to receive fees than to reject incompetence.

For the education of the people he esteems the Prussian system better fitted than any other, with its normal schools for training teachers, comfortable provision for them, suitable schools and school furniture, aid for needy scholars; and gives his decided opinion in favour of compelling parents to send their children to the public schools, unless they can show that they are educated sufficiently in private. When he wrote, the Reform Bill had just passed, and he foresaw that, with an uneducated people, that Bill would be a curse to Britain, as it would make its rulers an ignorant, dangerous mob. Now, that does not require to be *foreseen*, and some remedy must soon be found, whether in imitating Prussia and France or not. From few quarters can so valuable suggestions be had as from Sir William Hamilton's 'Discussions'; and they may be consulted with advantage by the politician who wishes assistance and authoritative opinion, or by the pamphleteer who wishes to appear original and cannot afford it, as he will there find thoughts little known, and capable of extension, illustration, and enforcement.

Besides his 'Review' articles, Sir William published several controversial pamphlets — one, in particular, bearing upon the Disruption of the Church of Scotland in 1843. It bore the significant title, 'Be not Schismatics; be not Martyrs by Mistake,' and proved

to the Free Churchmen, with an amount of learning
wasted upon them, that their pet doctrine of "spiritual
independence" had been given up by all Protestants
as dangerous to civil freedom, and was properly a
doctrine of the Church of Rome. Of course he could
not be listened to, and the magnificent dream of Dr
Chalmers had to be realised—not without benefit to
Scotland, and not without harm, for it has given rise
to a good deal of cant, lying, hypocrisy, and persecution on both sides, and it is difficult to find a strong
Churchman who will not prefer his own dogma to
investigation, and often to truth.

As a student, so long as the bodily and mental constitution of man is what it is, Sir William will have
few peers and probably no superior. To imitate him
would be impossible for most. His habits of study
are mainly fitted for warning to all who value a healthy
existence. To intellectual work he gave his nights
rather than his days. When in health he habitually
forgot the fact that he had a body which required rest
and sleep, and in his occasional fits of working dispensed with both. From all we know, his habits of
study were incompatible with longevity. A methodical Kant meditates and reaches eighty; a Goethe, who
rises early, may write poetry not unimpassioned, and
outlive that long term of years; but a Schiller, who
toils at midnight, overtaxing his weary brain, dies
early. Down to within a fortnight of his death—
Hamilton, though an invalid without hope of recovery,
and guarding the little residue of life that remained

with anxious but not very enlightened care, was up at his studies regularly until three o'clock in the morning. Shall we say this mode of acquiring wisdom was not wise, be it ever so calculated to move admiration?

As a professor Sir William Hamilton was the right man in the right place. Other places reckoned higher in popular esteem he might have filled equally well, but in none could he have given to the intellectual life of Scotland that impulse which he gave from the Logic Chair. No Edinburgh professor within human memory was ever more devotedly admired, and in his days of strength more attentively listened to; not even Professor Wilson himself so stimulated to activity, and sustained an interest and attention so steady; for to tell the truth, Wilson's preparation was not always quite satisfactory, and his notes, written on the backs of old letters and other scraps, sometimes got into a confusion which his flashes of eloquence and of fun did not conceal from the quick eyes of his young disciples. When Wilson was at his best, though he might be discoursing extempore, he was very great, probably the highest of Scottish academic orators. As Hamilton read all his lectures, he was never unprepared or unequal, and he read superlatively well. Whether his double course of lectures may not have been too closely stereotyped may be open to question; but it is not open to any question that his best students made the substance of them matter of memory, and this they could not have done had not notes of the lectures, added to and amended into completeness, descended from one generation of students to another. What Wilson had chiefly to communicate was something that could not be put into note-books, the sympathetic inspiration which emanates from a man of genius, contagious, indescribable, irresistible, enlightening, devastating, elevating like fire from heaven. Hamilton, too, was a fountain of this more than electric influence, but it differed from Wilson's as imagination differs from reason.

In his latter years Sir William had grown so feeble and powerless that he could not walk without assistance. Though unable to speak clearly, and with difficulty intelligible to a stranger, he was daily in his class-room at the appointed hour during the session which closed in April 1856. In spite of destiny, almost, he stood resolutely to his post, with mind and will vigorous to the last, regardless of the feebleness of the body, and knowing well that there was no rest for him but in the grave. A more touching sight than that of his appearance in the class-room is seldom seen. Two men helped him to his chair. He read for a time in a faltering, choky voice, changed and broken from the clear, deep, steel-ringing, decisive tones of his years of strength. He handed his MS. to an assistant to read to the end of the hour; and sat still, majestically calm—not unlike the statue of Aristotle in the Spada Palace at Rome—the remains of a strong, handsome person, at once elegant and compact; with round, firm shoulders, slightly bent; head not very large, nor like a poetic dreamer's, covered with white wavy hair, not much thinned; with Grecian

profile and serene forehead, fine as a woman's, rising
from arching, shaggy eyebrows, deep underneath which
glowed piercing dark eyes, as if lit up from some far-off
fire, burning in haste the gathered fuel of ages. When
will the centuries present mankind with such another
spectacle in Scotland? That venerable sage, prematurely old, was the last of the Scotch philosophers.
In him Scotch philosophy, so called, has culminated
and ended. With him it will be remembered or forgotten.

IDEALISM.[1]

For several years physical science has been the rage
of our country. To this fashion a just pride in Bacon
has helped a little, and a keen appreciation of material
comforts has helped a great deal. These physical
sciences are so useful! Chemistry prints calicoes for
us, and lights our streets; electricity runs our mes-
sages; steam has endowed man with gigantic strength,
carries him along roads of iron at a rate out-speeding
the tempest, and urges his vessels to port despite the
winds and waves; and physical science presents some
sensible amount of collected facts and solid materials—
be they geological specimens, wayside weeds, or cockle-
shells—which are more considerable in general estimation than the possession of invisible realms in cloud-

---

[1] Institutes of Metaphysic : The Theory of Knowing and Being.
By James F. Ferrier, B.A. Oxon., Professor of Moral Philosophy at
St Andrews. William Blackwood & Sons, Edinburgh.—[Reprinted
from ' Dundee Advertiser,' 26th Jan. 1855.]

land. So the practical comfort-loving British have
tortured matter to obtain her secret modes of operation, which they call laws, and forgotten to some
extent the Lawgiver, to whom they give the traditional
name of God. It has been the life-work of some
great men to preach against this God-forsaken era,
with its beaverish mechanics, mammon-seeking, and
body-worship. And against exclusive devotion to
positive science, metaphysics, as a methodical exposition of the aspiration of our highest faculties,
raise a vehement protest. For this is a highway to
atheism. In spirit we recognise God, not in matter,
unless we are preconvinced that He must be manifest
in His works. Never, by aught that we perceive by
the senses, will we attain an idea of the spiritual.
Therefore, human curiosity and human aspiration
demand some science of the super-sensible, some inquiry into the region of pure thought and true
essences; for there only can we hope for solutions
of those riddles which the sphinx of the universe
incessantly proposes. Our knowledge is begirt with
mystery, which retreats as we advance, like the distant
horizon. New regions open up before us, ever fresh,
extensive, and untravelled. Poetry saw them afar off;
science determined their reality; and the ways and
arts of common life at last find them a solid resting-
place. But still there is something beyond, and the
old questions rise again and recur *in seculis*—Whence?
How? Whither? What is existence in itself? What is
matter? What is knowledge? What is truth?—and

each metaphysician answers them in his own way. But we are children looking for cities in the summer clouds, and no one can clearly perceive the castle turrets and the cathedral spires pointed out by his comrade. So has it been from the dawn of speculation; will it not be so to the setting of its sun? But though man is not born to solve all mysteries, he is born to try; and the trial makes him wiser whether he fail or succeed; and it gives him the delight of intellectual activity, which is the truest reward of intellectual effort. It is training; and to train man does nature seem designed, with its grim difficulties and inarticulate speech, or in itself it might have been very different.

To solve certain old problems is the purpose of these 'Institutes of Metaphysic'; particularly to answer the questions, "What is Being?" and "What is Knowledge?" To effect this, Professor Ferrier seeks for a starting-point, and finds that the question What is? cannot be answered until we have determined what alone we can and must know. Getting his problem into shape, accounting for the difficulty of so doing, and describing the principles upon which the system is to be worked out, takes up a long beautifully written introduction. The system professes to be one of necessary truth, like mathematics, and to be entirely built up on one self-evident proposition or axiom. Necessary truth is defined to be that the opposite of which is inconceivable, nonsensical, absurd, and is reckoned essential to a system of philosophy, which is the "attainment of truth by the *way of reason.*"

Three divisions arise in the system, called by Greek-derived names—Epistemology, or the theory of knowing; Agnoiology, or the theory of ignorance; and Ontology, or the theory of being. In the Epistemology the questions are answered which concern knowledge: First, What is the one constant, invariable, and essential factor in all knowing? and second, What is the variable factor in all knowing? The invariable factor is found to be Self, the "me" the *subject*—mind; the variable factor is the not-self, not-me, the objective thing or thought. And these two are maintained to be inseparable in the fundamental axiom (Prop. I.): "Along with whatever any mind knows, it must, as the ground or condition of its knowledge, have some cognisance of itself." Hence it follows, by strict logic, that subject plus object is the least that can be known —that matter *per se* is unknowable—that mind cannot be known to be material—that the absolute can be known and is known—and that the only thinkable independent universe is the universe in synthesis with some universal mind.

Because our ignorance is confessedly great, an investigation as to what we can be ignorant of is entered upon in the Agnoiology, which is a novelty in philosophy. It is there shown, that since, by its nature, ignorance is a defect, not an impossibility in knowledge, that we cannot be ignorant of the unknowable—that we can be ignorant of the knowable only; but as the knowledge is fixed to be subject in synthesis with some object, so also must the unit of ignorance be subject in synthesis with some object.

Then, in determining what absolute being is, there are three alternatives to be considered. There is, first, what we know; second, what we are ignorant of; and third, the unknowable, the inconceivable, which we can neither know nor be ignorant of. The last can be rejected, because being is quite conceivable; and therefore it must be either of the two former; but since they are identical—expressed by the term subject plus object—absolute being is both what we know and are ignorant of.

Such is this shortest of metaphysical systems in the shortest possible space; perhaps too short to be intelligible. We hope not, if it be read with care and patience; but we could not do more than touch the bald mountain-tops of this chain of demonstrations, and we leave it to our readers with our best advice and most cordial wishes to go and cull flowers of rhetoric and poetry in the interjacent valleys.

The results of the system are too numerous to mention in detail. Among the most important is the effectual demolition of materialism, the logical enthronement of mind over matter, and the demonstration of the existence of a God (which Clarke had failed in), an infinite and supreme and everlasting mind, in synthesis with all things. Those natural theologians who have been reduced to search Paley for a reason for their faith have some cause to be

s

grateful to the author, for the God which Paley constructs has never been reverenced by any human being.

The method of the book can be ill understood from description, but it seems too perfect for any subject which is non-mathematical and cannot be based upon a few fixed definitions and axioms. The main body of the system is laid down in a series of demonstrated propositions, and forms a sort of metaphysical Euclid. Spinoza had adopted this method in those wonderful works of his, which many men have abused without seeking to master or even read. Of course, the result in the 'Institutes' is very different from the Calvinistic pantheism of this disprover of human individuality and free will. Then each proposition is explained in a series of observations, and each is set over against the erroneous counter-propositions of psychology and common-sense. Thus truth and error are set face to face and throw light upon each other, and the reader can choose which he prefers: his bane and antidote are both before him. In this way very many erudite and interesting disquisitions on philosophy and philosophers are introduced, so as to afford a fairly connected history of the progress of speculation. Plato is often appealed to and interpreted on the principles of the work with happy ingenuity. Great is the author's admiration of this greatest of Greek speculators.

" If Plato was confused and unsystematic in execution, he was large in design, and magnificent in surmises. His pliant genius sits close to universal reality, like the sea which fits in to all the sinuosities of the land. Not a shore of·thought was left untouched by his murmuring lip. Over deep and over shallow he rolls on, broad, urbane, and unconcerned. To this day, all philosophic truth is Plato rightly divined ; all philosophic error is Plato misunderstood."

The explanatory matter is adorned with the graces of poetry, rhetoric, and eloquence. We have nothing like it in English philosophic literature, except Brown's lectures, but they have not the same exactness, are very verbose, and not over-rich in thought. Nothing like it has been spoken from any Scottish chair except by Mr Ferrier's youthful inspirer and guide to literature—his relative by double ties, the unrivalled Professor Wilson. Whatever the ultimate decisions of a thoughtful reader may be, he must needs be dull, phlegmatic, and impulsive, who as he reads does not often find his admiration making free with his faith, and outrunning the decisions of his reason ; though they may follow tardily, for difficulties are thick. We do not ascribe them to the author but to the subject. Everywhere he is clear, definite, and precise, stating objections with fairness, refuting them with calmness, and testing his arguments with no undue and partial fondness for the offspring of his mind. He has no stock of that shuffling, hoodwinking, and confident assertion, which is of such vast service to unscrupulous argumentators ; but being convinced of the truth of his position, he takes his stand firmly and

believes that all nature will minister to prove it. The
sun of truth shines above him, and he is determined
to see it through the fogs of sense, the mists of error,
and the clouds of rash speculation. He has got raw
materials everywhere, and uses them so as to give his
work wonderful completeness. A careful reader does
not detect half-expanded thoughts or yawning chasms
fit to engulf realms of thought. But there is evidence
of the use of ideas gathered through long, studious
years, and well digested in a patient and subtle mind.
And through five hundred pages they are all directed
to the development of the one fundamental principle of
the 'Institutes.' The author's fancies and ingenuities
travel like bees over wide spaces, and come back laden
with the building-wax of argument and the honey
of poetic imagery, to elaborate, adorn, and render
stable the unique structure of one developed individual thought.

Though he has not refused to avail himself of the
labours of his predecessors, he has only done what all
original thinkers do. They are all more or less "dis-
posers of other men's stuff." Others quarry the stones,
but they build the house. Berkeley had an insecure
hold of the fundamental proposition of the 'Institutes';
Fichte threw it carelessly away; and it is closely akin
to Schelling's cardinal doctrine of the identity of subject and object. Probably the critical researches of
Sir William Hamilton, and the clear definite form he
has given to the problems of speculation, may have
contributed materially to enable Professor Ferrier to

discover its worth. In his famous article on the "Theory of Perception," Hamilton teaches that subject and object are perceived through mutual correlation and contrast—are set over against each other, as it were, and distinguished in consciousness. Mr Ferrier long ago tries, and fails, to perform this process; finds it impossible to separate subject and object in consciousness; cannot conceive how it is possible for any intelligence, human or divine, to do so; and so lights upon the basis of his system. After all, his work is as original and independent as any work of man can well be in these ages of large inheritance from the past.

His literary style is noticeable, and proves that he is accomplished in other than metaphysical walks. It is not perfect, if Kant's Critique and Locke's Essay are models; it is far from perfect if perfection consists in being bald, dry, unintelligible, illegible. For it is clear, simple, vigorous, elegant, varied, rich with the imagery and happy illustration of a poet, and, what is singular in philosophy, makes frequent use of the humorous. It approaches more closely to the style of Hume than that of any other philosopher, is less grave and more ornate: it is a medium between the terseness of Hobbes and Berkeley and the sonorous rhetorical fulness of Cicero and Dr Thomas Brown; and its wit is of a sudden Voltaire-like order. As a specimen of his manner, we give a few sentences from his critical estimate of Dr Reid's character as a philosopher; and it may amuse to note the mock-reverent way in which

he speaks of the venerable Aberdonian dry-nurse of
Common-sense.

"Dr Reid, honest man, must not be dealt with too
severely.   With vastly good intentions, and very excellent abilities for everything except philosophy, he had
no speculative genius whatever—positively an anti-specu-
lative turn of mind, which, with a mixture of shrewdness
and *naïveté* altogether incomparable, he was pleased to
term 'common-sense'; thereby proposing as arbiter in
the controversies in which he was engaged, an authority
which the learned could not well decline, and which the
vulgar would very readily defer to.   There was good
policy in this appeal.   The standard of the exact reason
did not quite suit him, neither was he willing to be
immortalised as the advocate of mere vulgar prejudices;
so that he caught adroitly at this middle term, whereby
he was enabled, when reason failed him, to take shelter
under popular opinion—and when popular opinion went
against him, to appeal to the higher evidence of reason.
Without renouncing scientific precision when it could be
attained, he made friends of the mammon of unphilosophy.
What chance had a writer like David Hume, with only
one string to *his* bow, against a man who thus avowed
his determination to avail himself, as occasion might require, of the plausibilities of uncritical thinking, and of
the refinements of logical reflection?   This amphibious
method, however, had its disadvantages.   At home in
the submarine abysses of popular opinion, Dr Reid, in
the higher regions of philosophy, was as helpless as a
whale in a field of clover.   He was out of his proper
element.   He blamed the atmosphere : the fault lay in
his own lungs.   Through the gills of ordinary thinking
he expected to transpire the pure ether of speculation,

and it nearly choked him. His fate ought to be a warning to all men, that in philosophy we cannot serve two mistresses. Our ordinary moods, our habitual opinions, our natural prejudices, are not compatible with the verdicts of our speculative reason.

We do not have much hesitation in giving it as our opinion, that this system is, beyond question, the greatest contribution that the genius of Scotland has made to speculative system-building. It is the only one which has the slightest claim to be thorough. Hume's universal exhaustion of realities and entities is not less so, but it only clears the field with sceptical earthquake and fire. Reid forswore and abandoned philosophy, retaining merely the name, and joining it to "common - sense." *Desinit in piscem mulier formosa superne.* Dugald Stewart spent his eloquence and varied accomplishments in aiding Reid to spread the delusion that Berkeley and Hume could be refuted without being understood. But then, with all his elegance and personal oratorical fascination, he had little original power. A misletoe, he was by nature fated to grow in some oak, however stunted. Dr Thomas Brown carried the day for a time with his acuteness, eloquence, and mild poetic fire; and these qualities will long render his lectures pleasant reading; but his philosophic reputation has been handled with just severity by Sir William Hamilton, and his authority is gone. As a critic and annotator Sir William has chiefly come before the public, but in his philosophical dissertations he has shown himself fit to

grapple with the hardest problems.   He has neglected
to elaborate a system of his own in his anxiety to learn
the doctrines of others; and he has been at more
trouble than enough with Dr Reid's dulness, ignorance,
and obtuseness, which are incurable.   Learned in many
languages, in universal literature, in all science, Hamilton appears before this age as the foreman of a metaphysical jury, composed of the philosophers of all
time.   And from each he gathers up what is wisest
and truest into eclecticism, and attempts to settle
questions by the numbers of votes.   This task is
not undignified, save when he goes round the great
shades of the past, and asks each in turn, "Do you
approve of common-sense?" and then sums up his
witnesses from every nation and clime, with a precision which is ridiculous, because their true opinions
are unascertainable, and would be worth little if they
could be ascertained.   Each petty quarry should not
be honoured by a swoop from the "great black eagle
of the desert."   Sir William is no dogmatist—rather
a doubter.   With Socrates, he sees that knowledge and
existence is poised amid irreconcilable contradictions,
and with him he would nearly say, "All that we know,
is nothing can be known."   To his erudition, Britain
has nothing to present as an equal or a second;
but perhaps he has read too much, and dissipated his
intellectual power too widely to be able to collect it
in sufficient intensity for any great or sustained effort,
and so it flashes over the realms of thought, like John
Sterling's conversation, "beautifullest sheet-lightning

not to be condensed into thunderbolts." He has no definite system; but he is far greater as a philosopher than
Reid, or Stewart, or Brown, who produced systems of
no intrinsic value. More widely learned than Ferrier,
he is less patient in solving the riddles of his own and
other men's thinking—less meditative, less acute, less
resolute; and therefore he has produced no work so complete, and compact, and consistent as the 'Institutes.'
It is not necessary to say which of these two philosophers we admire most; each is pre-eminent in a different sphere; and we cannot fix the relative amount
of admiration due to either, any more than to Bacon,
and Newton, and Shakespeare. But we admire them
both more than any others of our country, except the
"good David" Hume; and perhaps a respect for his
unshrinking boldness, and spotless life, through temptations without apparent restraint, help to bring up
our esteem to the level. Ferrier has the acuteness of
Hume without his recklessness, the eloquence of Dr
Thomas Brown; and he copies the stern logical manner
of Spinoza. With all these elements of excellence,
we do not think we seek too high a place for the
'Institutes of Metaphysic'; and we think they have
no chance to be either completely forgotten, or refuted,
or believed. Assuredly they will not tarnish the
honour of a country which glories in the names of
Hume, Hamilton, Adam Smith, Brown, Mackintosh,
Reid, Stewart, and Beattie.

POSITIVISM.[1]

These three books are all expositions of Positivism.
They are all favourable expositions, but not all equally
so. The last of the three is a translation from Auguste
Comte himself, by a zealous and intelligent if somewhat blindly devoted disciple, and is, of course (in
intention if not in fact), the most favourable of the
three. The second is the least so. It is characterised
by all its author's clearness of perception and vigour of
logic; and although M. Comte's absurdities and delusions are exposed with tenderness, they are not in-
effectually exposed. Mr Lewes has handled many
philosophies—some of them with enthusiasm, nearly
all with pretty thorough intelligence; but he has
deliberately, in his bulky work, treated them all as
rotten vegetation, out of which Positivism can extract
nourishment. His two large volumes are a third and
greatly extended edition of four small pocket volumes,
entitled 'A Biographical History of Philosophy,' published in 1845 by Charles Knight in his popular
shilling series. In 1857, a second edition of the work
was published in one octavo volume not quite equal in
size to either of the present volumes. Thousands have

[1] 1. The History of Philosophy. By G. H. Lewes. London:
Longmans. 2. Auguste Comte and Positivism. By J. S. Mill.
London: Trübner & Co. 3. A General View of Positivism. Trans-
lated from the French of Auguste Comte, by Dr J. H. Bridges.
London: Trübner & Co.—['Scotsman,' 13th Jan. 1868].

read the first edition with interest, for great was the fascination of its clear, rapid, dashing style, and of its eloquent talk about Spinoza and Fichte. We doubt if half as many will fairly go through the present bulky edition. The author, in his preface, says, regarding the two and their similarity and dissimilarity, their readers " will see the spirit and purpose still unchanged; but it will be like recognising in an iron-grey citizen the features of a third-form boy." And what if the liveliness of the boy has somewhat departed, and the iron-grey citizen has been an alderman and. grown ponderous with plates of turtle-soup, and has lost, if not the faith of his boyhood, at least the enthusiasm which was a good substitute for faith, and has taken to declaring that there is " positively " nothing substantial in the universe except turtle-soup ? We declare our partiality for a chat with the boy, whose brisk, sparkling speech, and juvenile want of veneration, were always rather amusing. The " purpose " above referred to is to show the futility of metaphysical speculations, and the falsehood of all philosophy except what is called the Positive philosophy.

'The History of Philosophy' is in substance, according to Mr Lewes, in the region of fact, an account of the lives and notions of intellectual visionaries; in the region of reason, it is a long *reductio ad absurdum* of philosophy itself. Thales and Plato, Spinoza and Descartes, Fichte and Hegel, were only cloud-compellers and dreamers of grand dreams. Their ideas all went to impalpable vacancy, like castles in the air.

Science, so called, is the conservator and discoverer of truth, and Auguste Comte is its prophet, priest, and king. For him all the speculations of philosophers were merely a preparation. So Mr Lewes seems to say; and if Dr Bridges were speaking in his own person, he would say it out with great plainness and perfect sincerity. In his opinion and that of Mr Congreve—another Oxford scholar—and a few other gentlemen, Comte has not merely superseded Moses and the prophets, but Christ and the apostles, and all philosophers from Plato to Hume. He has set science in order and abolished metaphysics; has preached up into practical prominence, if not invented, "the Positive method" of science; has done away with all the old religions, and invented a new moral code and a new religion—"the religion of humanity"—with nine sacraments and other apparatus, and a new "*Grand Être.*" He has done no one can exactly tell what, but, at all events, he has secured the belief of many men of a rather sceptical turn in favour of dogmas that, so far as we can see, can be believed in only by the force of miracle or of madness. The more sober and rational claims made on his behalf are,—(1) That he discovered or introduced the Positive philosophy; (2) That he discovered a law of evolution in all human knowledge —to wit, that every truth passes through three stages, the theological, the metaphysical, and the positive; and (3) A classification or hierarchy of the sciences. We are unable to give him credit for these claims, or any of them. So far as we can see, he did nothing new beyond coining a few names, by the process of inventing a few new words, or misapplying a few old ones. We do not deny that he invented the phrase Positive philosophy, and used the word "positive" a good deal in new senses, or without any sense at all. What Positivism really is—why it should be called Positivism and not Negativism or Superlativism—how much of it beyond the name was discovered or invented by Comte, and how much by other persons,—we do not pretend to define. We can see that the scientific method of it, so far as of value, is at least as old as Bacon. We can see that, though not called negativism, it denies a great deal, and is just a portion of the scepticism of Hume elevated out of doubt into dogmatism. We are utterly unable to see what good it can do, or even what good it proposes to do. Its essence and aim are exceedingly indefinite. Mr Mill and Mr Lewes are both acute thinkers and clear writers; and when it is possible to be precise and definite, they can be it. They disagree not merely in their estimate of the value of Comte's doctrines, but in their interpretation of their meaning, and neither nor both together give any exposition of a logical and rational system of thought.

Comte's own voluminous writings are far from intelligible. They have much of the vagueness, but little of the grandeur, of prophecy. Mr Lewes recommends — "Study the 'Philosophie Positive' for yourself—study it patiently; give it the time and thought you would not grudge to a new science or

a new language, and then, whether you accept or
reject the system, you will find your mental horizon
irrevocably enlarged." Truth can generally be put
into a more compact shape than six stout volumes;
and perhaps if Comte had been able to think a little
more clearly, he could have put his thoughts into fewer
pages, or what is more likely, he would have found,
in trying it, that the substance of his thought was the
mere steam and chaos of a restless, vain French mind,
simmering with self-conceit and madness, and that
it was not fit to publish as puzzles even for inquiring
and credulous mankind. The perusal of six volumes
of shorthand reports from Bedlam would indisputably
enlarge a man's mental horizon, if it did not send him
to the place the reports came from. We have looked
into Comte's doctrines a little, and have derived next
to no edification therefrom. We do not intend to
give a year's study to his six stout volumes until we
see that some one has been considerably the wiser of
them.

Mr Lewes exhorts that Comte's " doctrine will give
unity to life." What that means we do not know,
but can fancy that many persons do not care for unity
to their life, but feel, on the contrary, that unity is
just equivalent to dulness, and vegetative absence of
variety. The years of human life are too few to waste
one of them upon the study of the vague verbose
writings of a rapturous Frenchman, who was once
or twice mad in his prime, and who, in his latter
years, fell in love with another man's wife, and felt his

soul so much enlarged by the process, that from a dry
philosopher he became transfigured into the high priest
and inventor of the religion of humanity. The more
discreet and rational of his admirers—M. Littré in his
own country, and Mr Mill in this—while avowing
discipleship to the Positive philosophy, are disposed
to disown the Positive religion, and to hold that there
is a chasm of madness between them, and that the
philosophy and the religion are as distinct in character
as if they had proceeded from different minds—that
the one is pretty near the perfection of human wisdom,
and the other of human folly. We know that M.
Comte was at one time so insane as to require confinement in an asylum; and we are clearly of opinion
that his works throughout contain intrinsic evidence
of unsoundness of mind. No other theory can account
for their existence. We are not able to draw any
clear distinction between his earlier and his later
works. We think the religion a natural development
of the philosophy, and that it contains no exclusive
evidence of an access of insanity, as some Comtists
would like to maintain. We reckon both to be equally
irrational, in so far as original — and both inspired
by madness; though the absurdities of the religion are
more conspicuous than the absurdities of the philosophy, being indeed pretty much the same absurdities
exhibited by the help of a powerful magic-lantern of
mad self-conceit. In short, we believe that if Comte
had not been all along actively insane, neither the
Positive philosophy nor the Positive religion would

have ever been published to the world. Nothing
short of insanity could have raised him to such a lofty
point of self-conceit as he attained, and enabled him
at once to exhibit the ignorance of a smatterer in all
science while an adept in none, and the unfaltering
omniscience of a lunatic demigod.

We do not believe that M. Comte has added anything at all to the real stock of human thought.
Theories such as his can be sifted out of the vagaries
of every lunatic asylum. Though his votaries talk of
his profound knowledge of science, we declare ourselves convinced that he did not know any one science
thoroughly. Mathematics, at which he distinguished
himself before he was expelled from the *École Polytechnique*, and which he knew better than anything
else, do not seem to have been studied by him with
any remarkable zeal or success; and how highly he
valued or was capable of mathematical research may
be inferred from the fact, that to proscribe it as immoral is one of the duties assigned by him to his
" spiritual priesthood " in those blessed days of the
coming time when there is to be no God, and every
man is to worship his mother, or his grandmother, or
his wife, or some other body's wife. No doubt, worshipping other men's wives must be a nice philosophical and religious recreation; but it is a fact,
nevertheless, that most true mathematicians would
rather be working problems than worshipping women
of any sort whatsoever.

The opinion of Mr Mill in regard to political econ-

omy is valuable, for, in addition to knowing thoroughly
what has been done by others, he is an original discoverer in that field himself; and, in spite of his
Comtist discipleship, he says of Comte—"Any one
acquainted with the writings of political economists
need only read his few pages of animadversions on
them (iv. 193 to 205) to learn how extremely superficial M. Comte can sometimes be. . . . On the whole
question he has but one remark of value, and that he
misapplies." We have an idea that the opinion of a
truly skilful chemist or biologist would be to a similar
effect. He reviles chemistry as "metaphysical," because of the theory of chemical affinity; and he justifies
the putting faith in hypothetical substances for "pro-
visional" purposes, although these substances have no
actual existence—a course of conduct which is certainly not consistent with truth, whatever it may be with
"Positive science." All mental philosophy other
than phrenology he decried as deficient in certitude;
but the truth remains, nevertheless, that a man can
never be so certain of anything as he is of what passes
in his own mind, and that to disbelieve his own consciousness is to pass into an abyss of disbelief deeper
and blacker than the doubt of such a rational sceptic
as Hume, who went as far as reason can go without
becoming part of that "darkness visible" which it
refuses to see, as well as the light of conscious life,
which is a speck in the said darkness.

We grant that Comte invented the term "Positive
philosophy" by applying or misapplying the word

T

"positive." As three-fourths of his teaching is devoted to denial, we should have thought negative a more appropriate word. However, that is of little consequence. It is of more consequence to ascertain what is meant by the positive method. Does it differ from the methods insisted upon by Aristotle and Bacon? In so far as there is any soundness and substance in it, we do not think it does; so that Comte did not invent this method at all (he did less for it than Bacon), though he had intelligence enough, as many thousands since Bacon have had, to see that, when it can be applied, this is the only proper and trustworthy scientific method. Mr Lewes tries hard to explain it into a position of novelty and prominence. In his prolegomena (which are new and well worthy of his reputation), he contrasts the objective and subjective methods of search after truth, and disapproves of the latter, but without, we must say, making it clear what it is that he condemned; some of his illustrations—in particular, one of the style in which a subjective and objective inquirer would respectively examine a clock presented to them for the first time—being rather more ludicrous than lucid. He does, however, fairly and honestly seek after tests of truth—a duty which Comte neglected, being satisfied apparently that his *ipse dixit* was a perfectly sufficient test of truth. Mr Lewes's subjective or ideal test of truth is that its negative is unthinkable; and this, as set forth by him in his work on Aristotle, is condemned by Mr Mill as being of the metaphysical mode of thought and not of the positive, and as being a setting up of "the acquired necessities of thought of one or two generations as evidence of real necessities in the universe." What is truth? is a question to which Comte attempts no specific answer. Mr Lewes does try, and Mr Mill condemns the result. We believe Pontius Pilate would have listened to them both with total incredulity, and probably have sent them both to Rome to fight with wild beasts, or with each other.

The most important claim made on behalf of Comte is, that he discovered the "fundamental law" of the evolution of the sciences by passing through three stages — the theological or the fictitious, the metaphysical or the abstract, and the scientific or the positive. Both the race and the individual, he maintained, passed through the first two phases before arriving at the last. He asserted every man knew that he had been a theologian in his childhood, a metaphysician in his youth, and a natural philosopher in his mature years. Astronomy furnished an excellent illustration—for the stars were once gods, stationary or wandering in definite courses through the heavens; then whirling in the metaphysical vortices of Descartes; and then transferred to the "positive" department by the Greek geometers—and by Newton's proof of the law of gravitation. Every hill and tree had its guardian divinity, if it were not itself a divinity. The universe at last came to have one God; then to one metaphysical entity, "nature"; but, lastly, both these were abandoned,—nothing was to be matter of

science except "laws"—that is to say, the invariable
relation of succession and resemblance in phenomena.
So far as we can understand it, this is a fair account
of the alleged fundamental law of evolution—*loi des
trois états*—and we have now to ask if it be consistent
with fact. We have no hesitation in declaring that it
is not—that as an observation it ranks with that of a
visionary who sees a succession of churches, castles,
and spinning-mills in the summer clouds. It is not
true that all the sciences have passed through three
stages. Geometry, algebra, and chemistry were never
theological; and they are as much metaphysical now
as they ever were. The Positive method is not a
new method. Far from it; for it is as certain as can
be, that the savage who gives personality to a tree or
a mountain, reasons in strict accordance with his own
experience. Plato argued that the earth was an
animal, and alive. He was probably wrong; but
his arguments are for the most part relevant arguments, according to the Positive method. The theory
of gravitation itself is an abstraction as much as the
vortices of Descartes; only it happens to explain the
facts more incontrovertibly than they did. Then,
again, it is not the fact that the "theological" has
vanished from among mankind. Professed atheists
there may be in China, and out of it; and they manage to sink low enough some of them in the scale of
beastliness almost to justify their creed; but atheism
is confined to a small minority, and at this day the
belief in an all-wise Maker of the universe is as

strong, and perhaps as universal, as it ever was, the discovery of laws being no good reason for abolishing the Lawgiver. The universe is certainly very mysterious; but it does not become less so by denying or ignoring all that it is difficult or impossible to know with perfect certainty. But whatever the secrets of the universe may be, and whether the existence of a God may or may not be "the open secret," we feel as certain as it is possible to be of anything in this world of ignorance, that Comte's law of evolution is utterly and entirely false, and that it would be worse than useless even if it were true, while it requires a credulity greater than that of the poor pagan who believed in oreads and dryads to believe it to be. It is marvellous that there is no faith equal to infidel faith—no infinity that strikes one dumb like the infinity of atheistic credulity.

The third scientific claim pressed on behalf of Comte is that he classified the Positive sciences, or propounded a hierarchy of them, beginning with the most simple and ending with the most difficult. There were, as he thought, six Positive sciences to be settled in some order. They could be arranged in 720 ways; and he arranged them — 1st, mathematics; 2d, astronomy; 3d, physics; 4th, chemistry; 5th, physiology; 6th, sociology—the last being a kind of Pope in this hierarchy in which there was to be no holiness. There is not very much in this arrangement at first sight. It would seem that almost any one could have done it, that the philosopher's machine

in Laputa could have arrived at it; and that, whoever
did it, it was not much worth doing. But Comte had
wild views about this hierarchy. He asserted that the
sciences passed through the theological and metaphysical stages in the evolution mill afore-mentioned
in the order of their simplicity, and likewise of his
classification; that so his classification was the order
of history, and was also—from its placing the simplest
sciences first, and then those other sciences that were
dependent upon all their predecessors, and yet had
something distinct in themselves—the order of nature.
These assertions are as fanciful as all his other visions
about the law of evolution, and they are given up by
Mr Mill as "exaggerations confined to language, and
which the details of his exposition often correct."
This kindly critic should have used the word "destroy" instead of "correct"; and it may here be mentioned, as a common peculiarity of Comte, that he
frequently adduces details that demolish his whole
theory—a peculiarity favourable to his character for
honesty (which cannot be gainsaid), but destructive
to his title to be reckoned a consistent, or logical, or
rational thinker. Mr Herbert Spencer has effectually
demolished the Comtish classification of the sciences;
and Mr Mill's defence, that he "has not shown it to be
ill adapted for its purpose," is a defence of what was
not attacked, and a defence which Comte himself
would have disdained, for his claim was rested, not
upon a purpose of expediency, or any purpose at all,
but upon history and nature. His classification was

no ingenious arrangement which could be objected to
and improved, but it was an arrangement evolved by
time, and unalterably consistent with the subject-
matter of the sciences. Comte has excluded the law
of gravitation from his science of astronomy and
arranged it under physics, asserting that astronomy
does not depend on any of the four more complex
sciences that succeed it, although it is clear to the
student of the subject, who has at all come to comprehend it, that if the law of gravitation be left out,
astronomy is not a science at all. Mr Spencer points
this out. M. Littré and Mr Mill admit that Comte
is wrong here—the otherwise almost infallible philosopher and high priest; but they say it is a "slight
error in detail." That is a statement that does no
credit to their candour, and is, as we think, dis-
graceful to both of them. Newton's great discovery
was a slight discovery in detail! Was it? They give
up Comte, however, clearly because they could not
help it. The truth is, that he advisedly entered into
this slight error in detail. He held that astronomy
became a science when the Greek philosophers "referred the diurnal movements to geometrical laws."
No other date would suit his delusions as to the law
of evolution and the "hierarchy" of the sciences. He
was as consistent as possible for a visionary doing the
sciences into an absurd Papacy, when they are in fact
and truth a Presbyterian General Assembly (a kind
of body of which he was entirely ignorant), helping
each other forward age by age—never ruling, and

seldom going far in advance of each other, being so
linked together that they often cannot move a step
without mutual assistance.

His only other great claim in the realm of science
consists in his asserting the possibility of a social
science, inventing for it the name Sociology; and
then in his latter years quietly assuming that he
had erected the whole fabric of sociology, which
fabric existed only in his heated imagination. The
solitary real accurate work which has been done in
social science has been done in political economy;
and we have already seen Mr Mill's opinion of
Comte's knowledge of that only solid part of the
whole fabric which he had first named, and then
imagined to exist. His peculiar social notions are,
however, not by Mr Mill, or by M. Littré, or by Mr
Lewes, admitted to be scientific. Mr Lewes does
indeed declaim at M. Littré for excusing them on
the score of insanity, and asserts that there is no
sufficient proof of any second attack of cerebral
disease—as if the notions themselves were not sufficient evidence of a chronic madness which is not
less lamentable than one or two attacks of acute
mania. The notions are curious as those of an enthusiast whom much self-conceit and a good deal of miscellaneous and superficial learning had made mad—
who loved truth greatly but himself much more; who
had little or no logical faculty, no sense of humour,
and little common-sense, and who therefore plunged
honestly forward from sublime Alps of self-conceit

into all manner of contradictions, ludicrous bogs, and quagmires. He believed that he had reconstructed not only science, but religion, morals, and politics; and Dr Robinet the hippophagist, and a dozen Frenchmen, and a score of Englishmen, who, for that matter, could swallow camels, concur in this belief.

Love was the principle upon which M. Comte did all these miracles in his latter years. He preached it with endless reiterations; but his practice, like that of some other preachers of love, was remarkable. At school "he was intractable, tiresome, and argumentative with his masters." At the *École Polytechnique*, which he entered at the age of seventeen, he was an admirable scholar, and was petted by his professors; but as the manners of one of them were not satisfactory to the students, the students, with M. Comte at their head, decided that he was unworthy to continue in his office, and informed him of their decision; whereupon M. Comte was expelled, and sent home to vex his father and mother, which he did until he ventured back to Paris, to live by teaching mathematics, or to starve. Casimir Périer hired him as a secretary, and after three weeks' trial they parted, mutually disgusted. Philosophic St Simon next employed him. He was secretary and *collaborateur* for six years, when they separated as bitter enemies. In 1825, then twenty-seven years of age, he married Caroline Massin, a bookseller, in her twenty-fourth year. They led a cat-and-dog life. He became insane. She one day

kept him from drowning himself, and probably regretted it ever afterwards; for they agreed so ill that
she left him finally in 1842. Three years later, he
became acquainted with a lady named Madame Clotilde de Vaux, whose husband had been condemned
to the galleys for life, and he fell madly in love with
her. She died in a year, and for the rest of his life
he continued to shed tears about her like a Frenchman, to visit her tomb every week like a pilgrim, and
to say prayers to her or her memory, or her defunct
spirit, or rather the dissipated forces that had once
been her, three times every day like a saint. Had she
lived longer than a year, or been free to marry and
had married him, it is not impossible that they would
have quarrelled and hated each other sufficiently to
have saved the world from a new religion, more absurd
than any that has hitherto been promulgated out of
Bedlam.

It is very difficult to give in sane language any
adequate idea of the Comtian religion. When it first
broke out in Oxford, and a scholar there, who has since
been a prominent Positive apostle, declared for the new
religion, and carried along with him his wife and
sister-in-law, a wit, who was asked about the faith of
this new Oxford trinity, replied, "It consists of three
persons and no God." Douglas Jerrold also expounded it a little, by a slight adaptation of the Moham-
medan creed, to a lady who condensed Comte into
two volumes of not unreadable English—"There is
no God, and Miss Martineau is his prophet." The no-

God element of the religion was quite distinct in the early stages of its development; and to that element it is probable Miss Martineau and Mr Mill would still adhere. But Comte himself in his later years, after being softened and sublimated a little by the "divine Clotilde," and after having perhaps found leisure to read and consider the arguments of Voltaire against atheism, denounced atheism as more offensive and unreasonable than theism. He says (Dr Bridges' · volume, p. 50)—"The order of nature is doubtless very imperfect in every respect, but its production is far more compatible with the hypothesis of an intelligent will than with that of a blind mechanism. Persistent atheists would therefore seem to be the most illogical of theologists." So it is clear that, although M. Comte is of opinion that, like King Alphonso, he could have given the Creator of the universe a valuable hint or two, he did not in his latter years venture to deny His existence. He simply concluded that the theory of a Creator did not fit into his great law of evolution, which abolished the theological and dispensed with all causes, especially a First Cause, as being beyond the pale of being seen, and smelled, and handled, and therefore beyond the pale of knowledge and Positive philosophy.

The Positive religion, however, could not do without some substitute for the God which all ages and nations had worshipped; and, strange as it may appear, Comte invented a Supreme Being for himself — an invention by no means of the sort suggested by Vol-

taire, and hardly to be conceived in its ludicrous
aspects until some second Voltaire will be at the pains
to direct his ridicule against it.   The new deity is
called the *Grand Être* of humanity, and is to be a sort
of colossal ideal monster in human shape embracing
all mankind, past, present, and future; good, bad, and
indifferent; black, white, and grey—a sort of reduction
to dull prose of the old Norse ash-tree of existence,
Igdrasil, every bough of which was a nation, and every
leaf a human life.   It would be very curious to see
Voltaire's Candide set out on a pilgrimage to the
shrines of this *Grand Être*—this best of possible gods
manufactured out of the worst of possible materials.
Comte's own account of his creed and its performances
is exceedingly queer:—

"Sincere believers in Christianity will soon cease to
interfere with the management of a world where they
profess themselves to be pilgrims and strangers.   The new
Supreme Being is no less jealous than the old, and will
not accept the servants of two masters.   But the truth
is, that the more zealous theological partisans, whether
royalists, aristocrats, or democrats, have now for a long
time been insincere.   God to them is but the nominal
chief of a hypocritical conspiracy, a conspiracy which is
even more contemptible than it is odious.   Their object
is to keep the people from all great social improvements
by assuring them that they will find compensation for
their miseries in an imaginary future life.   All theological tendencies, whether Catholic, Protestant, or Deist,
really serve to prolong and aggravate our moral anarchy,
because they hinder the diffusion of that social sympathy

and breadth of view, without which we can never attain
fixity of principle and regularity of life. There are now
but two camps; the camp of reaction and anarchy, which
acknowledges more or less distinctly the direction of God:
the camp of construction and progress, which is wholly
devoted to Humanity.

"The Being upon whom all our thoughts are concentrated is one whose existence is undoubted. We recognise
that existence not in the present only, but in the past, and
even in the future; and we find it always subject to one
fundamental law, by which we are enabled to conceive of
it as a whole. Placing our highest happiness in universal
love, we live, as far as it is possible, for others; and this
in public life as well as in private, for the two are closely
linked together in our religion—a religion clothed in all
the beauty of art, and yet never inconsistent with science.
After having thus exercised our powers to the full, and
having given a charm and sacredness to our temporary life,
we shall at last be for ever incorporated into the Supreme
Being, of whose life all noble natures are necessarily par-
takers. It is only through the worship of Humanity that
we can feel the inward reality and inexpressible sweetness
of this incorporation. It is unknown to those who, being
still involved in theological belief, have not been able to
form a clear conception of the future, and have never
experienced the feeling of pure self-sacrifice."

If a passage like that were discovered in the hand-
writing of a man who had by will left his money past
his relations, it would be prized by them as containing
very strong evidence of insanity. There is no reason
in it at all, little coherence, and less than no truth.
Old phrases which have been the symbols of revered

ideas are made the vehicles of delusions of the most extravagant kind. In so far as Positive knowledge can be applied to the assertions in it, they are all, or nearly all, the reverse of true—untrue as to Christianity, and visionary as to the new Supreme. We do not recognise the existence of any such monstrosity either in the past, the present, or future; and feel sure that the " fundamental law " which renders possible such a conception as a whole must be a madman's dream. To worship the wholly conceivable, is impossible, even if it were wholly venerable; much more is it impossible to worship the contemptible and abominable, as the greater part of aggregate humanity is well known to be. But does this *Grand Être* exist except as a coinage of the brain ? Can it be subjected to the scrutiny of the senses or of reason ? Sense never perceived it, and reason rejects it utterly. The mystery even that is required to drape the falsest of divinities is here awanting. There is no scope for either doubt or credulity. There were mists about Olympus; but the Comtist Pantheon stands entirely open to sunlight, scoffing, and contempt. Only there is a kind of melancholy suggestion as well in seeing an old man who has in his prime abolished God and all religion, inventing a divinity and a worship in his old age, and publishing it as essential to the wellbeing of the world, he having found by more or less ample and rational experience that atheism would not suit love-stricken sages and other victims of strong emotion. Moreover, he says the *Grand Être* would hardly do for general adoration ; so he invented a compound of polytheism and monotheism. His polytheistic divinities are some of them living women. *They* clearly have a fair chance of being worshipped to some extent. He did not know about worship himself until he met with the lady whose husband was detained in the galleys. But after his experience in Platonic love, he arrived at the conviction that worship was not merely possibly for, but necessary to, man. Therefore he invented a divinity, a religion, a saints' calendar, and composed prayers and hymns more or less spiritual (chiefly with reference to the divine Clotilde), and expected the world to follow in the wake of his fantasies. The world has been rather slow about it, and we rather think that the world will allow the Comtist religion to pass like that of Joanna Southcott, and that of the wealthy old lady[1] lately deceased in London, who had her drawing-room expensively furnished for the Second Advent, and whose testamentary settlement had to fall because of her religious frenzy.

Comte's formula of faith, or substitute for a creed, is "love is our principle, order our basis, and progress our end;" and his substitute for making the sign of the cross, so important to French mechanical worshippers, consists in touching those bumps or regions of the skull which the cerebral theory assigns to the devotional and other propensities. Mr Mill cites this last as an illustration of Comte's total want of a sense of humour; and, to be sure, it is absurd enough. But

[1] Mrs Thwaytes.

what does the creed mean? Love for a principle may
be loosely applicable to a few purposes of life, though
in the course of time there has been a good deal of
unprincipled love. But how can order be a basis any
more than disorder? There must be something under
order or before it—something to arrange. This basis
is like that of the Hindoo philosophy for the world,
according to which the world rests on the back of an
elephant, and the elephant on the back of a tortoise,
and the tortoise upon nothing,—a most *orderly* arrangement, but no basis at all. And as to progress, it can
never be an *end*. It may be *motion* towards an end
more or less distant and desirable, but it cannot be an
end itself—unless, indeed, existence be a kind of tread-
mill, in which it is necessary to keep walking and
making imaginary progress to no end whatever, until
death and absorption into the *Grand Être* arrive and
demolish the delusive dream of progress. To say that
progress is an end, is like declaring that the highway
is our goal. This creed, like Comte's doctrines in bulk,
could not have been published by an exact thinker, or
by any man except a restless, vague enthusiast, who
could believe and assert almost anything that he could
put into words, and who was too conceited to scrutinise
the vapours of his steaming imagination.

There is undeniably a kind of moral elevation about
Comte's writings and doctrines. Novalis had styled
Spinoza a God-intoxicated man, and Mr Mill styles
Comte a morality-intoxicated man. The moral results
he desired to attain would, many of them, be worth

attaining. But we are afraid that they are unattainable by any means, and especially by the means that he proposed. He did himself live the life of an ascetic and enthusiast. But the self-assured "high priest of humanity" had a motive not applicable to those who are neither priests nor high priests. His pet doctrine was that of universal love. The ancient and well-known form in which this doctrine was enjoined was, "Love thy neighbour as thyself." But Comte could not be content with anything so reasonable as this, so his form of the injunction became in substance—"Love thy neighbour better than thyself, and thyself only for the sake of thy neighbour"—*vivre pour autrui.* Selfishness is, no doubt, a somewhat unamiable quality; but what is the use or the warrant for going so far against selfishness as Comte goes? There is no warrant for it in nature, "positive" or negative, and there is no use in any philosopher propounding dogmas which it is not in man or woman to obey. To "love thy neighbour as thyself" is quite enough to require of frail human nature. It is more than frail human nature is likely ever to be capable of rendering fully; so that there was little call for a dogma going beyond it into the impracticable and the inexpedient. Society will flourish if each individual begin by loving himself and minding his own business, and providing for himself and those of his own household, quite as well as if—perhaps better than if—everybody were attending to every other body's business, and embarrassing his neighbour's efforts, and destroying his independence

U

and self-reliance, by his officious, universal love. We
distrust the charity which does not begin at home, and
hope that the plague of *vivre pour autruism* will never
appear among our friends. We don't think it would
suit a latitude so far north as ours. Comte was once
in a lunatic asylum in France; and had it been his lot
to be confined in Scotland, we are rather inclined to
believe that he would never have got out. Upon the
whole, we are glad to think he was not doomed to be
tried by the common-sense of this country. And yet
we doubt if he has not done more harm than good.
The good that he has done we are unable to appreciate;
his countrymen obviously hold it as worth little; for
no Frenchman of intellect above commonplace, except
M. Littré (and he rejects the religion), has declared
himself a disciple of Comte. We do see, however,
that he has done harm in England; for we see that
his disciples are wasting their talents in the prom-
ulgation of doctrines that ought not to be accepted
as true, and that cannot be of use to the common-
sensical masses of mankind. Mr Lewes can hardly
employ his versatile talents and his clear style to a
worse purpose than preaching Positivism; nor can
Dr Bridges. Really, the waste of a life and intellect
like that of Dr Bridges upon Positivism, in its maddest developments, is almost as much to be deplored
as Comte's confinement for life in Esquirol's madhouse
would have been.

The politics of Comte were hardly what might have
been expected. They were not those of the Radicals

and atheists of this country, nor indeed those of any one in this country except the noisy half-crazed knot of his declared disciples—who accept all his dogmas as if they were a revelation from heaven, and, while professing to be free to think for themselves, manifest a blind faith equal to, if not surpassing, that of all the fanatics whose blind credulity they affect to despise. Comte's politics are very different from those of Mr J. S. Mill—the latter being an apostle of liberty and democracy, the former a contemner of both. He says: "For the people tŏ take a direct part in government, and to have the final decision of political measures, is a state of things which in modern society is only adapted to times of revolution. . . . Positivism rejects the metaphysical doctrine of the sovereignty of the people." He was clearly of opinion that the duty of the people was to be led like sheep by great philosophers like him; liberty of speech was the only liberty he was disposed to allow to men; and as for women, he seems to have thought them a very useless set of creatures, except for the purposes of worshipping and being worshipped. No Turk could have been less disposed to grant them the rights and privileges to which some of them aspire in the present day, and to the attainment of which Mr Mill is enlisted to help them. This is not much to be wondered at, seeing that the following is one of his dogmas: "Comparing sex with age, biological analysis presents the female sex, in the human species especially, as constitutionally in a state of perpetual infancy;" a dogma which must

have been exceedingly gratifying to Miss Martineau
when she was doing this English interpretation of
it, and which cannot fail to afford a criterion for
arriving at the value to be assigned to Comte's opinion as to a *matter of fact* upon which every rational
mortal can form his or her own opinion. Burns's humorous assertion that "Nature's 'prentice hand was
tried on man" is fully as like the truth as this serious
utterance of the founder of Positive science, a science
which is to eliminate all error and rash hypothesis
from the world. Another "positive" fact of a similar
character, and otherwise closely related, is—" In the
Positivist theory of marriage, the principal function
of woman is one quite unconnected with procreation."
Marriage lies at the foundation of civil society, and
the position of women in social esteem and in admitted right to justice indicates the point of civilisation
reached by a nation or by an age. Comte's " facts "
as to these perpetual children and their function throw
much light upon his *capacity* to arrive at truth, and as
to the improbability that any good can come to mankind out of his pretended science of sociology, which
starts from premisses so monstrously at variance with
the most obvious truth as to one-half of the human
race. We have no faith whatever either in the ac-
tuality or the possibility of this science. Actual it
certainly is not; possible it never can be, so long
as human nature continues what we, in our experience,
know it to be—a thing not of invariably fixed and
recurrent rule, and method, and uniformity, but of

vagrant caprice and unforeseeable variety. A wise
man comes out of the dark abysses over which human
society hangs as a visible exhalation, and revolutionises
the whole course of history; a madman or an impostor
arises—such as Mohammed, Peter the Hermit, or Comte
himself—and the results, whatever they may be, are
certainly not such as science can classify or foretell.
The deaths and births of men depend somewhat on
physical laws, and they have been brought within the
range of statistics; but who can form a rude guess
even of the peculiarities of the wise men or of the
fools that will rule future generations? Comte, to do
him justice—while boasting of his social science—had
an idea that he or his successors would require to
adjust the materials to the science, and not the science
to the materials. So he set himself to eliminate a
great many of the characteristics of individual humankind—a great many of the forces of society, so as to
fit the human race to be driven along his scientific
iron rails of progress to nowhere. The civilisation
desired by him, if allowed, would be as flat, dreary,
and arid as that of China—a kind of civilisation to
pick up the statistics of which is easier, and to pretend
to discover the laws of which would be more feasible,
more within the powers of finite intelligence and
infinite self-conceit, than it would be to gather the
statistics and generalise, and collate appearances of
succession and resemblance, so as to be able to talk of
laws of a civilisation such as we know in this free
country, where mankind are not forced into any fixed

models of theoretical perfection by either political
or philosophical tyranny.

Comte is always raving about order, and system, and
unity, as infinitely desirable in society for their own
sake alone. But why should they ? Nature does not
display these alone. It is interesting from its variety
—a variety which makes the world wider and more
interesting to look through and live in. Ah, yes!
but nature, it seems, is a metaphysical entity, and is
abolished ; and as the world was made without God—
that is, without wisdom—it was necessary for a most
self-assured high priest and philosopher like M. Comte
to tidy up this godless world a little, as an orderly
French draper's apprentice would do. He was the
first, and it is to be hoped the last, who saw how
to make amends for the want of a designer of the
universe. If the whole thing should require to be
rearranged, we should prefer that some less elevated
bedlamite would do it. In point of thoroughness,
however, Comte left little to be desired. He did not
shrink from details as modesty, or indolence, or prudence would have done. He devised his nine sacraments, the last to be transacted seven years after a
man's death; he set apart two hours a-day to say
prayers to some woman or her manes; he decided that
divorce should never be granted except when one
spouse had been convicted of an infamous offence, as
was the case with his divine Clotilde's husband; that
nobody should marry twice, but that widows and
widowers (let them beware) should go on till death

saying prayers to their deceased partners, instead of marrying again; that the father should resign in his son's favour at sixty-three; and that a spiritual power, consisting of Positive philosophers, supported virtually by public alms, should bully everybody, from the supreme civil power downwards, and give them good advices without being able to back their advices by miracles or any arguments more cogent than vague public opinion. One delightful little detail about a flag for the Western republic of the coming Comtist era—regarding which flag Comte says he had been talking in his lectures for two years—we give in the words of the pious Dr Bridges, thinking that any profane condensation would spoil the fine effect:—

" A flag suitable to the Western republic might be adopted which, with slight alterations, would also be the flag for each nation. The want of such a symbol is already instinctively felt. It should be painted on canvas. On one side the ground would be white; on it would be a symbol of Humanity, personified by a woman of thirty years of age, bearing her son in her arms. The other side would bear the religious formula of Positivists, " Love is our Principle, Order is our Basis, Progress our End," upon a ground of green, the colour of hope, and therefore most suitable for emblems of the future. Green, too, would be the colour of the political flag, common to the whole West. As it is intended to float freely, it does not admit of painting; but the carved image of Humanity might be placed at the banner-pole."

We are almost ashamed to have dwelt in such detail on such rampant folly. But we could not help supposing that there must be something in a philosophical system which Mr Lewes and Mr Mill have been at so much trouble to explain, and which they both in part espouse; in a religion which is professed by an accomplished Oxford scholar like Dr Bridges—the not unworthy son of a clergyman who has achieved fame and added to his fortune by his comments on the 119th Psalm, and who is himself of good intellect, and of a really lofty but impracticable moral nature, which might have found its use as a Puritan divine 200 years ago, but which, alas! in this age of vast scepticism and vaster credulity, is utterly wasted. The imperfections of an Oxford classical education afford a better excuse for him than we can conjecture for the other two. In truth we do not see any plausible excuse for them, for they differ very far from the inexact, illogical, half-infidel, half-mad smatterer in natural and mathematical science, who is by nature and culture fitted to be a disciple of the inspired apostle of the divine Clotilde. Perhaps they have been bribed by the Convention of Bishops to make scepticism ridiculous, which cannot be done more effectually than by preaching up Comtism. Had Mr Mill addressed himself to his critical exposition of Comte in the way in which he "examined" Sir William Hamilton, he would have arrived at less objectionable results. Mr Lewes's history is really, in many important respects, a great work. It is able, intelligent, earnest sometimes (unconsciously, of course, but not the less really so), and written in a clear, fascinating style. As a narrative of opinions, it is free from intentional bias. At all events, there are few philosophers named in it that it commends so little to a reader's affection and admiration as M. Comte, so that whatever the writer intended, his innate love of truth and the real nature of his hero have triumphed over any slight partiality which he might cherish. Comtism is not much the better of his partial discipleship, though the profession of that discipleship will not tend to improve his reputation for philosophic capacity and accurate scientific culture.

BIOGRAPHICAL NOTICES

BIOGRAPHICAL NOTICES.

LORD JUSTICE-CLERK HOPE.[1]

THE Right Hon. John Hope was the son of the long-lived Right Hon. Charles Hope of Granton, Lord President of the Court of Session, and Charlotte, daughter of John Earl of Hopetoun. He was born in Edinburgh in 1794; was called to the bar in 1816, was Solicitor-General from 1823 to 1830, and was Dean of the Faculty of Advocates from 1830 to 1841. He was appointed Lord Justice-Clerk in that year, and took the oaths and his seat on the bench on 12th

---

[1] 'Scotsman,' June 16, 1858. [The death of this judge had occurred suddenly, at his house in Moray Place, on Monday the 14th, half an hour before midnight, the probable cause of death being the bursting of a blood-vessel in the brain, which first gave the sensation of swelling in the face, then loss of sight, then of speech, and in a minute or two unconsciousness—deep, deeper, and deeper. The sentence following the quotation from Scott is Mr Russel's contribution to the article, to whom also, I think, is due the substance, if not the words, of the final sentence of the second last paragraph.]

November 1841, on the occasion of the retirement of
his father from the office of Lord President (which he
had held for thirty years), and the translation of the
Hon. David Boyle from the chair of the Lord Justice-
Clerk to that of Lord President. He never was Lord
Advocate, but it is believed he was offered that office
by Canning, and declined it in favour of Sir William
Rae. He was a strong Conservative in politics, and at
one time, when comparatively young, the hope of his
party. When he was Solicitor-General, Sir Walter
Scott, in his Diary, 13th December 1825, wrote of him
as follows :—

" Walked home with the Solicitor—decidedly the most
hopeful young man of his time ; high connections, great
talent, spirited ambition, a ready elocution, with a good
voice and dignified manners, prompt and steady courage,
vigilant and constant assiduity, popularity with the young
men, and the good opinion of the old, will, if I mistake
not, carry him as high as any man who has arisen here
since the days of old Hal Dundas. He is hot though, and
rather hasty ; this should be amended. They who would
play at single-stick must bear with pleasure a rap over the
knuckles."

On the whole, making allowance for Scott's devotion
to Tories and Dundases, this is not a very unfair estimate; but until the end there was an incapacity to
bear the "rap over the knuckles," along with an
increasing tendency to give it. In that passage much
of the man is revealed, partly as we have seen him,
and partly as we have learned his history. When at

the bar, he was very popular among his contemporaries.   It is doubtful if there ever was a more popular
Dean of Faculty, or an advocate whose services were
more generally and eagerly sought.   Business was
poured in upon him without moderate limit, but yet
he did not slight it and allow his reputation to gain
cases for him; he always did his work thoroughly to
the best of his ability, even when he might have
shirked it.   His appetite for labour was insatiable.
In his advocate days he toiled from three or four in
the morning till late at night.   Whatever was useful
was done, and much that was useless also.   He carried
industry to excess, and was given to amass rather than
discriminate.   Never content with slaying an argument, he must needs bury it too.   But that method,
which would in most cases be irksome and injudicious,
was well suited to his peculiarities of mind and tem-
perament.

The chief peculiarity of his mind was its strong recep-
tive character, or, in other words, the extent, power, and
retentiveness of his memory.   Probably he remembered more than any other member of the bar, and he
read incessantly through scores of volumes of history,
fiction, theology, and law.   He recollected minute
details about long-forgotten cases, who were counsel
in them, what turns the argument took, what was said
by remarkable witnesses, what were the grounds of
judgment, and numberless little matters which are in
general pushed from the mind by the crowd of new
thoughts that are day by day claiming their places.

That uncommon memory was his weakness and his
strength. It was always easier for him to remember
an old line of thought than to invent a new. Therefore he was incessantly searching for precedent, and
he found it somewhat too often, and occasionally
applied it amiss. He had a great respect for the
wisdom of those who are no more, and very little
respect for the wisdom of the living, for his contempt
for public opinion had a sort of grandeur about it.
"That no man is an authority till he is dead," was
with him an article of faith and not of reason. To
appropriate terms used by modern theologians, but
equally applicable to lawyers, he was a traditionalist
and not a rationalist. He has been heard to state on
the bench, "I would not care to disturb that judgment,
though I believed it to be wrong." His apprehension
was not ready, or rather he could not make a ready
and dexterous use of a new idea ; but that was chiefly
seen when he was a pleader. His mind did not turn
easily, and was not nimble. Its motion was straight,
crushing like that of a heavy-laden waggon, but it
could not alter its course quickly or gracefully. Hence
his opinions are very involved, full of not well-directed
force, running out in lines that do not converge to the
point in hand, but bear upon it very obliquely, if at
all. They have, however, the merit of being very
suggestive, and often indicate unsuspected sources of
information which the searcher for authority discovers
with delight. Of a similarly amorphous character was
his letter to the Lord Chancellor on the Spiritual

Independence controversy in 1839, which, with the exception of a few trifling articles in 'Brewster's Cyclopædia,' written when he was young, is, so far as we know, his only acknowledged publication as an author. He was, however, understood to be the author of one or more articles in 'Blackwood's Magazine' on Non-intrusion, which, though possessed of some force, were exceedingly heavy and indigestible. In truth he was utterly destitute of the literary faculty, and especially of good taste as well as of clearness in expression, and seemed to be quite unaware of the defect.

It may be doubted if he ever was effective as an orator. He was too tedious, and not sufficiently direct. To appeal successfully to the intellect and to the reason was quite within the scope of his powers; to stir the emotions as Cockburn did, was not. And yet he did not want genuine feeling. True pity for misfortune was in him; and if he was sometimes stern, it was not through hardness of heart, but from deficiency of perception and temper. If in a hasty mood he did an injury, he was not too proud to make a generous atonement with speed. To the bench he carried the indefatigable industry which he had manifested at the bar, examined every document himself, and every authority which could throw light upon a case, and never allowed himself to fall into error through negligence or indolence. That he was thoroughly upright and conscientious is beyond question, though his decisions were often questionable on equitable rather than strictly legal grounds. In many departments of the

X

civil law, and in medical jurisprudence, the soundness
of his opinions will stand unshaken, and continue to
be cited as authority second to none.   Having, however, spoken of his popularity as an advocate, we are
bound to add that, as a Judge, he was far from popular
either with the profession or the public—arising not
merely from his arrogance of manner, but from an
alleged tendency to form, and obstinately to adhere to,
foregone conclusions.   Whatever view he took, he took
strongly; whatever personal dislikes he entertained
(and they were not few), he manifested them beyond
mistake.   Probably no Judge on the English bench
could have taken the course and exhibited the demeanour he adopted without coming into collision
with the bar, and being mastered in the contest.   A
hundred times we have been asked to assail him for
his errors and impetuosities, and have always declined,
on the ground that he ought to have been confronted
in his own court by his own profession, and not by a
political journal, whose knowledge and whose rights in
the matter were imperfect, and whose motives would
have been suspected or evil-judged.

Over such a character as Lord Justice-Clerk Hope's
it is not possible to pronounce an unmixed eulogium.
He was arbitrary and capricious, strong in hatred as
in kindness; but he was upright, fearless, and unwearied
in the discharge of what he believed to be duty.   It is
a fact from which to divine the good in his character,
that those who knew him best esteemed and loved
him most.   And, standing by his unopened grave, let

us forget political and other antipathies, and think
lightly of the evil in the dead, from whom in life we
differed, yet could not cease to respect.   Let us sorrow
rather with a true human sorrow over the marvellous
in erudition, the strong in will, the imperious yet
generous, the honest and courageous, the indomitable
worker, sunk from the light of life untimely into the
darkness where there is neither work, nor device, nor
knowledge.   To-morrow will come, and those who
trembled at his look will forget him, with those to
whom he was helpful, kind, and generous; but by us,
who rank with neither of these, be it written down
as truth here and now, that his was an upright,
worthy, and noble nature, not faultless, but faulty
more on the surface than in its essence.

LORD MURRAY AND HIS COMPEERS.[1]

So far as the Faculty of Advocates in Scotland is concerned, and so far as it is safe to affirm or deny anything respecting the feet of a centipede not yet advanced into daylight, the affirmation may be hazarded, that this nineteenth century put its best foot foremost. In the first year of it, the year 1800, five young gentlemen became members of that learned body, and four of them bore, in the almanacs of several succeeding years and other documents, the not unknown names of J. A. Murray, H. P. Brougham, F. Horner, and H. Cockburn. The hopes and fears with which they began to walk the boards of the Parliament House—"the Salle de Pas Perdus"—have long been almost forgotten even by themselves, and are now forgotten quite by three of them; one alone surviving in the person of Lord Brougham, who has realised more of the hopes of ambition than any public man living, and who has hardly ever felt any of the fears of ordinary mortals. What their subjects of amusement and of talk might be on the old floor, more than fifty-eight years ago, is all dim and

[1] 'The Journal of Jurisprudence,' April 1859.

uncertain now. Yet in fancy it is possible to observe
them listening to some speech of their short, smart,
glib, prettily and confusingly eloquent friend, whom
they all knew in the Speculative Society—Frank
Jeffrey, a young man of a few years' standing and
no great practice, and of the political principles of
Whiggism, reckoned dangerous by those in high
places, but of the swiftest thinking faculty and the
most rapid dignified utterance, very certain to find
something to do in the world if Destiny have no
decided objections, and be not less thrifty of her
instruments than she used to be; or one can conceive
their laughter over some happy pun of Harry Erskine,
or some prurient joke of John Clerk, and their admiration at some finished statement of the classical George
Cranstoun, or some profound thought of the grave and
taciturn Solictor-General Blair; or see them mix in a
circle around the unknown magician, Walter Scott,
suspected of being a poet, but not yet aware of it
himself, a Tory in his creed, and made Sheriff of
Selkirkshire among the last days of last century
through the influence of the Dùke of Buccleuch;
to hear him tell some odd Scotch story, or with
protruded chin and disjointed phraseology mimic Esk-
grove, the absurdest being ever decked in judicial
trappings; or answer inquiries, when pressed, as to
the researches which then occupied him after that
Minstrelsy of the Scottish Border which he was born
to collect and transmute into those marvellous fictions
which, years afterwards, became the delight of all

civilised nations. How far they ventured to each
other to express sympathy with the principles of the
French Revolution, which, with the martial achievements of the "armed soldier of democracy," Napoleon,
the practical embodiment of them, then convulsed
Europe, or with the speculations of the French scep-
tics, Voltaire and Rousseau, may be conjectured, though
it is not left to conjecture that these principles had a
most decided influence on their living and thinking.
Whether they applauded in whisper the Consul
Buonaparte's letter to George III. urging peace for
Europe, or Lord Grenville's insolent reply to that
letter, or Talleyrand's spirited reminder that this
monarch held his throne by virtue of a revolution
and national choice just as much as the First Consul
of France, or rejoiced at his victory over Austria at
Marengo—who shall tell? That they all were eager
for the advancement of liberty, they showed long
after the ardour of youth had cooled; and it is not
difficult to imagine the strong mutterings of indignation with which they condemned the refusal of
stubborn, bigoted King George, to redeem the pledge
of Pitt, and afford his Roman Catholic subjects relief from unjust disabilities and the other politicial
oppressions of that day.

Certain it is that there never were more stirring
themes for discussion, and minds abler to discuss them.
For a year and upwards they were content to talk
about literature and politics in the Parliament House,
at private suppers and in the Speculative Society; but

in 1802, on the suggestion of Sydney Smith, a witty,
vagrant, and wise Englishman, afterwards nearly overwhelmed in the Church, they resolved to set up the
'Edinburgh Review.' Mr John Archibald Murray was
present at the beginning of that business; Cockburn
was not, having Tory connections, though he helped
it forward by his pen afterwards; while Murray gave
it his countenance only, being too comfortable and
contented to write; and Jeffrey, Brougham, Smith,
and Horner were its active and administrative spirits.
All about it and them is well known through the
biographies of three of them, and many other sources.
What glorious amusement it must have been to see the
astonishment of old Toryism, looking as if its sumptuous robes had been converted into fly-blisters, and gout
had entered its every joint! what excitement for men
nameless and unknown to watch the "paper pellets
of the brain" striking down time-honoured corruptions
and follies! what a delightful consciousness of power,
to feel that they were working changes for the good
of humanity which the obstinacy of all the royal
Georges in creation could not avert!

Very soon this consciousness of power drew Horner
and Brougham away to London, and left behind the
more easily contented Cockburn and Murray, who knew
that it is not in outward station, be it the very highest,
that happiness consists, and who chose to remain in
beautiful Edinburgh, and deserve, as they did, the
respect almost bordering on affection of an intelligent
though limited community, with leisure to enjoy life,

which was more valuable to them than the heartless and faithless applause of three kingdoms. For practical faculties, the result has proved that Brougham was the greatest of the four, though he was reckoned rash, and distrusted by wiseacres who would proceed gravely to measure the waters of the Forth with their quart-jug, intended only for small beer and other domestic liquors. In spite of their prognostications, solemn shakings of the head, and unsatisfactory measurement of his faculties in their quart-jug, he has made several brilliant reputations—the reputation of an unrivalled orator, of a philosopher both physical and metaphysical, of a *littérateur*, of a legislator, and of a philanthropist; having given the work of twenty busy lifetimes to the advancement of knowledge and liberty among his species.

Had not Francis Horner died 8th Feb. 1817, at the somewhat early age of thirty-nine (early for a lawyer and M.P.), his integrity and industry might have raised him also, in due time, to the Lord Chancellorship and the woolsack. But he overtaxed his constitution in the cultivation, to an extreme pitch, of faculties not much above common, and fell a victim to lung-disease at Pisa, leaving undone every one of his many tasks to be performed in his weakness, " under the auspices of opium and returning spring." Much was expected of him by his party and friends—a great deal too much —and especially by himself. His life is one long tale of aspirations after the impossible, not without interest, and valuable both for encouragement and

warning. It shows how much can be done with
resolution and morality—how much cannot be done
when there is no regard had to the limits of the powers
of mind and of body. Francis Horner did a great
deal that was honest and good—he never was known
to do anything else; but intellectually he never could
have done anything great. Many distinguished men
of immortal memory have not had so long to live as
he had; it was not time that he required, but talent.
His speeches in the House of Commons, bepraised by
Mackintosh and successful at the time, are rarely above,
though never below, elegant mediocrity. That he was
beloved by all who knew him, is the secret of his
reputation. Morally, he was unexceptionable. He
always kept his honour pure, and had the Ten Com-
mandments written on his face, as Sydney Smith could
see. His failing lay in mapping out for himself
courses of study fit for Methuselah, and laying down
rules of self-culture, in supplement of the Decalogue
written on his face, which no mortal could keep since
the Deluge. Sir Walter Scott perhaps undervalued
him a little, though his insight into character was
deep, when, in reply to Jeffrey's praise, he said,
"Come, you cannot say too much about Sydney or
Brougham, but I cannot admire your Horner; he
always puts me in mind of Obadiah's bull, who,
although, as Father Shandy observed, he never produced a calf, went through his business with such
a grave demeanour that he always maintained his
credit in the parish."

The truest genius of the four was Henry Cockburn; but, like the heathen gods, for whom he had a great respect, he was very lazy. Master of a beautiful style, clear, terse, and suggestive, he would have been a writer far superior to any of them, if he had been at pains to collect materials and thoughts to cast into it. His 'Memorials of his Own Time' are delightful. They have no fault, unless it be a slight inattention to facts here and there, which would have cost pains to be accurate about; but the humour, the graphic description, and the pathos, over scenes departed never to return, which cost nothing, and are not to be bought or forced by any bribery or bullying of the Fates, are there to delight generations to come, so long as Edinburgh and its history has any interest to any section of mankind. No judge ever expressed his opinions with greater clearness and neatness; and it would be a vast saving of time to posterity if all judges were equally inclined to brevity. Blocks of pudding-stone may be very useful in their day; but diamonds have a better chance of preservation. It is almost unnecessary to say, what has been so often said, that Henry Cockburn was the greatest forensic orator of his time in Scotland, and the only one who could with sure hand strike the chords of human emotion.

Like him, John Archibald Murray, was content with Edinburgh, and found ample enjoyment in its society, in its politics, and in its picturesque lineaments, better worth contemplating than smoky London. Unlike the others, Murray never sought distinction in literature or science, or he might have attained it. He was too happy ever to strive to be great. There was no spur of care or misery to goad him along the steep paths of fame. He was to the Edinburgh Reviewers what Dr Carlyle of Inveresk was to the preceding generation of philosophers and writers—to Hume, and Home, and Adam Smith—their friend, companion, and adviser. All believed that he could achieve distinction if he were driven to try. His speech in the General Assembly in 1805, on the Cause and Effect persecution of Sir John Leslie, shows that he could estimate with unanswerable acuteness the atheistical results to which the doctrines of the reverend inquisitors led, when they denied that sequence of phenomena is all that man can observe, and maintained a necessary connection between cause and effect due to an operating principle in the cause; a doctrine which holds one quality of matter adequate to produce another, and therefore does not require the agency of a great First Cause to begin a chain that might have no beginning. Horner wrote to him affectionately one of the last weeks of his life. Cockburn and he were intimate to the · end of Cockburn's days; and so was Jeffrey, whose despairing, doubting nature always found "great resources in Murray," who was genial and hopeful, a contrast to himself. With Brougham, too, the last and brightest of this bright band, he was on terms of brotherhood; and, since Cockburn's death, they two have been together and alone in the procession of

Advocates on the same arch of the Mirza bridge, all their compeers, nearly all their predecessors, and many of their successors, having dropped off one by one into the dark and unknown river.[1]

When it is written, Lord Murray's personal history will not be long. The current of it flowed too smoothly; it was hurried over no cataract, rippled by no tempest, and clouded by not more than one calamity. The second son of a judge, Lord Henderland, he was born with a silver spoon in his mouth; and if he exchanged it at all, it was for a gold one. His career was one continuous and easy success. Without being forced to toil like a galley-slave at endless cases upon cases, as is the usual fortune of those who attain the highest honours of the profession, he had always sufficient leisure to live a little for his own behoof, and not entirely for that of the public. Perhaps he went somewhat too leisurely about his business; and

---

[1] There is a doubt about the time when Lord Murray entered the Faculty, which it may be as well to settle. He passed his public examination on a title of the Pandects, as appears from the Minute-book of Faculty, on 21st Dec. 1799, and at present the date of this examination is the date of entrance. But up to 1812 the entrant had, on some legal subject appointed to him by the Dean, to perform a spoutation in public to the Court and the members of Faculty; and Murray did not get through this public speech until the beginning of 1800. He considered this the year of his admission himself; and there seems no doubt that he was correct, all the early almanacs of the century classing him under that year, though they went wrong afterwards. The dates of the public examinations of the other three are—Henry Peter Brougham, 7th June 1800; Francis Horner, 21st June 1800; and Henry Cockburn, 13th December 1800.

any man who has courage to do so is never oppressed
with work.   But he could work easily.   He had faith
in common-sense; and that saved him a great deal
of hunting after precedent, which is often of as little
value as the opinions of the old women who perished
in the siege of Troy.   When Jeffrey was raised to the
bench, he succeeded him as Lord Advocate, and was
the first M.P. for Leith after the passing of the Reform
Bill.   With his Leith constituents he was very popular,
as indeed he was a favourite with all, high and low,
with whom he came into close contact.   In 1839 he
was raised to the bench, shortly after he had received
the honour of knighthood.   He sat on it for twenty
years, and died at the age of eighty (7th March 1859),
having preserved his faculties to the end, and enjoyed
more unalloyed pleasure in life than is the common
lot.   His sorest grief was the loss of an only son, born
of a happy marriage, which he entered into in his
middle age with a lady who was for upwards of thirty
years his ally in every hospitable and benevolent work.

Opinions somewhat discordant prevail as to Lord
Murray's character as a judge.   There are some who
sneered at his abilities, and who asserted that he did
not seek to apply them.   We have not been able to
see much, except what was superficial, to justify the
sneer, or the imputation of indifference to his duties.
On the contrary, we believe that he was most conscientious in the endeavour to discharge his official
duties, and that he neglected nothing necessary for
their effectual discharge.   Counsel who had occasion

to speak before him, had often, by his puzzling questions and off-hand remarks, good reason to believe in the acuteness of his observation and the steadiness of his attention. He sometimes demolished a long-winded argument of an hour or two by one whisk of his mischievous banter, to the chagrin of the speaker, and the agent who had paid for the fruitless eloquence. Of that legal learning which consists in being a living 'Morrison's Dictionary' and 'Shaw's Digest,' and a host of other publications, he had as little as possible. He had objections to make his mind a lumber-garret, on which he could not move without stirring clouds of dust to blind those superstitious persons who cannot believe that the unmistakable common-sense of to-day is as well worth giving effect to as the mistakable and often-mistaken wisdom of "fifteen" jolly gentlemen in horsehair a century ago, who overturned one week what, under the influence of sobriety or port wine, they had set up the week before. He had excellent reasoning faculties, and kept a fast hold of first principles. He was never drawn away from common-sense by the authority of any great name; and in his judgments, that essential of all practical wisdom is never outraged, but is always, as it ought to be, the trusted guide. He never failed to seize upon the true point at issue; and if his opinions are not so lengthy as some, they are always distinct, and throw the condensed light of a mind which had mastered the entire subject into the learning which others had collected to illustrate it. The amount of his legal learning was a pretty minute acquaintance with Lord Stair, for whose dicta he had the highest veneration. In several famous cases, Lord Murray's opinion, though opposed to that of his brethren of the Second Division, prevailed in the House of Lords; and on some of these occasions (*e.g.*, as in Fleeming *v.* Orr, 15 D. 488), it will be observed that he places his chief reliance on the doctrine of our greatest institutional writer, which, in the course of a long practice to the contrary, had been entirely over-looked and forgotten. The story goes, that when he was raised to the bench, he carried with him to it regularly, a copy of 'Bell's Principles'; which story, true or false, proves two impressions in the professional mind—first, that his law learning was moderate, and second, that he never had the evil courage to pretend to be what he was not.

What Sir John Archibald Murray was as an orator, is a matter of tradition. Some say he was a great stirrer of passion, and so forth. We are slow to believe that. He was not sufficiently in earnest, not enough of an enthusiast, too indifferent and serene, not sufficiently self-willed, to have triumphed over the wills of other men. His intellectual ability was great, his knowledge extensive, his utterance fluent, his style rather happy, but too loose and rotund, and his wit ready. Altogether, the mental machine was admirable, fit for bright things; but the motive power, the fire of zeal, conviction, and earnestness, was awanting. Practically, he was a philosopher, half Epicurean, half Stoic; not getting into a passion about anything : taking the good of life with good-humour, and the evil without complaint; doing the best always when it required moderate trouble, and the evil only by omission. He would have made an excellent bishop, being free from fanaticism and full of good works; but would not have been popular with the congregation of the Rev. Habakkuk Mucklewrath. His faculty for banter—call it wit, humour, or whatever else—was his most formidable weapon. It did not require seriousness, only the semblance of it : the gravest countenance for the most absurd remark, the most bland and funny smile for the most cutting sarcasm. We can believe of his humbling almost any rival by that talent. It is a talent purely destructive, however ; most useful as an accessory, it can never be the chief of an orator's endowments, which must always be the faculty of serious and solid argument.

He was distinguished for his hospitality ; and in that virtue he would have put all the Mussulmans under the sun to shame. Whether he held his salt as sacred as they do, may admit of doubt. He had no rancour, and was at bottom a steadfast friend; but he had a constant supply of Attic salt, of which he was very liberal, as well as of condiments that cost him dearer, and, with the most perfect friendliness and innocent smiles, he used to powder it over the raw places of weak brethren and sisters without the least mercy. Perhaps it was a species of cautery, and meant to harden them for harsher usage. Ill-natured it certainly never was, and it never made him enemies; for where the perceptions were dull, it was not seen or felt; and where the perceptions were sufficiently keen to see it, the subject could scarcely help laughing, and never mistook mirth for malevolence.

Of his private table it would be wrong to write, had it not been almost a public institution to which every visitor to Edinburgh distinguished for science, literature, politics, good fortune in any walk, or even misfortune, was heartily welcome. Free conversation on all subjects, sometimes jovial but never coarse, and always far above the vulgar run of comment over the excellent wine and the bad weather, flowed around it; and it may be safely averred, that at no table ever known in Scotland have so many pleasant hours been spent by so many honoured and honourable guests. In that way his great wealth was made a blessing to others, as it was in numberless other ways in the support of charitable institutions: of the United Industrial School, and of every scheme (not sectarian) which promised to enlighten society, or advance science or art, or improve the city in which he had fixed his home. Sometimes, it must be added with reluctance, he was not very discriminating in his munificence. For instance, he paid, and has bound his estate to pay, £1500 a-year to a gentleman whom he considered unjustly turned out of a situation of that value. Some may admire this act, which has a princely air; but we venture to think such charity extravagant, and not

Y

well applied, for any man who could earn £1500 in
one situation ought to have been able to do something
for himself in another. Altogether, we cannot refuse
our admiration and respect for his entire character,
intellectual and moral, public and private; and to
those who have seen the venerable octogenarian, with
his silver hair, and eyes independent of spectacles,
twinkling keenly to the last, the image of his kindly,
happy, cheery face, and his sunny smile, will return
long hence, and be a witness to the blessings which
benevolence can spread around it, like sunlight, costing
nothing, but gladdening all.

PROFESSOR SPALDING.[1]

THE death of Professor Spalding, which took place on Wednesday morning, 16th November 1859, in his house at St Andrews, has not taken those who knew of his extremely delicate health by surprise; though it will startle as well as grieve those of his large circle of friends who were not aware that he had been for some weeks in a very precarious state, for the last six or seven days hanging between life and death. From his childhood a martyr to rheumatism, some eight winters ago he had a severe attack of rheumatic fever, which so affected the action of the heart that his recovery was looked upon as almost miraculous. Ever since he has believed he would die suddenly, and avoided all excitement, taking especial care of cold, and teaching in his house in winter, besides keeping himself very retired, chiefly to his study and his garden. His presentiment as to the mode of his death has been partly verified. Unlike most victims of heart-disease, he died of a lingering illness, the action of the heart growing feebler day by day— so feeble, that the pulse was scarcely perceptible,

[1] 'Scotsman,' November 18, 1859.

and the blood circulating so languidly in the lungs as to cause choking, and asthmatic sensations, and violent fits of coughing. His shattered nervous system, also, was racked by painful rheumatic spasms; and the stoical resolution which enabled him to snatch the work of a very long life out of a short and feeble one, was never more needed than in the slow agonies of the close.

Mr Spalding was about fifty years of age, and twenty of these he was a Professor — holding first the Chair of Rhetoric in Edinburgh, and then the Chair of Logic and Rhetoric in the United College, St Andrews. He was an advocate, called to the Scotch bar in 1833, after graduating at Marischal College, Aberdeen, and spending several laborious years in the office of a Writer to the Signet in Edinburgh. He knew both the principles and practice of Scotch law well, having a mind excellently fitted to master principles, and an untiring industry which could conquer any details; but he never obtained extensive practice at the bar, and his attention, not being required in the domain of law, was gradually drawn off to literature, at which he worked unweariedly and extensively all his days, and not a few of his nights. When in Edinburgh he contributed to the 'Edinburgh Review,' then edited by Macvey Napier, and besides wrote his elaborate work on 'Italy and the Italian Islands'; and at that period, as throughout his life, his pen was also extensively active in unacknowledged composition. Lord Jeffrey's friendship helped him to his chair in

St Andrews; and when Jeffrey died, he told his
students, with tears in his eyes, how much reason
he had to be grateful to that distinguished man, who
was never too busy to lend a helping hand to struggling merit. He entered upon his St Andrews Professorship in 1845, having succeeded Dr James Hunter,
the son of the celebrated philologist. Here he pursued
his literary labours, writing his well-known 'History
of English Literature,' and, among other articles for
the present edition of the 'Encyclopædia Britannica,'
one on Logic, which has since been published as a
separate treatise, and which is indisputably the best
practical treatise on that science in the English language, and most probably in any language, Archbishop
Whately's very popular, but shallow and occasionally
inaccurate book, being absorbed, and all its errors corrected, with additions of a valuable kind from the profound speculations of Sir William Hamilton, De Morgan,
John Stuart Mill, and others, all fused and run into
a consistent whole by a mind which, if not powerful
enough, or too self-distrustful to originate theories, had
sufficient fire in it to eliminate the dross from other
men's theories, sufficient acuteness to detect what was
not dross, and sufficient constructive sagacity to dis-
pose it into the form best fitted for the purposes of
mental culture. In fact, the aim of all his writings,
and of all his teaching, was to educate the mind by
giving it the largest possible amount of information in
the smallest possible extent of type, or of time; to
surprise with ingenuity, or claim credit for originality,

does not appear to have been a motive of much strength with him. Accordingly, his style is clear and elegant, relieved by a neat illustration, comparison, or metaphor, when it will help the sense— always rising to the dignity of the subject, but perfectly unambitious, and never wearing ornaments for their own sake ; while the matter consists in very closely compressed facts, and doctrines collected from all quarters, with an industry evidently indomitable, and a care which thought nothing beneath its notice.

To all his three chief works above-mentioned this remark applies, and the marvel of the reflective and studious reader will be, first, how any one could have had the patience to gather together so much information ; and, second, how human ingenuity could have crushed it into so small compass. We say the "studious reader," and we speak of that sort of reader alone, for Professor Spalding's writings, being the fruit of very careful study, all require to be carefully studied. To the careless reader who can give no concentration of thought above what is required for a fashionable novel, with little or no thought in it, they are dry reading ; but no one who has patience, and the sense to learn, can fail to find in them whatever information he may be in search of, and which can reasonably find a place there.

Nor was his class-room a place for amusement, for listening to lectures in a sleepy, self-satisfied frame of mind, as most sermons are listened to, and forming sleepy opinions, complimentary or the reverse, thereon, but a place for giving rigid attention to his teachings, either oral or read, and for steady note-taking; the conduct of every student being under his quick grey eye, the most tricky being restrained by it, and the laziest being fascinated, incited by his praise, or stung by his censure, to do the utmost possible, to obtain some words of commendatory criticism before the class or on the margin of examination paper or essay. Every production of this kind, and they were not few (some eight or ten of each a session), was gone over carefully and repeatedly by the Professor, and corrected down to the spelling and punctuation. In the matter of hard work (without which there is nothing to be done in any useful art or science) he set all his students an eminent example, and it is asserted by many, is perhaps denied by none, that no Scotch Professor ever did so much work for his students, or obtained so much work from them. He did not simply point out the way, and in his easy-chair express his satisfaction with the account they gave of their journey when they returned from having professed to travel it, but he went every step of the way after them, and saw for himself whether they had walked as wise men or as fools. For this he deserved the higher praise, that such course is so unusual in our universities that no one is blamed for not following it; and he certainly deserved and obtained the life-long gratitude of all his students—dull as well as clever—for his unexampled pains to do them all the good he could, and give them that acquaintance with the philosophy and literature of their country which all educated gentlemen ought to possess, and, at least, that rudimentary mastery over their language (not so common as may be supposed), without which neither wealth nor station will secure from ridicule and contempt.

In his own intellectual culture he had neglected and despised nothing. Neither science, nor languages, nor philosophy came amiss to him. He taught the Greek class in Marischal College, Aberdeen, when he had just completed his own college course; and in his curriculum he stood first in mathematics, though he rather eschewed that branch of study in after-life. Of the physical sciences, botany, which he cultivated in his garden and in his walks, was his favourite, but he could have written an excellent popular treatise on almost any of them; and indeed his industry knew no favourite subject except the one in hand, which he worked at until it was exhausted in all its branches, with the zeal of an enthusiast. To leave nothing half done, or with any fraction undone, was the rule of his life; and of all his works, the distinguishing characteristic is their thoroughness. He slighted nothing, however insignificant, and whatever he did was thoroughly well done.

That the mind which was capable of so much—so well furnished with the wisdom of past times—so willing to work in the present — should have been taken away in the prime of intellect and of ordinary human life, will not fail to stir deep emotion in all

who feel for frail mortality, and lament over work
undone because years have been denied; but there
will be especial grief for their unforgotten Professor
among those old students—in heart old friends, and in
intellect almost sons—scattered, it may be, over many
lands, to whom the tidings of his death will be tidings
of the loss of a benefactor who never spared himself to
render their youth wiser, or to help them in manhood
by encouragement or counsel; whose genuine worth
won their confidence, though hidden under an indifferent and sometimes even impatient manner; and whose
moral example of discharging every duty with unhesitating honesty, no less than the results of his intellectual teaching, have proved invaluable to them in
the struggle of life.   Nor among the mourners will St
Andrews appear last; for, learned and highly gifted as
almost all her Professors are, to the oldest University
in Scotland—standing remote in classic dignity from
the hurrying market-places of the modern world, and
inviting those only who desire learning itself, and not
the name of it—his death is an irreparable calamity.

SIR HUGH LYON PLAYFAIR.[1]

THE death of the Provost of St Andrews had not been unexpected. He himself has known for a year or more that his sands were nearly run. Last winter he had a severe bronchitic attack, which kept him in his chair for seventeen days and nights almost without sleep; and when he was again seized, about the first day of this year, with the affection of the lungs, complicated with heart-disease which speedily developed itself, his recovery became next to hopeless. He had over-lived the Psalmist's term of threescore and ten by four years, and he had never been an idler.

His father was minister of the parish of Meigle, and afterwards Principal of the United College, St Andrews, to which office he was translated in 1799. Sir Hugh was born in the manse of Meigle on the 17th November 1786, and was educated there, at Dundee Grammar School, and at St Andrews University. He chose the army for a profession, and, before entering at Woolwich, studied under his relative, the celebrated Professor Playfair of Edinburgh.

[1] 'Scotsman,' January 24, 1861 [being the third day after the death].

In 1805 he became an officer of Artillery in the East
Indian army; and for some fifteen years, without interval, performed his military duties with uncommon
vigilance and energy, and in such a way as to secure
not merely the obedience, but the affection and loyalty,
of his men. Abuses he corrected with firmness, but
with that agreeable pleasantry which always took
off the edge of even disagreeable orders. He seems
to have encouraged among the soldiers competitions
in professional skill, and to have established libraries
and reading-rooms, and a theatre, thinking that such
recreations were among the best ways of relieving the
tedium of life and avoiding dissipation. A year or
two before 1820 he returned to Scotland, and in that
year he was presented with the freedom of the city of
St Andrews, and married to the estimable lady who
is left to mourn his decease. He returned forthwith
to India and his military duties, besides which he held
the civil appointment of superintendent of the military
road, telegraph towers, and postal arrangements between Calcutta and Benares, his tact and energy well
fitting him for such a responsible post. In 1834,
having obtained the rank of major, he resigned the
service of the H.E.I.C., and took up his abode in St
Andrews, occupying his leisure with mechanical and
mathematical pursuits, and the furnishing of his garden with those instructive curiosities, and whims, and
oddities, which have made it one of the shows of the
city, and to which, with characteristic generosity, he
welcomed all. In 1842 he was elected Provost, and

his fertile invention found full scope for itself in transforming it into one of the cleanest, trimmest little towns in Britain, a sort of miniature Oxford and Brighton combined; and regenerated St Andrews must be his monument.

Great natural advantages St Andrews no doubt has, the want of which no genius could have supplied. The sea and sea-breezes, the long hard sea-shore, and the spacious Links (so attractive to golfers) were all there before the Culdees, waiting for men of less grim type than these early devotees to enjoy them. All the religious buildings were there also, at least their foundations and ruins were, and their time-hallowed associations. The streets had once had a sort of metropolitan spaciousness, but the wind alone swept them. They were unpaved, full of mud-holes, and adorned with patches of green grass, on which goats and asses fed, and their straightness and breadth were broken up by outside stairs, porches, small garden walls, and all manner of offensive projections. The ecclesiastical buildings had been a quarry from the time of John Knox, and half St Andrews had been built out of their desecrated stones. Probably pious provosts had encouraged this dilapidation, and it is pretty certain some of them had practised it, assured that whether they did service to any one else or not, they were serving themselves. But all that has been changed, and the ruins of the Cathedral, the Castle, and Blackfriars Chapel have been put as far as possible beyond the reach of decay, and certainly beyond the reach of dilapidation. Sir Hugh Playfair, or "the Major," as he used to be called in the heyday of his career of improvement, waged a war of extermination against all manner of projections, and most successfully. Often he had to wait for the death of an old maid who would not consent to give up the porch of her great-grandfather; but sooner or later he carried his point, which was the carrying away of the obstructive stones some morning before the respectable citizens were out of bed. He jeered, and bantered, and bargained until he abolished those eyesores, and now there are not above three or four ugly projections left in the whole town. To render the streets passable, he had a line of pavement laid along their length, and he taunted the proprietors of houses who would not for comfort's sake pave out from their houses to the line until they did it; and now the streets are as well paved as can be, and are a model certainly which Edinburgh might do well to imitate. The Madras College owes him much, the Infant School owes him its existence, and so we suspect do the City Hall and the new Town Hall. Some of the United College class-rooms were in a state of frightful disrepair, and a wing that was to contain new ones had stood for nearly twenty years half built. The Treasury had been often tried, but they would not give the money until he took to dunning them in his irresistible, pertinacious way, and of course succeeded; and indeed there is almost no material improvement in St Andrews during the last eighteen years which he did not either suggest or

carry into execution. The finances of the town were
embarrassed, but he managed them well; and he had
a great talent for obtaining subscriptions to carry out
any scheme of public improvement. As a beggar, he
was probably equal to Dr Guthrie, and much in the
same humorous style; and, as a ruler of free men, it
would be difficult to name his equal.

At all public places his erect, middle-sized, military
figure, with voluminous muffler, faithful walking-stick,
imperious, self-reliant, intellectual face, ruddy complexion, white hair, shaggy grey eyebrows, and light-
blue twinkling eyes, were conspicuous always in the
centre of the business, encouraging and carrying it
forward; and wistfully and sorrowfully, in imagination, will those who have known and loved St Andrews
wander back to the scenes where they have seen him,
and where he will be seen no more.

A most frank, unaffected, soldier-like manner, ready,
careless, jocular speech, rendered him no stranger to
any one in St Andrews, and a great favourite with
most, although there were some obstructors and detractors who professed to dislike, and probably disliked more than they professed, his sarcastic speeches
and his imperious ways. But the humblest could not
reproach him with pride, or say that he was ever deaf
to the claims of pity or justice. He was generally
professing with his lips the philosophy of selfishness,
and with his hand and head working for others. On
the surface, his character was full of contradictions,
but his deeds showed that underneath it was genuine,
and far better than he cared to make it appear. His

light, "chaffy," diplomatic talk, the sincerity of which was a puzzle, while its grotesque humour was always apparent, and its purpose hidden until he saw whether or not it was worth while to disclose it, induced in shallow observers the belief that he reckoned life a jest, and mankind no wiser or better than they should be. But he could be serious, and he had a true, kind heart, though he veiled it carefully. He did more benevolence than twenty talkers about benevolent schemes; and though he had no objection to throw a little dust in the eyes of decorous dunces, he could tell the truth to those who could understand it with the candour of an enemy, and advise with the kindness of a friend.

He was a Conservative in politics, and indeed professed ultra-Toryism as his political creed. A chronological table stretched round the wall of his garden gives, as its final item, his opinion of the Reform Bill, —"Britain having attained a position of power, glory, and respectability never enjoyed by any other nation, it required a mighty effort to subvert her stability. This was effected on the 7th June 1832, from which we may observe the decline of the British empire!" But in spite of his Toryism he has often supported the Whigs; and at the last St Andrews election, when Francis Brown Douglas, Esq., went in to oppose Mr Ellice, Sir Hugh proposed Mr Ellice, and with his provoking banter told Mr Brown Douglas, who had been professing everything, Toryism included, that he would make "an excellent member of Parliament for every place except St Andrews." In all matters of social reform he was almost, if not altogether, somewhat more than a Whig, and the antiquity of any abuse or obstruction was a vain plea with him. Altogether, he had too much originality and native independence to be bound by opinions or creeds; and to do or say with a grave face things that have a tendency to cause old women of both sexes to shake their solemn heads was one of his amusements, which he prosecuted also for the higher object of putting cant out of countenance.

Since not many modern provosts are worthy of remembrance after they are gone, and some of them cannot be too soon forgotten, it is a rare pleasure and duty to testify to the virtues of this famous Provost of St Andrews—a sort of born king, gifted to conquer gnarled circumstances, ordained to rule anywhere, either in regiment or city, for good—and who had an energy and a resolution and a clearness of insight that could bring order out of chaos wherever Providence might send him. And for long years to come thankful may St Andrews be that he was sent to her. For the Reformation, in breaking up the ancient ecclesiastical era, left her among ruins which, crumbling down for centuries, had buried her in her desolate and forsaken sleep, and to awake her from her living grave required no common faith, or zeal, or courage. She waited, and they came, fulfilled their mission, and they have gone amid countless regrets, and she will wait long before she obtain (may she never require!) such another patriotic restorer.

PROFESSOR FERRIER.

NOT unexpectedly, but yet prematurely, has the distinguished Professor of Moral Philosophy in the University of St Andrews gone the way of all living flesh. He was only fifty-six years of age, and belonged to a long-lived family, many of whom had survived fourscore; but he had pursued his metaphysical studies with too great eagerness at all hours of the night and day, neglecting sleep, and fresh air, and exercise; and so, by disregarding the physical laws, used up his vital force too soon. He never slept so long as he could keep awake, moving about his library or lying on the sofa reading Plato or Hegel, or musing upon the great problems of Being until three or four o'clock in the morning, and taking almost no exercise beyond walking backwards and forwards to the University library and his class-room. The evil effects of these habits of life showed themselves first several years ago in occasional breathlessness, his lungs being inadequate for their task under any slight accession of exertion or excitement; and in December 1861 he was attacked by violent rheumatic spasms of the heart.

Z

He recovered so far, and taught his class during the latter part of that session and all the next. In November 1863, he was again attacked by heart disease, and was occasionally insensible. Dropsical appearances supervened, and his physicians gave up all hope of his recovery. He did, however, partially recover, and set his house in order for the inevitable end, which his philosophical serenity, original strength of constitution, and the affectionate care of his wife and family have warded off for these six months past, which must have been dreary enough in his sick-room in spite of his calmness and constant occupation in reading, writing, or listening to others reading, with which he whiled away the lingering hours.

He died on Saturday, 11th June 1864, at St Andrews. He was born in Edinburgh in 1808. His father was John Ferrier, W.S., one of the Clerks of Session, and his mother was a sister of Professor Wilson. His aunt, Susan Ferrier, was the authoress of three novels that are still deservedly popular — 'Marriage,' 'Destiny,' and 'The Inheritance'—and in each of them she worked out thoroughly and in wondrously ingenious ways a central idea, upon which her thoughts and the acts and observations of her characters are brought to bear and converge in a manner that, for literary works necessarily dissimilar, reminds the reader of her nephew's metaphysical speculations and their unique central ideas, to illustrate and fortify which all the others were expended. She was a friend of Sir Walter Scott, and so was her brother. Mr Ferrier married his cousin, Margaret, eldest daughter of Professor Wilson.

In his childhood James Frederick Ferrier was surrounded by literary influences. When a boy he had sat on Scott's knee; the Ettrick Shepherd had told him stories of ghosts and fairies, and recited Border ballads for him in the broad dialect of Yarrow; and Lockhart had drawn portraits and caricatures for his amusement. He very early adventured upon verse himself, and with no mean success, though his mind was too keenly and compactly philosophical for poetry. A poem of his gained the prize in the Moral Philosophy Class; and some classical translations found their way into 'Blackwood's Magazine.' On leaving Edinburgh, he went to Oxford to prosecute his studies, where he was a contemporary of Sir Roundell Palmer,[1] the present Attorney-General of England, and well known to him and the brighter spirits of these college days for his humour, his elegant classical culture, and for his verses. In 1832 he passed to the Scottish bar. From his connection with Edinburgh men of business, he had a fair share of junior counsel's fees; but could not harness his intellect to the hack-work of the ordinary legal tradesman, and he had no ambition to be great in the Parliament House. The bent of his mind was towards philosophy and literature. He aspired to cultivate fields which, though less fertile in money than is the busy practice of law, are more productive of permanent results of a kind that are

[1] Now Earl of Selborne, Lord High Chancellor of England.

not valueless or incapable of yielding enjoyment because they cannot be lodged in the bank or invested in the funds. To a mind saturated with the idealism of Berkeley, and its scepticism regarding the outer and material world, a few guineas more or less were a matter of supreme indifference. He contributed to 'Blackwood's Magazine' a series of papers on the "Philosophy of Consciousness," written in a more ornate, eloquent, and highly poetical style than any strictly philosophical speculations in the English language, or perhaps in any language except the German of Fichte and Schlegel. In that periodical, also, he expounded the idealism of Berkeley with an ingenuity, clearness, and eloquence that has secured for this paper the reputation of being the best exposition of Berkeley in existence. Another famous paper is his exposure of the extensive and barefaced plagiarisms of Coleridge, especially from German writers, which his extensive German learning—not surpassed among his contemporaries, except, perhaps by Sir William Hamilton, De Quincey, and Thomas Carlyle—enabled him to detect. Among his last, if not his last, contributions to 'Blackwood,' was a series of papers on the various readings and emendations of Shakespeare, *apropos* of Collier's edition, in which he adopts the conservative view of holding by the established readings when they are not plainly nonsensical.

On the death of Dr Cook, he, on the recommendation of many men distinguished in literature and philosophy—among them, Sir William Hamilton, for whom he had read lectures one session when he was ill, and with whom he used to spend every Sunday afternoon in walking, and more or less transcendental talk—was in 1845 appointed to the Chair of Moral Philosophy in the University of St Andrews, in the discharge of the duties of which he has since laboured with universal approbation. His old students are scattered everywhere—through all countries, professions, and churches. To many of them the world of faith and action has become more narrow and less ideal than it seemed when they sat listening to his lofty and eloquent speculations in the little old class-room among earnest young faces that are no longer young, and nearly all gone dim to memory; but to none of them can there be any feeling regarding him alien to respect and affection, while to many there will remain the conviction that he was for them and their experience the *first* impersonation of living literature, whose lectures, set off by his thrilling voice, slight interesting burr, and solemn pauses, and holding in solution profound original thought and subtle critical suggestion, were a sort of revelation, opening up new worlds, and shedding a flood of new light upon the old familiar world of thought and knowledge in which genius alone could see and disclose wonders. Not merely were the ideas of Leibnitz, Descartes, Malebranche, Spinoza, Berkeley, Hume, Hobbes, and Bishop Butler expounded and rendered intelligible—probably for the first time—but well-remembered passages of Milton and Byron were shown

to contain undetected and noble meanings, and the
shrewdness, wit, and half-merry half-melancholy *carpe
diem* philosophy of Horace, "with Cocytus trailing in
the background" of his gaiety, were unfolded and
touched into life and beauty, so as to free his thought
from the mummy wrappages of pedants and peda-
gogues, and justify his literary immortality.   His
reading of the Ode, *Eheu ! fugaces Postume, Postume,
labuntur anni,* his prose translation and his metrical
translation of that ode, all introduced into a lecture
to illustrate the association of ideas, can never be
forgotten by any intelligent auditor ; and now that
he has himself passed the dark river, they sound like
his dirge to the ear of memory.

The subject-matter of his metaphysical course was
changed year by year, for he was always reading and
working.   In the early years of his professoriate he
taught the philosophy of Consciousness.   Then he
developed year by year the ingenious and beautiful
speculations on Knowing and Being that he afterwards
expanded into the 'Institutes of Metaphysic,' published by him in 1854; and since then he has been
extending his ethical course, which was chiefly historical, and, in so far as it contained any dogmatic
teaching, consisted of an exposition and enforcement
of the views of Bishop Butler, as contained in his
sermons on morals ; and also introducing into the
metaphysical part of his course lectures on the history
of philosophy which, had he been spared, no doubt
would have grown into a most readable and valuable

book on that subject, and which we should hope may even in its imperfect state be published as a book; for as an expositor of the views of others, he was if possible more successful than he was in the elucidation of original thought.[1]

No St Andrews professor was ever more popular or more deservedly so. Dr Hunter was run after from all quarters by eager students of philology, Dr Chalmers by the admirers of living eloquence, and Professor Spalding by those who were prepared to work· hard in studying exactitude of thought and expression, and receive the full benefit from a teacher who with many higher merits was perhaps the most effective "intellectual grindstone" ever known in any Scottish university. Professor Ferrier was different from all these in many, and like all in some respects. He had a patience and a persistence in speculation equal to Dr Hunter; a keenness of apprehension equal, if not superior, to Professor Spalding; and an eloquence not so strong and overwhelming as that of Dr Chalmers, but more fine, subtle, and poetical in its affinities, and revealing thoughts more splendid and transcendental, or at least more free from the cloudy steam of sensationalism, from earthly impurities, from

---

[1] Two volumes of his literary and philosophical Remains have been published, under the editorship of his son-in-law Sir Alexander Grant, and Dr Lushington, formerly of the Greek Chair, Glasgow. They contain his philosophical papers contributed to 'Blackwood,' and the lectures regarding which the above hope is expressed. The best of them is that on Heraclitus and the unpausing flux of existence.

illogical inaccuracy, and the taints of a materialistic philosophy. In person and in manner, Professor Ferrier was the very ideal of a professor and a gentleman. Nature had made him in the body what he strove after in spirit. His features were cast in the finest classic mould, and were faultlessly perfect, as was also his tall thin person,—from the finely formed head, thickly covered with black hair, which the last ten years turned into iron-grey, to the noticeably handsome foot. Sir John Watson Gordon, whom he has so swiftly followed out of time, painted his portrait for his friends and former students about a year ago; but the likeness, though moderately faithful, does not at all adequately express his keen intellectual look. A better conception of it can be obtained from the portrait of Lockhart, or from that of Bishop Berkeley in Trinity College, Dublin, which latter is an aid to understand the man to whom Pope ascribed every virtue under heaven. Those who knew Professor Ferrier intimately would not think that character which was applied to Berkeley misapplied to his expounder and disciple. A human being less under the influence of low or selfish motives could not be conceived in this mercenary anti-ideal age. If he made mistakes, they were due to his living in an ideal world, and not to either malice or guile, both of which were entirely foreign to his nature.

His personal friends and students will, no doubt, always remember him; but they will not live always, and his reputation with posterity must depend upon his 'Institutes of Metaphysic.' He has built up by the geometrical method a system of philosophy upon the proposition, "Along with what any mind knows, it must know itself," and ending in the result that God is the universal mind in synthesis with all things. He wrote his book in the evident belief that it contained not only philosophical truth, but the whole of philosophical truth. Without this conviction he could not have done it. But the conviction is only based on truth to one-half of its extent. It is true that mind can know nothing without knowing itself; but there is a great deal beside that is true, and to rest the universe of truth upon one proposition is a splendid enthusiast's dream. It is to set a pyramid with an infinite base upon its vertex, and such a pyramid is Professor Ferrier's philosophical system. It is beautiful, logical, self-coherent, ingenious. It is true as far as it goes; but that is not very far— certainly not to infinity — which alone is the limit within which can be embraced all philosophical truth. Still it will bear comparison with other philosophical systems; and as a piece of readable philosophical literature, this book expounding it and condemning other systems is not surpassed. Its pages do not contain Sir William Hamilton's crushing weight of thought; and it is doubtful whether, if Sir William Hamilton had not cleared the field by his learning and destructive speculations, they could have been written, and the theory contained in them been built up. But they possess a clearness almost equal to that of Hume and Berkeley; an eloquence and poetry not inferior to what formed the charm of the lectures of Dr Thomas Brown; and a variety and brilliancy of expression and a fertility of illustration to make plain, and of humour to render ridiculous, not to be found elsewhere in the writings of metaphysicians. Perhaps the world is too old now for systems of philosophy. Amid the deafening thunder of machinery, it almost seems so. But to those who escape or can withdraw themselves into quiet regions afar from this distracting noise, and are curious about the half-solved or insoluble problems of existence and thought, Professor Ferrier's 'Institutes of Metaphysic' will, we believe, continue long to be a work of interest both for what it does and for what it leaves undone.

REV. JOHN ROBERTSON, D.D.[1]

THE death of the Rev. Dr Robertson, minister of the parish of St Mungo's, took place at St Andrews on Monday, 11th January 1865. He had suffered long from an affection of the heart, which manifested itself at the beginning in slowness of pulsation—the rate of his pulse being often so low as twenty-five per minute —and towards the close in rapid irregular action and fainting fits. For the last eight weeks he suffered from sickness, loss of appetite, and intense weakness, and was confined to bed. His recovery, which was from the first as doubtful as recovery always is in cases of obscure and uncommon heart complaint, had during these late weeks of weakness and illness, begun to be despaired of; and while his death among those who were in the habit of inquiring after his state of health could not excite surprise, it will be felt by all who knew him, and most deeply by those who knew him best, to be a great calamity.

Dr Robertson, who was, we believe, forty-two or forty-three years of age, was a native of Perthshire. He was educated at St Andrews, passing through the

[1] 'Scotsman,' January 12, 1865.

arts and theological classes at the University there.
He was a distinguished student in every class, and,
according to the tradition among St Andrews students,
he carried away more high college honours than any
student at the United College within human memory.
He was first, we know, in all the three mathematical
classes, and we have heard that he was first in every
other class at the United College during his curriculum.

The Non-intrusion or Disruption fever was raging
over Scotland during his early college years. He had
too great a preponderance of intellect over enthusiasm
to be affected by it, so he remained faithful to the
Established Church; and in 1848, within a short time
after he obtained licence, he was ordained minister of
Mains and Strathmartine, a country parish near Dundee. For ten years he continued to discharge his
pastoral duties there, visiting occasionally, and rather
as a homely friend than as a clergyman; reading
ravenously when he could, and writing, chiefly on
Saturdays, sermons which riveted the attention of his
country congregation from their simplicity and sincerity,
and which charmed audiences in cities by these qualities, as well as by their elegance, their completeness,
and their depth and force of thought. The best heads
of Dundee always gathered to hear him. In St Andrews he never failed to draw a crowd, and during the
college sessions the students flocked to hear "John
Robertson," as they called him, as they flocked to hear
no other minister whom they had a chance of hearing
frequently. Before these ten years had ended, he was

well known in Edinburgh, and at one time was all but
appointed one of the ministers of St Andrew's Church.
He had many opportunities of leaving his quiet country parish; but, caring very little for money, he declined them all, until in 1858 he was selected as
minister for the Cathedral of Glasgow. To select a
country minister to preach regularly in the most beautiful church in Scotland was a bold act; but it was
justified by the result in a manner confidently anticipated by those who knew the Rev. John Robertson,
and were capable of forming a judgment. He preached
in Glasgow Cathedral, so long as health was left him,
to overflowing audiences; and they were audiences
that did not cough and yawn, or sleep, or exhibit that
pious stupidity and vulgar vanity that are too visible
in too many churches in Glasgow and elsewhere. They
were obviously audiences of very high intelligence and
culture, drawn together by their intellectual and moral
affinities to the preacher,—whose unpretending plainness veiled his merits to the artificial, the insincere,
and the dull, but did not conceal them from those who
had insight into the realities of manhood and a gospel-
preacher's mission.

To name the precise secret of Dr Robertson's success as a preacher would be a difficult, indeed an impossible task. He was not a man of any striking
special faculty. There are many ministers more brilliant in rhetoric, more dexterous in logic, more copious
and splendid in fancy, more ardent in emotional eloquence. But he was strong in all his faculties. No

one of them was allowed to run away with him, or
with his subject. Whatever topic he took up, he
handled it so easily that to a careless or an incapable
observer it appeared that what he did could be done
(as it was done) without effort; but those who had
themselves grappled with the same topics, and seen
small rhetoricians toiling at them to no useful purpose,
were astonished at his enormous unpretending strength.
Many of his sermons were written at a sitting. He
had almost always difficulty in making a beginning,
and often wrote the first paragraph five or six times
over. But when once his thoughts and illustrations,
long treasured in a memory that remembered everything at the right time, were fairly heated and molten,
they poured out into the mould. There was no longer
any hesitation or difficulty in expression. The right
words and thoughts came like an inspiration, and the
sermon thus hastily written seemed to have the completeness and the finish of a composition over which
weeks and perhaps months had been spent. But its
parts had, when closely examined, a coherence and a
unity not to be found in those sermons that are composed upon the method of writing down all the fine
things that occur to the mind in its best moods over
a course of weeks or months. Some specimens of his
sermons were published by him a month ago under the
title of ' Pastoral Counsels,' along with a very affectionate and touching letter to his congregation. They
are in his more homely and quiet style, and only indicate by little casual touches the immense latent power

of his mind; but we have rarely read any volume so marked by freedom from every shadow of cant and affectation, by earnestness, love of his fellow-men, and unpretending—apparently half-unconscious—intellectual strength, and in which the doctrine that " God is love " is so fervently enforced.

Personally he was beloved by all who came to know him, whether high or low. The liking of his people for him in his old country parish of Mains was quite wonderful. They did not comprehend how he was reckoned a great preacher in Edinburgh and Glasgow, but they knew his homely kindness to them; and we doubt not that in most cottages in that parish to-day he is lamented as a brother. As a man there was no pretension or self-assertion about him. He was never known to have a quarrel. He did not care for controversy, except for the humorous aspects of it, at which he could laugh very heartily. He seemed almost destitute of ambition. Though he gained college honours he did not toil for them. In fact, he did not toil at all. His desire for knowledge led him to gather it as a pleasure; and he had a memory that allowed nothing once known to escape. The extent of his knowledge was not suspected, except by those who drew him in conversation to disclose his curious stores of information, or who noted the velocity with which he read a book, and the accuracy with which he remembered it after two or three years, and who knew that he spent a great part of his time in reading. He took little or no part in religious controversies, looking upon the majority of them as very small matters, and of next to no importance at all in the presence of death and eternity. But he was strongly in favour of toleration as the rule in those controverted matters that seemed to his mind so supremely indifferent. He was liberal in his views both regarding theological questions and forms of worship. He preached against making Sunday a disagreeable day to the young, and against all extreme puritanic views of Sunday observance. He approved of the use of a partial liturgy, and of instrumental music. But he did not magnify any of these points of controversy into essentials of religion. He treated them as nothing compared with charity to men and love to the Father of all. His moderation, tolerant wisdom, and devotion to duty, are worthy of imitation in all the Churches; and his premature death is a loss to all, for it is a loss to the cause of religion itself. Especially is it a loss to the Church of Scotland; for probably Dr Robertson was its most massive intellect of this generation.

JOHN HUNTER, LL.D.

THE natural life of this excellent man closed at Craigcrook on Friday afternoon.[1] His official life closed three years ago. Since then he has been, as it were, dead to the public; but in consideration of what he was, not merely as Auditor of the Court of Session, but as a man of letters and friend and adviser of literary men (in which vocation he had use for far higher and rarer faculties than those required for Auditor), he ought not to be allowed to pass into silence and forgetfulness without an attempt being made to tell what manner of man he was, and how it fared with him in labour, learning, and friendship, in his quiet but not uneventful or inactive life.

John Hunter was born in the manse of Dunino, near St Andrews, in March 1801. He was a grandson of Dr John Hunter, who was in early life secretary to Lord Monboddo, and his ally in classical studies; in his prime, a celebrated professor of Latin in the United College, St Andrews; in his green, long, old age, the Principal of that College, a scholar and philologist of great acuteness and philosophic

---

[1] 'Scotsman,' Dec. 6, 1869 [being the third day after the death].

2 A

power, likely to remain for ages one of the most
notable of Scottish grammarians. His father, at the
date of his birth, was minister of the parish of
Dunino. Afterwards he was appointed Professor of
Logic in the United College of St Andrews and minister of the College parish; and is remembered by
old students as a gentleman of a military rather
than professorial bearing and figure, both in person
and mind, a man with force of intellect fit to carry
him triumphantly through great and difficult occasions, but of a disposition to push aside ordinary
duties—such as preaching routine sermons—with a
very moderate amount of effort and care. His wife,
John Hunter's mother, Jane Wilson—a clever woman,
whose strokes of wit are still laughed at in St Andrews,
but were trembled at by some of the prim people there,
two or three generations ago—was a daughter of the
Professor of Hebrew, and afterwards of Church History, in St Mary's College, St Andrews, and author
of a Greek Grammar, which in its day had a high
reputation not confined to Scotland. Another of Professor Wilson's daughters was the first wife of Lord
Jeffrey. John Hunter was thus in a manner born
to a heritage of learned associations. He would almost have required to have been born with a stock
of antenatal knowledge, for he was, after passing
through the classes of the Old Grammar School of
St Andrews, entered a student at the United College
at the early age of ten, and in his little red gown
went forth in the twilight of the winter mornings

when this century was also young, to stumble through
the big holes of the then unpaved streets of the venerable city, and take his seat in small confined class-
rooms, nearly as dark as cellars, to prove what his
much-meditating grandfather and his colleagues could
put into so juvenile a head. Incredible as it may appear from such a too early beginning, he was really
a successful student, and obtained a respectable or a
high place in all his classes. He got prizes for
classics and mathematics. He was second in the
natural philosophy class, which was taught very
effectively in those days by Dr Jackson—a hoarse-
voiced, severe, impartial teacher, and universal scholar;
and he would have been first had there not been in
the same class with him George Lillie Craik, his
senior by some years, whose abilities are otherwise
attested by his 'History of English Literature,'
'Romance of the Peerage,' and many other books.
Hunter took the degree of M.A. at the age of fifteen,
which is certainly some years too early. Hard brain-
work from the age of ten onwards may be interesting
to the unconcerned observer, but to the delicately
organised human worker it is all too likely to secure
a stunting of the mental powers and their premature
decay. John Hunter turned out a remarkably able
man in spite of it. How much greater he might have
been but for excessive mental toil begun too early, and
continued too uninterruptedly, may be conjectured, but
cannot be known.

Mr John Hunter, A.M., of St Andrews, was, at the

age of sixteen, apprenticed to the late Walter Cook, W.S. He wished to be a clergyman, but his father had shrewdness to see that his talent could be carried to a better market than that of the Church. In the autumn of 1826 he passed as W.S., and commenced business. He was successful in business beyond his modest expectations. He was a partner of the well-known firm of Lockhart, Hunter, & Greig, and did a great deal of that severe, not very interesting, intellectual work which falls to the lot of a busy law agent. He never loved his profession very much. He had faculties for, and aspirations after, far higher things; but he, day by day, in business hours, and after them when necessary, stuck to his desk, and did his duty as punctually as the most prosaic of legal mortals. He rose early, and enjoyed the luxury of cultivating literature from six to nine in the morning, when his mind was clear of the worry of small, selfish squabbles, and that anxiety which besets all who are destined to strive against injustice. In 1848, Lord Advocate Rutherfurd, who did not distrust a lawyer because he had a liking for literature, appointed him Auditor of the Court of Session, telling him that he did so "entirely on public grounds;" which unstated grounds we can conjecture to have been his unquestionable talents, his knowledge of business, and the experience he had derived from acting as occasional substitute for Mr Guthrie Wright, his predecessor in the office. How punctually, faithfully, and rationally he discharged the irksome duties of Auditor is well known to the profession in

Edinburgh. To him most of the disputes about whether 6s. 8d. or 3s. 4d. should be allowed as the proper charge for writing a letter swollen with verbiage, or how many pages should be deducted from the length of a "memorial," because of quotations and irrelevant nonsense, must have been both wearisome and contemptible. But he adjusted himself to settle a question of 3s. 4d. with unflinching resolution; he heard a deal of talk thereanent, with more or less impatience, and more or less amusement, and then he gave his decision in no great profusion of words. Arguments were for the most part apt to be lost upon him. He thought for himself what was just, and after he had once done so he was nearly as obstinate and inconvincible as Fate, and kept his place like a rock among currents of attorney-brawling and eloquence—some of them pretty muddy with seething selfishness and not over-honest desires. That he was always right cannot be said of him or of any man, especially a man who is hard-worked; but that he always tried strenuously to do right, will, we believe, not be gainsaid by any intelligent, much less by any charitable man, who had an opportunity of discerning the truth.

In his prime, Mr John Hunter renewed his connection with the University of St Andrews, and was for three years a member of its University Court. The degree of LL.D. was conferred upon him by the University of Edinburgh in consideration of his literary attainments. He published little compared with what he might have done; but a volume of poetical translations from the Italian testify to his fine taste and power of poetical expression. From his early years he was devoted to poetry. He was a worshipper of Wordsworth when it was not fashionable to worship Wordsworth. Leigh Hunt and Charles Lamb were among his friends and favourites. His old fellow-student, Professor Craik, continued his friend through life, and consulted him about all his literary undertakings, down to many of the details. Many literary men were accustomed to take the benefit of his advice, which, both in praise and censure, was as candid as could be desired from the most trusted of friends. He was full of encouragement to young men; and to talk an hour with him was a stimulus to intellectual endeavour not readily to be forgotten.

Few men knew and remembered the best books as well as he. His critical insight was of the finest edge and penetrating power in the regions of poetry and quaint humour, and he could repeat for hours and hours the best passages from the best books. Why he should have known and understood so much and written so little was a mystery to those who saw what great capabilities lay in him. Perhaps it was self-distrust, though in other matters of action he was not deficient in self-reliance; but more probably it was an over-cultivation of the critical faculty which has a tendency to stifle originality, seeing that most new thoughts do not start into birth perfect and full-armed like Minerva, but, on the contrary, are strange

and clumsy of aspect, and apt to be incredible in the
eyes of the critical faculty, which has little mercy
and no parental affection. Had he read and scanned
less, he might have written more. The shadows of
the well-remembered thoughts and utterances of great
thinkers and poets stood between him and the sun,
and darkened his native possibilities.

Owing to failing energy, both of body and mind,
Mr Hunter resigned his appointment of Auditor about
three years ago, and since then he has been gradually
decaying. He, during his busy days, looked forward
to a period of leisure when he could give his whole
time to books, and to those studies which he loved so
well. The time of leisure arrived, but the intellectual power to enjoy it was denied him. He sat like
Southey among his books—"The mighty minds of
old" were on the library shelves as formerly, but the
eye of the earnest admirer was dim and his natural
force abated. The tide that was to lift him to their
level had ebbed for ever in this world. His early
years and his prime were full of worthy labour, of
much mental enjoyment—and it may be of some
sorrow—and of warm friendship with men of talent
and genius. His latter years were nearly a blank, a
sad illustration of the vanity of those human wishes,
and the hopes that are confined to this life and this
mortal lot.

LORD BARCAPLE.[1]

THE illness of this esteemed Judge terminated fatally shortly before noon yesterday, 23d February 1870 When the Court of Session rose for the Christmas vacation, he went home to his bedroom, which he was never again to leave alive. His malady, whatever it was, had been gathering for a considerable time. Want of outdoor exercise and want of ordinary rest aggravated it, and not improbably gave rise to it. His vacation came too late.

Edward Francis Maitland, whose loss we now deplore, was born in Edinburgh in 1808. He was a son of Adam Maitland, Esq. of Dundrennan, and a younger brother of Lord Dundrennan, one of his predecessors on the bench. He was educated at the High School and University of Edinburgh, and passed to the Bar in 1831. For many years he had little practice, and at one time meditated abandoning the profession of advocate. He was gifted with an intellect of no common order—strong far beyond the requirements of either junior or senior counsel work, sure-footed in matters of logic, and swift to run down big fallacies,

[1] 'Scotsman,' Feb. 24, 1870.

but rather too heavy to turn lightly upon small fallacies, and deal neatly with trifles. His great qualities were beyond the appreciation of small men. He was no fussy smiling flatterer, no cringing courtier, no adroit artist in hiding his contempt for the contemptible. On the contrary, he spoke out the truth gruffly, stamped upon every first appearance of falsehood or deceit, and duly earned the hatred of all pettifoggers, and vulgar votaries of tact and untruth. During his era of enforced idleness and neglect, he solaced himself with literature, and for a time edited the 'North British Review,' of which he was one of the originators, with much ability and the most anxious care. At last, the summer of his professional good fortune came, and all the ice-barriers of wintry years suddenly dissolved. He required but to get an opportunity to disclose what lay in him, hidden to dull plodders, and hoary disbelievers in justice, and indiscriminating worshippers of the fashionable and the shallow, to rise for ever above their power to exclude him from that work which he was as fit as any, and fitter than most, to do thoroughly well. Adversity had allowed him leisure to study, to fill his mind with ready knowledge, and had supplied him with antidotes against the intoxication of prosperity. Indolence could hardly steal upon an honest worker who had been so long waiting for his work.

He was for some time, when the Liberals were in office, an advocate-depute; and indictments drawn by him in uncommon cases are among the best models of style to which the modern Crown lawyer (occasionally somewhat helpless as to style) can look back.   In 1851 he was appointed Sheriff of Argyleshire; in 1855, and again in 1859, he was appointed Solicitor-General; and in 1862 he was raised to the Bench, and known by the title of Lord Barcaple.   In that calm and dignified position he probably expected some leisure; but instead thereof he had laid upon him far more labour than he underwent at the Bar—at least as much labour as at the Bar would have produced an income of more than double his salary as Judge.   And then this winter a burden already too heavy was greatly increased by the failure to fill up Lord Manor's vacant chair.   The result was that he, the hardest-worked of Judges, broke down under the load.   And now at last his death has come as one of the blessings which demagogues who fancy themselves to be patriots have secured for their country.   Very sad it is to see the strong true man, that could ill be spared, destroyed before the weak, cunning, and unscrupulous; but, somehow or other, the towers of Siloam never fall where they ought to do.

What was the intellectual faculty strongest in Lord Barcaple's mind, it is not easy to specify, the truth being that all the essential faculties of his mind were strong and peculiarly well balanced.   He had singular powers of observation, of accurate retentive memory and of reasoning—the latter, of course, being those that were called into greatest prominence and most con-

stant exercise by his professional avocations. He had
humour also of a subtle and refined but genuine kind,
and his beautiful smile and faint blush, lighting up
and tinging his pale, usually grave face, at some
irresistible joke, were in their combination a singular
tribute to energies that cannot be judicially recognised.
His oratory was of a very high order, and in some
respects it was not surpassed by that of any of his
contemporaries. Speeches more convincing than his
could occasionally be heard if the hearer knew nothing
of the matter of controversy except what was contained in these speeches, seeing that to pass by unanswerable difficulties in silence was not one of his
oratorical tricks. He resolutely fronted the strength
of an adversary's position, having too much courage
and honesty to slip gracefully past the flank, waving
above his head all manner of standards and streaming
banners, as if he had swept the whole field bare of
all obstacles to his progress. His speeches in the
Maciver divorce case and in the Yelverton marriage
case were among the finest forensic efforts of this
generation, and were in their substance an outpour-
ing of the red-hot earnest conviction of a lofty pure
mind, in which unclean suspicions could find no resting-
place, and out of which the practice of the law had
not banished the poetry that belongs to the ideal of
woman. He had not ceased to believe in the grace
and beauty of human life. Truth and virtue were
dear to him, and were dearly cherished, and his

charity did not permit him to suspect the worst of mankind and of womankind without any evidence beyond the mere fact of humanity.

The duties of a judge were discharged by him faithfully—too faithfully, as his end has proved. He was an excellent listener to a good argument, and a dangerous critic for a bad one. Long-winded palaver and laborious arguing beside the question did not meet with much tolerance from him. He was impatient of most of the evil that is done under the sun, and it may be, also, of some of the good that was so clumsy and awkward as to look like evil. From the path of integrity he never wittingly swerved. The dictates of his conscience were sacred to him. His errors, which were few, were those of the intellect, and were due to a tendency to excessive refinement, and to put faith in some kind of fitful illusive light that led him astray into what may be thought dangerous transcendental regions. To restrain him therefrom he had not the common check of weak men who cannot think for themselves, and who have a prudent horror of whatever is singular and uncommon. The opinion of the majority was nothing to him. He trusted to the operations of his own mind, and gave expression to his own convictions, regardless of the talk and the opinions of the multitude. Intellectually he was of a rigid unbending nature, like an oak which had grown for long centuries alone, and had at last become fixed, knotty, and twisted and gnarled by wrestling with all the winds of heaven. But though this was his attitude to his fellow-men and their opinions, he was at heart one of the truest, kindest of men. No duty did he neglect; no act of charity did he leave undone. Free Churchman though he was, he was no bigot. With him the petty interests and animosities of the sect had not superseded the essentials of Christianity. He was, so far as we can judge, worthy to be a member of the Church invisible, the temple of which is not made with hands, the worshippers in which look upwards to a God of truth through the mists and vapours of this life, and hope for a clearer light and a surer vision after the sun of Time has set for ever.

GEORGE MOIR, LL.D.[1]

THIS well-known lawyer and literary man died at his house in Charlotte Square, rather suddenly, on the afternoon of Wednesday, 19th October 1870. Five years before, when he resigned the Professorship of Scotch Law, he was seriously ill, and did not expect to recover; but he did regain tolerable health, and though he had been complaining for a few days before the unexpected end, was in the midst of arrangements to remove permanently to London; and had resolved, after consultation with his medical adviser, to travel all the way to London by train without stopping, in the course of the night. On Wednesday, he took lunch heartily, and was cheerful and feeling pretty well. Between two and three he had an interview with his old confidential clerk, and showed no signs that the end was near. Shortly after, he was found lying on the sofa pallid and dying, and by four o'clock he was gone upon the longest and darkest of journeys, it having been decreed that London should never be the home of his old age.

Though he had been for several years in delicate

[1] 'Scotsman,' October 21, 1870.

health, he was not, among veterans of the legal profession, what could be called an old man. He was born in Aberdeen in the year 1800, and was educated there—at least he had the benefit of a good deal of Aberdeen education, which is probably equal to the best that Scotland can give; but he was one of those uncommon men that require to get beyond all that schools and colleges can do, and are constrained to acquire knowledge as they best can by the force of their own inner lights and impulses, and such outer aid as fate permits or good fortune supplies. He came to Edinburgh early, among his twenties, and spent some time in a lawyer's office and in cultivating literature, probably upon a sufficiency of oatmeal, for he had a moderate patrimony that raised him above care for daily bread. In 1825 he passed as advocate; and though he had previously been a contributor to the 'Edinburgh Review,' he threw in his lot with the Tories, and became a pretty frequent and greatly esteemed contributor to 'Blackwood's Magazine.' He was not a fanatic in politics. Had he been a man of half the intellect he possessed, but a political bigot and a stout hater of Whiggery and suchlike, the Tories would most likely have felt bound to promote him to the Bench, which he would certainly have adorned as much as the ablest of his contemporaries; for in point of logical force and clearness he had few superiors, and in point of easy, fluent, elegant precision and crystal lucidity of style, whether oral or written, he had no superior and scarcely an equal.

He was not, however, utterly neglected by his party. He was appointed Professor of Rhetoric in the University of Edinburgh in 1835. On Lord Jerviswoode's promotion to the Bench in 1859, he was translated from the Sheriffship of Ross, in which he had succeeded Lord Mackenzie, to the Sheriffship of Stirling, which office his critical state of health, and the still more critical state of the Tory party's tenure of office, induced him to resign in the fall of 1868, shortly before that party's surrender of their lucky *cornucopia* of judicial and other patronage. In 1864 he was chosen by his brethren of the Faculty of Advocates to fill the Chair of Scots Law; but that office a sudden attack of illness compelled him to resign in about a year after his election. He had written his course of lectures, not without great labour, and it is an incalculable loss to the legal literature of Scotland that he did not enjoy health and strength for a few years to enable him to mature and perfect his exposition of Scotch law. Had he done so, his lucid, graceful statements, would, we feel certain, have been not unworthy to take rank with the bold, sweeping, philosophic generalisations of Stair, and the elegant dignified dogmatisms, and cautious subtle doubts (which are generally dogmatisms in disguise), of Hume; and would, we do not hesitate to assert, have deserved to take rank above the lucubrations of Erskine, which are often weak in logic, being self-contradictory, and not satisfactory as specimens of literature or of philosophy, nor altogether creditable to the age that produced them, nor to the generations since that have accepted them with the reverence due only to inspiration or the utterances of some infallible oracle.

Mr Moir had in his prime a very fair practice at the Bar, for no man, could "open" a difficult, complicated case more simply, clearly, and beautifully than he; and the race of men and of lawyers who had worshipped Jeffrey could hardly neglect the pleader who had nearly all Jeffrey's elegance of expression, and a far fuller knowledge of law. On the other side, however, it is not to be concealed that Mr Moir was not so successful in replying to the arguments of an adversary, or the incisive questions of some judges, as he was at expounding those arguments that had recommended themselves to his own mind, or that it was necessary for the interests of his client that he should place reliance upon. His mind was not so nimble and shifty as that of most successful debaters. Moreover, he was naturally a shy, modest man. He could be happy and most lively, suggestive and free in conversation, with a friend, or a knot of intelligent friends; but he shrank from the public gaze—it seemed to make him nervous and unhappy.

We believe he was better known as a literary man than as a lawyer. For nearly half a century the name of Mr George Moir has been familiar and admired in the literary circles of Edinburgh, and indeed of this country. Though a Tory, he was a familiar friend of many Liberals, and among them Sir William Hamilton, whose acquaintance he made in 1824 (as he has himself

2 B

told in interesting notes printed in Professor Veitch's recent life of Sir William), when, before passing to the Bar, he was employing his leisure in writing an article on the ballad-poetry of Spain for the 'Edinburgh Review,' and got introduced to Sir William, in order to draw information from his enormous and heterogeneous stores. Two or three years later he dedicated to Sir William his elegant and faithful translation of Schiller's " Wallenstein," Sir William himself revising the proof-sheets nearly to the end, when his mother's illness interrupted his friendly aid. Mr Thomas Carlyle also counted him among his friends during his sojourn in Edinburgh about forty years ago. After Mr Moir's appointment to the Chair of Rhetoric, he wrote treatises on Poetry and Modern Romance for the 'Encyclopædia Britannica,' which treatises were published in a separate volume, along with Professor Spalding's treatise on Rhetoric. Whoever would know what Mr Moir could do in literature should read his treatise on Poetry and his "Wallenstein." The latter indicates his singular command of poetical expression — the former his extensive knowledge of poetic literature, and his sound genuine critical faculty. Both indicate a mind with a great deal of light in it, and not much heat; a mind fitted to illuminate the definite, and to rise into the ornate, the fanciful, and even the beautiful; but not a specially sincere, original mind—not a mind fitted to burn up human impostures or delusions, or to melt down the impassable adamant into the true seer or poet's pathway into unknown worlds. Still he achieved various literary successes amid the difficult conditions that surround a practising advocate. In literature his success was less disproportionate to his merits than it was in law. But it matters little now. His writings will excite human interest and keep alive his memory long after the names of most of his successful rivals have perished utterly, or survive only in the dusty mummy-wrappings of law reports and session papers.

LORD STAIR.[1]

LORD STAIR is one of the most noteworthy characters
in Scottish history, but one of the darkest, not in the
sense of being bad, but in the sense of being mysterious,
dim, indefinite, and self-contradictory. He has been
a great deal written about, and has fallen within the
range of study and discussion of various masters of
insight into human character, but none of them have
done much to restore him to daylight, and send him
forth as credible flesh and blood. Sir Walter Scott
had him in a manner forced upon his attention as the
father of the Bride of Lammermoor; but he could not
use up all the realities of his character for the purposes
of his fiction, and he warns his readers against supposing that "there was any idea of tracing the portrait of
the first Lord Viscount Stair in the tricky and mean-
spirited Sir W. Ashton;" adding significantly—"Lord
Stair, whatever might be his moral qualities, was certainly one of the first statesmen and lawyers of his
age;" which means, or at least suggests, as we read it,

---

[1] Memoir of Sir James Dalrymple, First Viscount Stair. By Æ.
J. G. Mackay, Advocate of the Scotch Bar. Edinburgh: Edmonston
& Douglas. ['Scotsman,' June 27, 1873.]

that in Scott's opinion it was not conscience but intellect and prudence which prevented him from exhibiting all the vices of Sir William Ashton and probably a few more—and leads us to infer that had Scott not been educated as an advocate to reverence the name of Stair, the portrait he would have painted of him would have been pretty black and not very comely.

Macaulay, whose political leanings were in favour of Stair, has in his 'History of England' drawn a portrait of him in which Scott's view of his deficiency in point of moral principle is fully accepted, and touches of doubt as to his fidelity to justice and the sincerity of his religious professions and weekly fasting and humiliation are skilfully laid on. Having been one of Cromwell's judges, appointed by the silent, diplomatic, non-fanatical General Monk when overseer of Scotland, Stair fell within the scope of Carlyle's 'Life of Cromwell,' and would, no doubt, like Paul Jones in the French Revolution have had a " word spent or mis-spent " upon him " for country's sake," had it seemed possible to do it truly and effectively ; but the greatest living delineator of human character has found nothing worth printing to say of the greatest of Scottish jurists. His silence is all the more suggestive, because of the reputation for heroism and magnanimity he has accorded to his military grandson, Marlborough's pupil, in the 'Life of Frederick the Great.' It is presumable, therefore, if not quite plain, that there do not exist materials for constructing a character of Stair that could fascinate the creative or reconstructive powers of a great historical or dramatic genius. His *sacer vates* has been, and always will be, wanting. Yet his name will not be forgotten' for centuries. His worthiest title to be remembered is his 'Institutions of the Law of Scotland,' published in 1681, which is probably the most masterly, clear, methodical, compendious, philosophical exposition ever produced by any man of the laws of any country, embracing as it does the best results of the combined experience of a Professor of Philosophy in Glasgow, which he was in his youth, and of Lord President of the Court of Session, which he was in his prime and in his latter years, and singularly free alike of the perplexing wiredrawn speculative pedantries of the professor, and of the still more irritating and confounding pedantries of the mere practical lawyer who has had no philosophic or general culture, and who knows little or nothing beyond the sordid cunning technicalities and tricks of his trade. But the time may come when, in the march of assimilating Scotch with English law, Stair's 'Institutes' will be forgotten, and it may then be his undesirable destiny to be remembered for having permitted his clever ambitious wife to sacrifice his daughter in the way detailed, with more or less ideal truth, in the 'Bride of Lammermoor,' and of having failed, through indifference or malice, to prevent his eldest son John, the Lord Advocate, and one of the Secretaries of State for Scotland in 1692, from urging and largely contributing to the perpetration of the memorable and execrable massacre of Glencoe.

For these current generations, especially in Scotland, he is manifestly a man worth knowing about, and Mr Mackay has assiduously collected all, or nearly all, the facts regarding him that have not sunk irreparably into oblivion. He does not give, he does not profess to give, a biography of him. He has undertaken to write "memorials," and to give the results of "a study of the history of Scotland and Scotch law during the seventeenth century," and he has faithfully fulfilled his undertaking. The merits of his work are not of a very high historic order, but they are many and genuine, and they seem to us to be due to the author's catholic sympathies, his industry, his extensive and diversified reading, his capacity for seeing the truth, sharpened a little by professional experience in sifting evidence, and his candour in stating the truth, preserved perhaps in spite of professional temptations. We are not quite sure that he fully believes in his hero, but we rather think he disbelieves pretty stoutly in nearly everything that every writer of note has written against him, and can give reasons for his disbelief. Into Macaulay's estimate of him, for example, he pricks a number of footnotes that go into the tissue of Macaulay's facts like so many needles, and show that to a great extent Macaulay's picture of Stair is drawn from the ideal, and from satirists who were not very particular about the real unless when it consisted in some deformity, which in the special case of Stair was a wry-neck. But notwithstanding of these sharp critical footnotes, and our inclination to accept the most of them as accurate in point of fact, we feel inclined to believe that Macaulay did his best to understand and fairly and even not unfavourably to portray the character of Stair. If he required to borrow from his imagination and from satires, it was because other and more unexceptionable materials were not to be had. Mr Mackay's strictures upon Macaulay do not prove that Macaulay was wrong. They only prove that he introduced elements of fiction into this portraiture, and they help to prove that, apart from fiction, it is henceforth impossible to fill in any detailed human character of Stair.

Of only a few facts is it now possible to be sure, and these chiefly dates. He was born in Kyle (and not the last or the most remarkable "lad" born there) in May 1619, and died 25th November 1695. He was educated at Mauchline Grammar School and Glasgow University, was an officer in Glencairn's Regiment during the war of the Covenant, was a regent or professor in Glasgow University from 1641 to 1647, married in 1643, and passed as advocate in 1648; he was appointed a Judge by Monk on the death of Lord Balcomie, which took place suddenly on the bench in the Parliament House on that very 26th of June 1657 on which Cromwell was for a second time solemnly installed in Westminster Hall as Lord Protector; was a second time appointed Judge by Charles II. in 1661, and a third time by that same monarch in 1664, his place being declared vacant in the interval, because he refused to sign "the Declaration." The tragic marriage of his daughter Janet took place in 1669. He was appointed President of the Court of Session in 1671; he resigned it ten years thereafter rather than take the test. Shortly after, his wife having deserted the Episcopal parish minister, and his eldest son, the bailie of the regality of Glenluce, having fallen into a dispute with Claverhouse about jurisdiction and the fining of Covenanting old wives, the ex-President's position became uncomfortable, and indeed perilous, in this country; so he betook himself to Holland, and there made the acquaintance of William of Orange, with whom he returned as a cherished adviser in 1688, and by whom he was next year appointed to his former exalted post, of which he was notably well worthy—that of Lord President of the Court of Session. He published his 'Institutions' in 1681, his 'Decisions' in 1683, his 'Physiologia Nova Experimentalis,' a book showing a fair knowledge of the crude natural sciences of his day, in 1686, an 'Apology' for or rather a defence of his public life in 1690, and a 'Vindication of the Divine Perfections,' just before his death in 1695.

These books and a few letters form the most solid materials upon which to base inferences as to what manner of man Stair really was. And they indicate a clear, calm, expansive, rather than intense or subtle, a serene imperturbable kind of intellect, carefully cultivated chiefly with reference to the practical business of life, and steadily controlled by considerations as to

the *cui bono*, but not naturally disinclined to speculate and interrogate the mysteries of existence if such
work could have been made to yield any kind of
adequate profit; a moral nature not equal in fineness and power to his intellect, but good enough,
indeed too good, for his age, distracted and overwhelmed as it was by irrational religious fanatics on
the one side, and inhuman persecuting atheists on
the other, and a genuine but not intensely earnest or
aspiring religious spirit. His last book of meditations
upon the Divine perfections, could hardly have been
published by a hypocrite at any period of life, and
least of all within sight of the brink of the grave.
There is plenty of absurdity in it, not so much or so
glaring, however, as in the religious writings of Newton of a somewhat later date; but the absurdities
even are, if closely looked at, evidence of sincerity.
There is also in it, to his credit be it told, a free use
of that right of private judgment to which Protestantism lays emphatic claim, and a bringing of such doctrines as the baptismal washing away of original sin,
and eucharistic purification from actual transgression
—both miraculous, of course,—to the test of reason,
and the quiet casting of them aside as unbelievable,
with an assured confidence which shows that Stair
was a very early and pretty advanced specimen of a
Christian *rationalist*, who would not have talked or
written such childish nonsense as has proceeded from
most of his successors on the Bench who have treated
of such subjects. That he knew the Bible well is

manifest from the Scripture instances and illustrations
that abound, and even superabound, in his 'Institutes,'
generally apposite enough, but some of them far-
fetched, and some of them so odd, that only a sincere
man with next to no sense of humour could have used
them; for no scoffer or humorist would have introduced them into a serious, dignified treatise such as
Stair's unquestionably is, both in conception and execution. But then, though his religious and moral
convictions were in all probability quite genuine, it is
clear that they were those of a philosopher with sceptical hesitations, rather than the fiery irresistible convictions of a prophet or a martyr.

He had insight into the right, and all but certainly
wished it success; but he, unlike the zealous, fervid
Covenanters of his day, could distinguish between the
desirable and the practicable, and he did not care to
throw away either his life or his chances of ambition
in the pursuit of an enthusiast's dream. The world
that lay around him did not admit of the working out
of any high ideal: he tried to make the most of it,
but did not seek to quarrel with it and waste his blood
like some of the more noisy, and not the least noble,
of his contemporaries. Both his philosophical exer-
citations and his professional experiences must have
taught him to bear the misfortunes and the villanies
of others with a sort of equanimity. If a lawyer of
his powers were to fret at all the evil he sees done
even in the name of law, through stupidity, or worse,
he would be among the most miserable of men. No

other profession, not even the medical, is so adapted to teach uncomplaining endurance of ills that cannot be cured. Stoical indifference or passive obedience to the inevitable, seems to account for all Stair's sins of omission, whether in submitting to domestic or royal or Cromwellian tyranny; whether in neglecting to save the lives and limbs of the poor Covenanters to whom he had kindly leanings—or the wild Highlanders of Glencoe, for whom hardly any civilised man cared—or his own daughter, whose tragic story is written more indelibly upon the memory of humanity than her father's fame.

LORD WESTBURY.[1]

His lordship's death took place at four o'clock yesterday morning [20th July 1873] at his residence, Lancaster Gate, London. He succumbed to the effects of a paralytic affection of the spine, with which he had been afflicted for five or six months.

Richard Bethell, who became Lord Westbury, was the son of a physician at Bradford-on-Avon, Wilts, and was born on 30th June 1800, so that he has attained to only three weeks more than seventy-three years of age. He was educated privately at Bristol, and at the early age of fourteen entered Wadham College, Oxford, where he soon obtained a scholarship, and in 1818 took his B.A. degree, gaining the high honour for one so young of a double first class. After that for some years he acted as resident private tutor, and studied for the Bar, to which he was called by the Middle Temple in 1823. He soon obtained a considerable business, a successful suit for Brasenose College, in which he was employed as counsel through the eminence of his University career, having brought him into notice. He was created a Queen's Counsel

[1] 'Scotsman,' July 21, 1873.

in 1840, was elected M.P. for Aylesbury in 1851, and
held that seat for eight years, when he was elected
for Wolverhampton. He was appointed Solicitor-
General for the Aberdeen Cabinet in 1852, became
Attorney-General under Lord Palmerston in November
1856, and held office to February 1858. He was reappointed in June 1859, and was created a Baron
and Lord Chancellor in June 1861. When in Parliament he helped to carry through many measures
of reform, and among others a bill for the reform of
Oxford University. He took the chief part in establishing the Probate and Divorce Courts, and helping
to destroy the English superstition about the sacredness and indissolubility of a marriage which had been
desecrated by the wife's infidelity, or by the husband's
infidelity, *plus* cruelty or bigamy or a few other
crimes which are necessary to bring unfaithfulness
up to the mark of rendering a profligate English husband unworthy to possess an innocent wife who desires to be rid of him. Though Oxford had done her
best to educate him, and had succeeded in teaching
him the classics and a great deal of English literature,
she had failed to make him superstitious; and though
he sometimes made goody-good speeches, and talked
like an oily Pharisee of the advantage that Christianity had been to him, and got persistently sneered
at by the 'Saturday Review' as an "eminent Christian," he was in religious ideas evidently a man of
liberal views, to which he gave effect in the Privy
Council judgment in regard to the 'Essays and Re-

views,' which was quizzically summarised by Cockney
wits as having "abolished hell with costs," and in
some sarcastical speeches in the House of Lords, by
which he excited the wrath of the then Bishop of
Oxford, Samuel Wilberforce (whose death, by a curious
coincidence, is likewise announced to-day), describing
a manifesto of the clergy, believed to be drawn by
Wilberforce, "as a series of saponaceous and well-
lubricated propositions," with little meaning in them,
and no legal efficacy except what they might have in
rendering the authors of them liable in some of the
ancient penalties of treason inflictable upon those
who did not respect the headship of the Crown in
matters ecclesiastical. Lord Westbury, from his love
of sarcasm and other causes, had excited the enmity
of others than bishops; and on 3d July 1865, when
Scotland was chiefly intent on Dr Pritchard's trial
for poisoning his wife and mother-in-law, his personal
enemies, combined with the enemies of the Government of Lord Palmerston, and a few conscientious
and honourable persons, carried against him a vote
of censure in regard to an appointment made in the
Leeds Bankruptcy Court, and the granting of a re-
tiring pension to Mr Leonard Edmunds, and declared
that by his laxity of practice and want of caution
"great encouragement has been given to corrupt practices;" and that they were "highly reprehensible, and
calculated to throw discredit upon the high offices of
the State." On the second day thereafter, he, in the
House of Lords, with a good deal of calm dignity,

announced his resignation of the office of Lord Chancellor, and its acceptance by the Queen, and stated that if he had followed the dictates of his own judgment, he would have resigned several months before, he having of course seen the coming storm. How far he was to blame for the causes of the Commons' censure will never be known. Like some other eminent men, he appeared to be unfortunate in one member of his family, if not in more than one. That he had been careless was pretty certain; but then a Lord Chancellor, overwhelmed with work, must trust a great deal to the industry and the statements of others. It was, however, doubtful, and was often doubted, if he was quite scrupulously conscientious. Many of his political compeers openly avowed their distrust of him; and it was insinuated that he was not guided by any high principle. We do not pretend to judge him further than to doubt if many of his detractors would have been any better than he if placed in the same position of power and temptation. We are inclined to suspect that there was a laxity about his moral nature not often found in minds of such commanding power. But then he had been acted upon by the deteriorating influence both of his profession and of political life, and he had had to struggle upwards, probably sometimes in an attitude not very different from creeping, and not very pleasant either to a proud nature or a sensitive conscience. Add to this that there was in his veins a pretty large admixture of Jewish blood, which means for the most part strong

money-making earthly instincts, and it will be fully
as easy to excuse as to condemn him. But whatever his conscience might be, his intellect was such
as might well excite the envy and the hatred of
the mobs of small creatures who clamour about conscience, and who are certain to show that they possess it whenever a chance arises of finding fault
with any one who is cleverer or otherwise better than
themselves.

That Lord Westbury was a very great man in
intellect, and in public affairs one of the greatest of
his time, is certain, but it is difficult to determine and
set forth the peculiar elements of his mind and character. With all men this is difficult, with legal men
and politico-legal men it is especially difficult, because
it is so hard to find out when they are expressing
their personal convictions or merely arguing ingeni-
ously to convince or mislead others, or to defend
foregone conclusions propounded by policy or individual interest irrespective of principle; and with
Lord Westbury it was in somewhere about the highest
degree difficult, because, in addition to being a man of
law and of politics, he wore a mask consisting of a
smooth, formal, lofty, affected, artificial manner, under
which he could play the part of calm, acute, exhaustive
legal pleader, incisive, sarcastic, insolent parliamentary
debater, and solemn, counsel - posing, dignified Lord
Chancellor, but which seldom, if ever, allowed to show
through the workings of the inner man—a mask more
rigid and impenetrable than wax, for it involved both

voice and gesture as well as feature. An occasional
indignant flash of a rather fine darkish eye, in which
ice and fire seemed strangely mixed—the ice for the
most part superabounding; an occasional irrepressible
insolent curl of a handsome upper lip,—were almost
the sole indications of real manhood that burst through
the actor's veil, and they showed what was truly in
him,—a hot, fierce temper, the manifestations of which
could be hidden rather than controlled, a towering
magnanimous self-esteem, an unconcealable, unlimited
scorn for all or nearly all the rest of mankind—a
scorn so vast, and conscious to itself of being so well
justified, as to be not worth putting into words except
upon rare voluntary occasions, or upon occasions when
he had been fee'd to make a speech of some kind.
These occasions he found in Scotch appeals more
readily than otherwise when he thought it necessary
or expedient to criticise the decisions and opinions of
the Judges of the Court of Session. It was characteristic of him to say, in his oiliest tones and most
pleasant mincing manner, as he once did of an opinion
of the late Lord Justice-Clerk Hope, that it was "a
melancholy collection of erroneous sentences. It is
hard to say whether the law or the grammar is the
worse;" or to ejaculate, as he once did *sotto voce* when
interrogated by a noble and learned Lord as to what
he meant to say the Court of Session had decided,
before proceeding to give a polite, audible, and plausible answer—"Stupid old fool; just fit for being a
Judge in the Court of Session yourself." Elsewhere

in the English Courts, he, if gossip and numerous stories can be trusted, was often supremely contemptuous,—so much so as on one occasion before Baron Maule, one of the few men in England intellectually his equal, to have provoked the Baron to beg him to remember that "the Court is a vertebrate animal, and ought not to be addressed in the style that God Almighty might be expected to use to a black beetle." This story may be apocryphal, but it ought to be true, and it is really true to the ideal individuality of both parties to it. The late Lord Campbell was a special mark for that contemptuous chaff of which he had generally ready a large store for all Scotchmen, it being his way, imitated in part from Dr Johnson, of expressing his friendly regard for our country—a respect which has been fully reciprocated north of the Tweed, though our manner of showing it has been different. For many years he was counsel in every important Scotch appeal, and for not a few of them obtained more money than was paid to Dr Johnson even for his Dictionary, upon which he expended the labour of years.

The speeches of Sir Richard Bethell at the Bar and of Lord Westbury on the Chancery Bench and on the Woolsack were utterances of the highest merit, looked at from a legal point of view—that is, the point of view which recognises coherent logic and clear complete expression as the first requisites, and all sensational colouring as likely to distract attention and lead the reason to illegitimate results. They would not

have had much effect upon juries. The manner of the
speaker was too affected, too like that of a prim precise dowager of last century. It had hardly in it the
semblance of earnestness. The passion that had
burned in those for whom he spoke, that had sometimes burned under close cover in his own mind, had
cooled, and the lava once molten and capable of kind-
ling conflagrations was presented not merely cold and
rigid, but polished. The appeal was to the intellect,
and in its ideal conception to the intellect alone.
From that ideal there were very few deviations into
the region of feeling or emotion, hardly any invoca-
tions to conscience or whatever else it may be that
discriminates the right from the settled or the expedient; in short, not many deviations from the sphere
of pure intellect, and these almost all falling under
the category of dexterous parenthetical oblique appeals
to those prejudices that are apt to be generated in the
atmosphere of London, and affect small minds, those
prejudices from which Lord Westbury himself was
not entirely free, though few intellects could soar so
high above the fogs of Cockneydom, and look down
upon the seething swarming maggots underneath with
such contempt as he. Professional opinion placed
him first among the forensic pleaders of his day, and
we believe that in that matter the verdict of professional opinion was right, though it is often nothing
more than a rush like a flock of sheep in a track upon
which two or three knowing bell-wethers have had
the intelligence and the courage to venture. The

marvel was that the herd of Cockney solicitors could be found to believe in mental qualities which few of them personally could have had the capacity to appreciate. We are inclined to believe further, that in the field of *pure* law he was one of the greatest pleaders that ever lived, perhaps the very greatest—for it is not long since civilisation progressed so far as to permit of a field of "pure law," in which bribery and corruption, and partiality to counsel or clients, had no place. All the world has heard of Bacon's bribes as well as Shakespeare's deer-stealing; but though before his age in many particulars, Bacon was of his age in that particular, and not alien to some subsequent ages.

The judicial opinions of Lord Westbury scarcely gave an adequate idea of his powers. And yet they are most of them the manifest outcome of a mastermind. One of his longest opinions, and the one best known in Scotland, is that delivered by him in July 1864 in the celebrated Yelverton case. It is perhaps not too much to say of it that no other Lord Chancellor of this century could have written it—so lucid, terse, compact, carefully balanced it is, so skilfully touched with the graces of unobtrusive but real eloquence. It may be, however, that its merits appear greater than they really are, from the necessity of contrasting them with the manifestations of intellectual weakness that appear in the opinions of the majority of the noble and learned Lords who took a different view, and who, in consequence of Lord Brougham's absence from illness, left him in a minority of one. But there are a number of his opinions on points of strict law that are marvels of metaphysico-legal exposition. They weigh the *pros* and *cons*, meet the difficulties, eliminate the fallacies and expound the principles, or more probably principle (for he struggled always to arrive at one principle if possible), of decision, in the clearest, fewest words, in a style of English so perfect that it seems impossible to improve it by transposition or alteration, by subtraction or addition. Lord Lyndhurst alone of modern Chancellors approaches him closely in perfection of legal style; but then Lord Lyndhurst had not Lord Westbury's courage, he was always more anxious to state legal doctrines safely than to state them completely. The facility and precision with which Lord Westbury could throw into spoken words the most puzzling legal question, the most complicated proposition, omitting no essential qualification, and expressing neither too little nor too much, was altogether. wonderful, and in the House of Lords compelled the admiration of all except the unhappy counsel who might be expected to answer the question or refute the proposition. We are inclined to believe him to have been the best stater of legal propositions the world ever saw; and that by his death, not early in life and yet untimely for a successful lawyer who has reached the serene leisure which he had reached, the further services of the best of legal intellects appointed by Providence for the use of this age are lost to mankind.

HENRY GLASSFORD BELL.[1]

THE Sheriff of Lanarkshire died at Glasgow on the
7th January 1874. He had, for a considerable time,
been suffering from a disease in the right hand, called
epithelioma, and conjectured by some medical authorities to be cancerous in its nature. On the 8th of
November 1873, in order to remove, and, if possible,
extirpate this disease, he underwent amputation of the
hand, being hopeful, as his friends and his medical
advisers were, of a complete cure. A few days before
the operation, he wrote notes to two or three of the
dearest of his old Edinburgh friends, expressive of
calm and fearless outlook for the issue, whatever it
might be. It was pretty confidently expected that
his originally robust constitution would carry him
through; and until three or four days before his death,
it appeared likely that these expectations would be
realised. The wound actually healed, and yet, through
causes unforeseeable, inscrutable, his constitution collapsed in sudden ruin. Probably the transition from
the full strain and multifarious occupation of his
active, much-enjoying, all-engrossing Glasgow life, to

[1] 'The Journal of Jurisprudence,' February 1874.

the quiet and dreary abstinence of a sick-room, may
have thrown it out of gear, so to speak, and involved
it in that destruction which compulsory lethargy often
brings upon the most important machinery in all the
higher planes of vitality. The bear and the bat may
go to sleep for months, and so may, in a kind of way,
some human creatures that resemble them in hiber-
nating faculty; but Mr Bell was not one of these.
In almost all respects he was a gigantic kind of man,
doing the work of three or four common men, and
to all careful observers of him, stagnation must have
seemed difficult; the event showed it to be impossible.
Five days after death, his "mortal coil" was laid in
that grand old Cathedral which adorns the commercial·
metropolis of the west, and which few of the earnest
and busy and eager eyes that for centuries have looked
on it, could venerate so sincerely and so intelligently
as he, and which shelters few sleepers so worthy of
so magnificent a last resting-place.

In that city where he has found so illustrious a grave,
he also found his cradle, like the most of Nature's
nobles, in comparative obscurity. He was born there,
on the 8th of November 1805, and received, it is
said, his early education at the High School there.
His father was a member of the Scottish Bar, and
at one time, and we rather think for a considerable
period of years, was town-clerk of Greenock. He
did not manage to agree with the civic despots of
Greenock, and he removed to Edinburgh, and sub-
sisted in part by literature, being editor of the 'Edin-

burgh Observer,' to which paper, in due if somewhat
early course, the subject of this notice became a
contributor, having latterly a special page for himself and literature, which, by - and - by, attracted a
good deal of attention in the Edinburgh brilliant
literary world of that day—a literary world about the
most brilliant possible, if its own estimate of itself
be accepted. After he had passed through the University of Edinburgh, at the early age of twenty-two
or thereby, he became editor of the 'Edinburgh
Literary Journal,' and continued in that position for
three years, when his periodical was extinguished by
being merged in the 'Edinburgh Weekly Chronicle.'
It was from want of money, and from no fault of
Mr Bell's, that his journal did not succeed. He did
the editorial work very well, and much more carefully
than could have been expected of any literary enthusiast just escaped from his minority ; and his original
contributions, both in prose and verse, were constant
and varied, and of high merit. The six octavo volumes
of the 'Edinburgh Literary Journal' stood in some
libraries, pretty certainly carrying on their upper ends,
until recent events revived an interest in them, a thick
deposit of dust. Yet they will bear close dipping into, and even reading from end to end, and the perusal
of them will give, we believe, a higher estimate of the
mental range and capacity of Mr Bell than can be
gathered from all other quarters,—far higher, certainly,
than could be obtained from the thousands of interlocutors and notes which, during thirty-four years, he

wrote for the Sheriff-Court of Lanarkshire. These Sheriff-Court writings are wonderful in their way,—we believe, taking them as a mass, of merit hardly if ever equalled. In point both of quantity and quality they are a splendid monument of the force and industry of a single judge; but, as performances of mind, they compare with his early literary efforts as the strong, steady, rough pulling and ponderous tread of a tame sedate elephant compare with the gambols of a young race-horse aspiring to be a "courser of the sun." The contrast is instructive, and would be melancholy if it were of the least use either to reiterate Ecclesiastes, and assert "that all is vanity," or to forget that hunger and thirst are inevitable in this world, and that the bulk of the work of it is the most prosaic of prose with no poetry in it that is not hidden in thick darkness, or allied to the heroic only in the doing of duty not because it is pleasant, but because it must be done. And whoever would understand Henry Glassford Bell's accumulated work in its best aspects, will keep steadily in view what his natural gifts were and what his early ambition was, and try to understand not merely the amount of labour he went through, but also and chiefly the amount of self-denial he must have practised in renouncing poetry and most of its fascinations, except on rare holidays, and in toiling out his life in listening to dreary wrangling logic and settling twopenny-halfpenny quarrels.

The chair of the Sheriff of Lanarkshire was a very different sort of chair from the editorial chair of the

'Edinburgh Journal,' and except in point of emoluments, the differences were probably in favour of the
latter; at least so it would appear to a young man
with traces of the rosy-fingered morn still hanging
about his life, and perhaps even to an old man with
his eyes fixed "beyond the sunset and the baths of
all the western stars." We can well believe that the
old Sheriff, looking back occasionally during his last
twilight of seclusion, may have thought the time of
his editorship about the happiest, and probably not
the least useful, time of his life. The squabbles of
Glasgow which he saw burning and hissing and sput-
tering before him one after another for weeks and
months and years, have mostly gone into darkness
like bad lucifer-matches or wretched farthing candles
—even the nasty smell of them is utterly gone; but the
pages of the 'Edinburgh Journal' are still luminous,
and in them can be read the literary history of 1829,
1830, and 1831, and various utterances of talent, and
even of genius, which are capable of cheering a vacant
or lonely hour, and lifting the reader above the cares
and sorrows of everyday life, from the sensations of
the animal to the aspirations of the immortal. His
own contributions to these six volumes are the most
diversified, and they are certainly among the best; and
that is no mean praise when it is remembered that
among the contributors were the Ettrick Shepherd
and Professor Wilson, Thomas Campbell and Thomas
Aird, Professor Tennant and Dr Gillespie, Robert
Chambers and Robert Carruthers, Sheridan Knowles,

and Alaric A. Watts, Dr Moir, best known as Delta,
G. P. R. James the novelist, and David Vedder and
Robert Gilfillan, two of our minor vernacular poets.
But then some of these gave only fractions from their
scrap-books, while he gave the strength of his mind.
Selections of the best of these pieces were published
by him in two thin separate volumes—one entitled
'The Portfolio,' and the other 'Summer and Winter
Hours.' The latter volume, which appeared in 1831,
is entirely in verse, and contained the best of his
poems. They were marked by a good deal of imitation, especially of Byron, and there are detectable, also,
traces of Moore and of Scott. Many of the isolated
verses are excellent, and there are occasional lines
with flashes of the true poetic fire in them. Here and
there, however, there are lines and even verses the
excision of which would probably improve the poems
in which they occur; but of what verses published at
twenty-five may not the same be said? Their faults
are due rather to want of patience than want of power,
and throughout they indicate rather the giant who
could pile up pyramids than the artistic dwarf who
could polish a cameo to perfection. The most popular
of his poems, but by no means his best, is his blazing
rhetorical panorama of the life of Mary Queen of
Scots; and the child of his inventive faculty (we
believe his ingenious and accomplished friend, Mr
George Monro, advocate, is entitled to a share of the
credit) which has travelled furthest is " The Cork Leg,"
the story having walked over sea and land as swiftly

and extravagantly as the leg itself is said to have done. His only extensive prose work is his life of Mary Stuart, which was published in 1830 as part of ' Constable's Miscellany.' It is an out-and-out vindication of her, evidently most sincere. To the last his belief in her never faltered, and he often expressed it with no inconsiderable zeal and warmth. He could sift and weigh evidence as well as most of those who denounce her, and his unhesitating verdict of Not Guilty may probably induce others less capable of forming a judgment to join in the safe verdict of Not Proven.

The last number of the ' Edinburgh Literary Journal' was published on the 14th of January 1832, and on the 20th November of the same year he was called to the Bar. In the previous year he had married Miss Stuart of Sheerglass, Glengarry, a Roman Catholic in religious faith, and the daughter of a family of Jacobites, whose political faith was older than Killiecrankie, and had at that battle testified to its sincerity by the claymore; in all human probability a most suitable wife for the eulogist and worshipper of Mary Queen of Scots. He did not pass as advocate so soon as he might have done, having expectations of obtaining employment in the diplomatic service, and being fonder of literature than of law. His practice was of course rather slender to begin with. The race of agents that would have allowed Walter Scott and Wilson and Lockhart to starve because of their inclination to poetry and other kindred abominations,

could hardly be expected to do much for the enthusiastic admirer and follower of these men of genius.
Fortunately, however, there were then—there are
always—people in Edinburgh of deeper insight and
more generous sympathies than the common herd of
law agents, who trot after each other in the ruts of
fashion like imitative sheep; so that Mr Bell, in
spite of, and perhaps because of, his literary frailties,
was not left without friends. He had cases sufficient
to keep him from despairing and sinking out of sight,
and he had influence enough to get into the Town
Council, and pluck enough to try in that arena to set
his broad foot upon the anti-Church radicals when
they were dodging and whisking about amid the
complicated straw and rouped-out furniture of the
Annuity-Tax controversy. That he hated Radicalism
and was a good sound Tory was beyond doubt. That
he could make a fair argumentative speech was proved
by his Town-Council deliverances, and also that he
had nerve to make a speech before an audience likely
to appall most young men, for he had done this in
1827, at that world-famous dinner of the Edinburgh
Theatrical Fund, at which Scott avowed himself to
be the author of the Waverley Novels. Such considerations, and probably also his literary abilities,
recommended him to the favourable attention of Mr
Archibald Alison, then Sheriff of Lanarkshire, and in
1839 he appointed him to be one of his Substitutes
for Glasgow, an act the practical wisdom of which
is much more undoubted now than it probably ap-

peared at the time. This appointment harnessed Mr
Bell to the big, judicial machine of big, growing
Lanarkshire, and he set himself to the doing of his
work in the most thorough, determined manner. If
he did not carry much law to Glasgow in his memory,
he learned there whatever was necessary for the discharge of his duties, and he carried with him a powerful well - balanced intellect, which was capable of
weighing facts and applying law, and without which
cyclopædias of legal learning, bound up in human
skulls and white wigs, are so much chaotic rubbish.
To the praise of Glasgow be it remembered, his merits
and his steady labours were fully appreciated there.
He has been lauded greatly in that city since his
death; but the laudation began long ago, and was not
less hearty though less outspoken when he was living.
How many Scripture proverbs he reversed we know
not, but he certainly reversed that one which is almost
universally true—"A prophet is without honour in
his own country." The esteem in which he was held
in Glasgow took shape and activity, in 1852, when
there was a proposal to raise Sir A. Alison to the
bench of the Court of Session; it was then indicated
to Lord Advocate Inglis that, in the opinion of the
best heads of Glasgow, Mr Bell should be appointed
to be his successor. In 1867, on the death of Alison,
effect was given to this opinion, which in the interval
had been yearly gaining strength; and it is an opinion,
we feel sure, which no intelligent man who ever expressed it ever felt reason to recant.

In 1866 he published a third volume of verse, entitled 'Romances and other Poems.' In the previous
year he wrote an able biographical and critical introduction to an edition of Shakespeare, which exhibits
most of the merits of his prose style, and we should
think all its defects, of which the most serious is
a tendency to stilted and spasmodic ponderosity of
phrase. His touch was occasionally light and graceful in his earlier days, but latterly it was much less
so, especially in prose. His latest verses also, to a
considerable extent, want the flow and flexibility of
the productions of his youth, but they are more
mature in thought, and more sober and precise, though
more stiff in expression. There is a deep sadness
though a resolute courage in his reflections on death
and kindred subjects; and nothing that moralist or
sage could preach or write about him, now that he
is gone, could be more touching than his own poem
on "The End," unless it may be the last of the two
poems called "The Return after Death," in which he
goes forth, in fancied sadness and desolation, to re-
visit, after a sleep of centuries, the old familiar places
where the kindly hearts of yore were still, and cold,
and dust.

The character of Henry Glassford Bell cannot be
expressed in an epithet, nor yet in a large number of
epithets. The most readily apprehended peculiarity
about him was a sort of unusual indefinite bulk. He
was a six-foot man in stature, and intellectually, even
more than physically, he towered above the crowd.

But there was no mark by which he could be described as if for the police, and no eccentricity or oddity or abnormal specialty in the way of either strength or weakness that defined him conclusively from other clever men. Among the best qualities of his mind was its massive stability, its healthy tone, its broad, deep common-sense, its wide, catholic sympathies. There was nothing narrow or biassed or eccentric about it, such as is often the case with men who are actually born (as he was), or who fancy themselves to have been born, with an endowment of genius. When he arrived at the conclusion that prudence forbade him to make literature the business by which he was to earn his bread, he indulged in no weak repining, but applied himself to the business of law with the energy, if not quite the zeal, of a narrow-souled sharp-beaked human creature that had been constructed by the destinies for that vocation and no other. He fell back upon literature to gladden his leisure and ennoble his toilsome days. He did not look upon the garden of the Muses as a paradise from which he had been expelled, and waste his time idling about the walls and uttering imprecations at sight of the gates. Like a strong healthy nature he did not utter imprecations at all, but set himself industriously to exterminate the weeds outside the garden of the Muses, to do the duty that he knew himself to be fit for, and which lay before him requiring to be done. Guided by this principle he did his work as a judge through the long term of thirty-four years, and few

2 D

men have better realised than he the ideal of what
a judge ought to be. He had a clear sense of the
difference between right and wrong, and he reverenced his conscience as his king. Of intellect massive, hard, and penetrating, he had enough to furnish
out a large number of ordinary cautious sheriffs who
tremble to be wise beyond the letter of the law, and
who have seldom if ever any cause for trembling.
His judgment was probably worth that of all the
living sheriffs of Scotland put together, with perhaps
one or two exceptions. Then he was free from those
crotchets which cunning pleaders are apt to waken up
to serve the purposes of individual cases. He was
attentive and patient, and his good-nature was such
that youth or modesty was not confused or struck
into silence in his presence. As a man he was not
insensible to the applause of his fellow-men, and he
received it, and deserved it. All his friends loved
him, and, though many of them are no longer young,
their affection for him was more like the warm affection of boyhood than the polite calculating attach-
ment that prevails among mature men of the world.
He had managed to keep his own heart young and
susceptible, and so he was able in a notable degree
to shut out from the circle of his influence the cooling,
ossifying influence of advancing old age. In conversation he was brilliant among clever men, and
still more brilliant among clever women. Those who
have seen him teased by sharp female wit had an
opportunity of seeing signs of a geniality and playful-

ness which otherwise has left little or no sign. So far as is known, he had but one superstition, and that was his devotion to the memory of Mary Stuart. Her influence, radiating across the "chill chasm of centuries," was to him what the influence of living beauty has been to some of the greatest of poets and some of the maddest of philosophers. What his religious creed may have been, lies open to inference and conjecture. His latest poetry shows that before him the sceptical spirit of the age had been sweeping over the dry bones of ancient confessions, and asking, "Can these dry bones live?" as also, "Ought they to live?" And he returns no express answer. Certain it is that he believed in God and immortality, though not so sure about the latter as he evidently wished to be; and believing in these, he, by the necessity of reason, believed in all the utterable and unutterable ideas that are implied in God and immortality, — truth, justice, and the love of humankind being among the chief of those that are utterable and reducible to practice; and certain also it is, that he, in his life of unflinching, unwearied well-doing, revealed a religious creed of a beauty and excellence far surpassing that of many noisy professors of religion, who act as if they thought that dogmatism and self-delusion may be more acceptable in the eye of the Judge of all the earth than the patient doing of plain duty and the candid speaking of plain truth.

LORD COLONSAY.[1]

THE life of this noble and learned lord, which had
comprised within it every variety of work and every
variety of honour falling to the legal profession of
Scotland, closed after a course of eighty years at Pau,
on the 31st January 1874.   He had for several winters
past been subject to attacks of bronchitis, and he went
to Pau in the first week of January, in the hope that
the genial climate of the South might enable him to
escape in whole or in part the periodic attack.   But
it was otherwise decreed, and the last week of January
from Monday to Saturday, witnessed his seizure by
the disease and his end, it being difficult for any constitution that has stood the tear and wear of eighty
years to withstand the assaults of lung disease.   His
body was brought to Edinburgh after his death, and
on Wednesday, the 11th February, was laid in War-
riston Cemetery beside the remains of his brother
Archibald—one of the principal Clerks of the Court
of Session, who died in 1870—in presence of ten or
twelve mourning relatives and friends.   His private
funeral was in keeping with his lonely life, which

[1] 'The Journal of Jurisprudence,' March 1874.

eschewed most of the splendours and vanities and unreal pomp of the world. It matters little where the worn-out innermost visible vesture of any man, however great, may lie; but we could almost have wished to think of Duncan M'Neill, a strong son of Nature, fond of the wild hills and the bleak sea-shore, having found his last earthly resting-place afar from the hum of the city in some grassy hillock by the beach of lonely Colonsay, with the moan of distant Corryvreckan, and the sea-birds' shriek, and the wail of the Atlantic surges mingling round his grave for evermore.

He was the second son of John M'Neill, proprietor of Colonsay and Oronsay, and was born in the latter island on the 20th August 1793. His older brother perished in the wreck of the Orion in 1846. His next younger brother is Sir John M'Neill, also a man of striking presence and high intellect, who has made himself a name in the world. These two were educated at the University of St Andrews. Duncan went thither at the age of twelve years. When on his way to it, in passing through Glasgow with his father, he heard the victory of Trafalgar, which was gained on 21st October 1805, announced from the top of the mail-coach by the guard to an eager large crowd, whose ready cheers for Nelson were arrested by the intelligence that he was killed,—a crowd all vanished like smoke long ago, and leaving no trace of themselves and of the news they then heard, except what had dropped into the quick ear and retentive memory of the young Highland boy from Oronsay, who used in after-years to tell of this his first introduction to the current history of the big world with its cannon and its war-ships, but few newspapers and no telegrams. The St Andrews to which he went was a kind of city of the dead, grand and barren, its streets green with weeds and grass, and its great ecclesiastical ruins covered with wild wallflower and lichens. Almost the only thing about it then connecting it with the living world was the fame of Dr John Hunter, once the secretary of Lord Monboddo, then Professor of Humanity, editor of Livy and Horace, one of the most accurate of scholars, and one of the most profound, subtle, and original of reasoners on philological subjects. The two M'Neills were boarded with his son, Dr James Hunter, who was Professor of Logic, and a man of considerable natural ability, but of no inconsiderable indolence, and not a very successful teacher of logic, though a commanding kind of man, of a fine military manner and figure, much more like a colonel of dragoons than a man of books and syllogisms. His wife, the sister of the first Mrs Francis Jeffrey, was among the wittiest ladies of these early years of the century in St Andrews, and for sixty years later; and his family were all clever, and some of them endowed with literary talents—one daughter having acquired a reputation as a novelist, and a son, John, the late Auditor of the Court of Session, being a poet, and one of the most highly cultivated minds of his time in or about Edinburgh. Upon the whole the home was a fortunate one for any lad of brains to be placed in. Duncan always spoke of the Hunters with marked kindness, and of his St Andrews College days with evident pleasure. Though young he was a diligent student, good at classics, and *facile princeps* in mathematics. But his teacher, Dr Haldane, afterwards Principal of St Mary's College and first minister of St Andrews, was a poor mathematician. He had been appointed through influence, and he required to learn nearly all his mathematics after he obtained his appointment, which he did, however, most conscientiously, as he did everything else. To the last the old D.D. was proud of his old pupil; and no name in St Andrews could evoke a kindlier smile and flush on the expressive face of Duncan M'Neill than the name of Dr Haldane.

After being three years at St Andrews, Duncan came to Edinburgh, where he attended College classes for three sessions. One of the classes he attended was that of Dr Brown, designed as the Moral Philosophy class, but really, as worked by that celebrated and subtle professor, a class of metaphysics and psychology; and into the studies of that class he entered with great zeal and ability, that would have enabled him to outstrip his teacher in everything except faith in his own speculations. For several years he paid great attention to metaphysical subjects, and had so far yielded to their fascination as to have given a good deal of labour to the preparation of an edition of those philosophical works of Hume which Adam Black published several years afterwards in four volumes. It has been suggested, and not without reason, that this early affectionate study of Hume coloured the whole course of his intellectual life. Those who have seen with the requisite eyes how the delicate sceptical balance wavered in his hands as a judge, rejecting no fact, and with the most perfect veracity giving full effect to all, could readily infer how much of his intellectual method, how much subtle strength, how much hesitant weakness he had acquired from the truth-loving king of doubters. The oscillation of the balance had a positive charm for him. He strongly preferred uncertainty to probable error, indecision to positive injustice. Therefore he fixed nothing that could be left free, and he did not kindle admiration in those shallow dogmatic natures that are almost incapable of suspense of judgment, and would dash headlong into falsehood rather than wait and watch patiently for truth.

His physical education was that of an athlete, especially in the different modes of locomotion. Few men could run or walk or leap or swim with him. He was tall, lithe, and muscular; and the two deer-hounds that support his coat-of-arms, in their unencumbered wide-springing swiftness, were no bad emblems, in so far as the animal can represent the human, of the action both of his body and his mind. He could always reach conclusions in the smallest possible number of steps, and he always did so reach them, unless when it was thought expedient to gambol and make gradually nar-

rowing circuits around some quarry, vital perhaps with
stupidity, or knavery, or conceit, and so expose it and
frighten it out of its wits (if it had any), or its life,
rather than dash into it and end it at once. He was
upwards of six feet high, and very handsome, as his
engraved portrait by Thomas Duncan, taken thirty
years ago, when in his prime, and that other portrait
of him by John Philip, taken in his latter years, and
hung in the Parliament House, can show, but not
quite adequately either of them, more particularly
the latter; for Philip's portrait, though a recognisable
likeness, and in some respects a great painting, does
not catch any of the finest and grandest expressions
of his mutable face, being sleepy and homely, and not
at all like what he was when his intellect was effectually roused, as it was occasionally at an "advising"
in the First Division, or a charge to a jury. Three
photographs, by Rodger of St Andrews, disclose higher
phases of expression than Philip's picture, but they
too fall short of the reality, as it could be seen at
times when the irrepressible fire of a born Celtic
orator was flashing through and irradiating the lineaments of his face, and disclosing, as in a mirror, the
rush, struggle, and explication of his thought, the
evanescent visions of a moment, to be long remembered, but not to be recorded or reproduced any more
than the changeful glories of a sunset upon which a
Turner's eye has not chanced to look with ecstatic
watchfulness. He had such an abundance of white
hair that it was difficult to be sure of the exact shape

of his head, but it appeared to be one of those long, well-balanced, practical heads, of which Burns possessed one of the best specimens, if not *the* very best. His face, in profile, looked like a notched battle-axe; and the whole aggregate expression of head, face, and figure, when his mind was lively, was that of a splendid incarnation of velocity, directness, massiveness, and cautiously directed, carefully adjusted power.

Duncan M'Neill passed as advocate in 1816. As an element by no means unimportant in his varied and liberal preliminary education, he served an apprenticeship to Michael Linning, W.S. The same year that witnessed his admission to the Bar witnessed also the admission of John Hope, afterwards Lord Justice-Clerk; E. Douglas Sandford, who wrote on Entails; A. Earle Monteith, afterwards Sheriff of Fife, and trusted in the councils of the Free Church; Robert Whigham, afterwards Sheriff of Perth, and an exception to the rule that the Sheriff of Perth never dies; William Menzies, afterwards Mr Justice Menzies; James Ivory, afterwards Lord Ivory; and John Gibson Lockhart, the biographer of Scott, and author of the larger part of 'Peter's Letters to his Kinsfolk,' and a great deal beside. 'Peter's Letters' were published in 1819, and they give "The Scorpion's" views of the Edinburgh which then lay around a young Tory advocate. They are said to be full of libels, and the ink of them is no doubt largely mixed with *aqua fortis;* but they give a better, or at all events a more vivid, idea of the Edinburgh of 1819 than can be got out of any other book,

though they may require to be corrected by Scott's
Life, and Jeffrey's and Cockburn's Memorials, which
are themselves not quite free from romance, and the
'Scotsman' newspaper, which began to chronicle facts
and teach politics in January 1817. The more notable
figures of that time are fast fading into dimness and
oblivion. Jeffrey and Cockburn were then in the full
blaze of their fame, as were also the far greater lawyers
bearing the names of John Clerk, George Cranstoun,
and James Moncreiff. In the First Division Hope sat
as president, in the Second Boyle, and in the Jury
Court Lord Chief Commissioner Adam. Walter Scott
sat in the clerk's seat of the First Division, writing
interlocutors when required, and poems or Waverley
novels in his pretty copious intervals of leisure. Sir
William Hamilton, the most learned of all Scotchmen
of his time, was then walking the old Parliament hall
in a briefless condition, with the contents of whole
cyclopædias of metaphysics, published and unpublished, in his mind; as was also John Wilson, with his
flowing locks and broad shoulders, carrying about him
such definite fame as the 'Isle of Palms' could give,
such indefinite notoriety as the Chaldee MS. and
'Blackwood's Magazine' did give—and in him whole
volumes of eloquent 'Noctes Ambrosianæ,' some to be
published, but most never to be published. And there
were Forsyth, with his dark and his light eye, and
other "jog-trot lawyers," as Lockhart calls them, when
proceeding to describe a class that have become super-
abundant since. He refrains from expatiating upon

" the expanding energies and rising reputations of such
men as the acute and energetic Skene, Walker, Hope,
Macniell, and many others," purposely, of course, mis-
spelling the last name, in case he should discover himself by disclosing too much knowledge on the part of
the fictitious Dr Morris, and too much kindness to his
young contemporaries at the Bar, a species of frailty
into which he very seldom fell.

Such honourable mention of the owner of the mis-
spelt name would not have been made had he not been
really a rising young man. He had been distinguishing himself in the Criminal Court, and in 1820 he was
appointed an Advocate-Depute. In that capacity he
drew some of the best indictments ever seen, perfect
models for clearness, terseness, and precision. As
A.D. he signed the indictment charging Stuart of
Dunearn with the murder of Sir Alexander Boswell
—son of Johnson's biographer, and author of " Jenny's
Bawbee " and other sarcastic songs and verses—in a
duel at Auchtertool, on 26th March 1822, the duel
being provoked by some rhymes in the ' Beacon '
newspaper about " stot-feeder Stuart, a muckle fat
cowart," who in truth was nothing worse than an offensive Whig. In 1824 he was appointed Sheriff of
Perthshire, and resumed his practice as counsel for
the defence of persons accused of crimes, the reports
of the Justiciary cases for years after showing that no
counsel was more frequently employed, or was more
successful in obtaining acquittals, than he. He has
been pronounced by a highly competent authority to

have been " a most able criminal advocate, and indisputably the greatest criminal lawyer of his day." In
November 1834, after some years of wavering professional success, in which he ran the risk of being out-
stripped by smaller but bolder men, he was appointed
Solicitor-General, and held that office until April 1835.
He was reappointed to it in September 1841, and continued in it till October 1842, when, on the death of
Sir W. Rae, he was appointed Lord Advocate. He
was elected Dean of Faculty in 1843, on the elevation
of Patrick Robertson—the Falstaff of Scottish lawyers
—to the bench. He was Lord Advocate from 1842
till July 1846, and in 1843 he was elected M.P. for the
county of Argyle. The most memorable of his legislative labours is the passing of the Poor Law Amendment Act of 1845, unless it may be the 9 Geo. IV.
cap. 29, amending criminal procedure, of which he was
the actual, though the weakish Sir W. Rae was the
nominal author. In May 1851 he was appointed a
Lord of Session and of Justiciary by Lord Russell's
Administration, no doubt because he best deserved such
promotion, but perhaps partly also because he was a
very sharp thorn in the legislative side of Lord Advocate Rutherfurd, and had made havoc of his schemes
for overturning the Scotch marriage law, as he did
likewise of Lord Campbell's crotchets and blunders on
the same subject, which is so vexatious to the ignorant
uniformitarian mind of those who hold London to be
the centre and the larger half of the universe. In
May 1852, Lord Derby being then in office, he was

appointed Lord Justice-General and Lord President of
the Court of Session; and that high post he held greatly
to the satisfaction of all Scotland for fifteen years, the
" fierce light " that beats upon the head of the bench
having shown nothing so clearly as that he of all the
Scottish advocates of his day was the fittest to sit
there, regulating by his mature wisdom—restraining
by his caution—correcting and aiding by his accurate,
retentive memory, full of logically coherent, judiciously subordinated principles and facts, which had been
gathering through a long harvest of experience, or
specially acquired by diligent study in anticipation of
the expected work of day after day—lightening dulness
and weariness by his cheery humour—extinguishing
trickery, cunning, conceit, and prosy self-assurance by
his ready far-shooting wit—relieving the confusion of
nervousness and helping into expression thought that
was genuine and true but in want of appropriate language—and in all things acting the part of an ideal
judge, who held truth and justice to be sacred, and
felt nothing in his position so embarrassing and so
lamentable as the difficulty of finding truth and justice
amid the stupidity, falsehood, and impatient selfishness
of this unreflecting, untiring, undoubting, lucre-loving
age.

In 1853 he was created a Privy Councillor, and on
26th February 1867 he was raised to the peerage under
the title of Baron Colonsay. Since then he has sat as
an Appeal Judge in the House of Lords, and has exercised a vigilant control over proposed legislation which

affected the affairs of Scotland. By the constitution of
his nature he was a Conservative, and disliked change.
Whether in the House of Lords he did not act too
much by virtue of the Conservative instinct we do not
here venture to say. Still less do we venture to doubt
that he did not act quite conscientiously and for what
he believed to be the best interests of his country,
which were almost as dear to him as the interests of
wife and children are to most other men. At the time
of his elevation to the peerage we paid a not unwilling
tribute to his worth both in prose and verse, and we
then recorded also a eulogistic address delivered to
him by the then Dean of Faculty in the name of his
flock and of himself, which address was greatly admired at the time for its delicate compliments, and its
graceful eloquence, and of which the weight is not
diminished by the subsequent promotion of its author
to the Lord Justice-Clerk's chair and to the peerage
under the not unknown but newly decorated name of
Lord Moncreiff.

Lord Colonsay's life has been a long, varied, and
honourable course. He obtained in succession all the
honours that fall to the most successful of Scottish
lawyers—Advocate-Depute, Sheriff, Solicitor-General,
Lord Advocate, Outer House Judge, Lord Justice-
General, as also the unprecedented honour of being
raised to the peerage. In every position of his public
life he conducted himself with great prudence and
ability; and whatever work was to be done, he did it
as well as it could be done. At least he never failed

for want of intellectual insight, or of industry, or of
care. If he failed at all, it was because of cautiousness
or modesty. If he lacked anything it was the courage
of his opinions. He could see most clearly into the
right or the wrong of any question—no man more
clearly than he; but he had a kind of constitutional
inclination to leave undone whatever did not imperatively require to be done, to evade every question if
it could be put aside. This shrinking from accepting
responsibilities does not appear so much, or indeed
noticeably, in his reported speeches as a counsel, but
it does appear in all or most of his opinions as a judge.
He seldom if ever lays down a principle an iota more
extensive than is necessary for the decision of the
special case, and he makes his legal doctrine sit so
close to the facts that his judicial opinions do not
afford quotable authority so often as could be wished
—a peculiarity which is greatly to be deplored; for if
he had boldly put out to sea a little, instead of hugging
the shore like a steersman before the compass was
discovered, he could have expounded legal principles
with a clearness, just balance, and accuracy which few
of his predecessors on the bench could have equalled.
Indeed there is hardly a predecessor of his on the
bench that has left traces of greater intellectual power
than he has done. What Braxfield, and Blair, and
Stair, and Forbes of Culloden may have been, is rather
mythical and uncertain. Unluckily the printing-press
has not sufficiently recorded their thoughts; but we
doubt if any of them were intellectually superior to

Lord Colonsay; and we feel pretty confident that there
is no specimen of Scottish forensic oratory that sur-
passes, we should almost say that equals, his speech
to show that David Yoolow was not an idiot, and his
speech to show that the Glasgow cotton-spinners, or
'Thugs,' had not conspired to commit murder.   In
point of argumentative wit, we certainly do not know
any speech that is superior to the Yoolow speech; and
much as Patrick Robertson was admired as a joker,
his speech on the other side is dull, pointless, and
feeble in comparison.   His speeches in the House of
Commons—laying out of view, of course, their *political*
errors—were excellent, practical speeches; and one or
more of them, pounding to pieces some of Lord Campbell's blunders and nonsense about the Scotch marriage
law, were most effective pieces of combined argument
and ridicule.   His charges to juries were most masterly,
clear, and impartial groupings of facts, every little circumstance being dropped into its place out of a memory
that seemed to hold everything till the right time, with
the most perfect skill and apparently negligent ease.
His statements, as Lord President, of the facts of a
case, were also very complete, perspicuous, and able;
and he generally held the balance so steadily till near
the end, that in difficult cases it was impossible to tell
how his opinion was tending until he announced it in
a few terse sentences.   His opinions in the Cardross
and Yelverton cases were among his most elaborate
efforts as a Judge; and the former was delivered with
great animation and a vivid play of feature, which

2 E

showed that in the days of his oratorical efforts he did not depend on cold logic alone for his effect upon an audience. His oratory, we believe, used to be marked by the animation that prevails among the Celtic race; and it had one peculiar individuality—namely, the use of long pauses after specially emphatic passages or sentences, for the purpose of allowing them to sink into the minds of his hearers. He was one of the most direct of thinkers and of pleaders, going, as Jeffrey used to say, through the core of a subject like a knife. And both at the Bar and on the Bench, and even as President of the late Law Commission, he exhibited a singular faculty for examining or cross-examining witnesses, beginning always at such distance from the point to which he wished to force the witness as not to excite suspicion, and then gradually and conclusively shutting him up to it. Often, too, in the First Division he would listen with the utmost patience to a long, specious, plausible bit of argumentative talk, and when the speaker was resuming his seat well satisfied with his own cleverness, astuteness, and tact, he would demolish the whole castle of sophistry by a question or two. He was, as a Judge, one of the most punctual of men—never too late for any appointment, never absent from his judicial duties, except on two days, when the Queen required him to be elsewhere; and for fifteen years never absent from the chair of the First Division but on one day when he was in the Court of Justiciary trying Bryce for the murder of a young woman at Ratho.

His success in the House of Lords was matter of
dispute before he entered it, and may be still. Many
evils. were supposed likely to accrue from it,—that
he was to usurp the whole functions of the Court
of Appeal, and suchlike. Not one of these fears
was verified by the result. He may not have done
much in the House of Lords, but he certainly falsified
all the objections that were taken to his promotion,
and has smoothed the way to other eminent Scottish
lawyers obtaining that promotion which he was the
first to obtain. We believe he did not make a great
mark, as the phrase goes, in the House of Lords. He
was seventy-three years of age at the time, and that is
rather a late age for any man to be transplanted to a
strange new scene. He was, as we have said, a modest,
shrinking man, and the Houses of Parliament in modern
busy England have no leisure to find out the merits of
the modest. But we dare to assert, most deliberately and
with emphasis, that not one of the noble and learned
lords among the peers, except Lord Westbury, was his
equal in intellect; and even Westbury, though a far
more skilful stater of legal propositions, could not have
written the speeches that we have mentioned of Duncan
M'Neill. As for Cranworth, Wensleydale, Chelmsford,
and Hatherley, they were mere pigmies in comparison,
and hardly deserve to be named in the same breath.
Whatever Cockneydom may have thought of the grand
old man, there was in the House of Lords no finer
specimen of venerable manhood than he. His patent
of nobility—physical as well as mental—came from a

more unquestionable source than that of most members of the House of Peers; and if that House be to survive as part of the Constitution, it cannot have in it too many minds furnished and cultivated like his. For long he has lived a lonely kind of life. The friends of his youth and of his prime had all gone before him. Yet he was no cynic or hermit, shunning mankind. He was an admirable talker, and full of information on nearly all subjects. He had read all kinds of books; and, though never parading his knowledge, seemed always to remember the right literary allusion or the appropriate scientific fact at the right time. Wherever there was intelligence, he could find society, in which he gave himself no airs, leaving his mental rank to assert itself. It was impossible to see much of him in public without coming to admire him; and those who knew him in private seem to have got attached to him with that fidelity that heroes always ought to, but seldom receive. As an orator and judge he will be long and justly held in honour. He was truly great in what he did, but he was potentially much greater than anything that he did can adequately show.

LORD BENHOLME.[1]

LORD BENHOLME died at his house in Great King Street, Edinburgh, on Tuesday, 15th September 1874, after a brief and painless illness. On Sunday morning at eight o'clock his man-servant on entering his bedroom found him insensible, the seizure being apparently of a paralytic nature. Since then he has been gradually sinking, though he continued to talk quite rationally until within a short time of his death. For a few years past he has been the oldest acting Judge in any Supreme Court in Britain, and may be said to have died in harness. During all last session he was in his place in the Second Division, obviously feeble in body, but alert and vigorous in mind, and as devoted as ever to his duties. Ten days ago he concluded his fortnight's vacation work as Lord Ordinary on the Bills, and showed no signs of the end being so near. But he has long been so fragile in health, so emaciated in body, that it was plain his constitution could not stand any serious attack of illness, and that for him the fabled thread of life was spinning so close to the ultimate fibre of it that it seemed

[1] 'Scotsman,' September 16, 1874.

ready to sever at a touch. Rumours of his resignation have for years been epidemic, especially when the Tories were in power—and they were renewed during the recent summer session; but we have heard it whispered that he intimated to some urgent Tory or other—perhaps to more than one—that when he resigned his judicial appointment for any reason except inability to discharge his duties, he would resign it into the hands of the Whig party, from whom he, although a Conservative, got it.

The deceased was born in Edinburgh in 1796, so that he had reached to about seventy-eight years of age. His mother was Isabella Scott, the heiress of Benholme and Hedderwick, and his father was George Robertson, who, after his marriage, took the name of Robertson-Scott. After a course of education at the High School and University of Edinburgh, he passed as advocate in 1817, the year before Lord Colonsay, the year after Lord Curriehill. About this time he must have given very close attention to the decisions of the Court, for in his place on the Bench he was sometimes able to adduce from his memory, and corroborate by the session papers, points of law that had been settled in the early years of his advocateship, but omitted from the reports. He acquired a fair but not a large practice, he having no arts wherewith to fascinate the vulgar herd, and few of the essential, but sometimes questionable, gifts of the fashionable counsel. In 1829 he married Lord President Hope's youngest daughter, who died in 1842, leaving a family, one of whom is a well-known engineer, and another of whom is now one of the Sheriff-Substitutes of Forfarshire. In the same year he was appointed Sheriff of Renfrewshire; and after holding that office for eleven years, he was, in 1853, appointed a Lord of Session by the Earl of Aberdeen's Administration, Lord Moncreiff being then Lord Advocate.

Few of Lord Benholme's contemporaries or predecessors have stood so high as a Judge in the esteem of all who are capable of forming an opinion—a class, it may be observed, much more limited in extent than those who are ready, very ready, to express an opinion, and who set no value upon intellectual and moral merits of which they have little conception. Intellectually he had superiors—men of greater subtlety, comprehensiveness, and power—but in the matter of a good conscience he had no superior, and, we are afraid, but few equals. A man more resolutely determined to be just, we believe, never sat on any bench; and the strong moral sense of him came to the aid of an intellect of a high but not of the highest judicial order, and raised into a great Judge a man whose intellect, without the kingly moral sense, would have left him in the desert of commonplace, dealing in platitudes and plausibilities, supporting judgments by false pretences, and weighing hollow considerations of expediency against each other in the vain attempt to strike at some feasible balance of right and fact. For him justice still had a reality, difficult it might be to attain, but still to be resolutely sought after; and

he sat day by day, pale and withered to a living
shadow, striving to dispense it as if he truly recognised that there was a just God above him, whom he
was bound to serve as long as life was left, in the
endeavour to put down wrong and set up its contrary.
Not many men who have been so long familiar with
the arts and practices of courts of law have been able
to preserve so genuine and fierce an aversion against
falsehood. For all manifestations of that not unknown
though generally disguised weapon in the professional
armoury, he had an unquenchable hatred; and to the
last it was beautiful to see the glow of indignation
that sent the blood to his pale cheeks at the suspicion
of a lie. Manifestly he was that rare kind of man,
and that still rarer kind of lawyer, who believed and
acted as if this world had a moral Creator and Ruler,
who had not merely turned men out into it to grow
rich and drink wine, and hang up pictures, and beget
similar hungry, thirsty insects, and then die, and be
utterly extinguished. He judged as if he himself
expected to be judged, which in these days of deifying
matter, and pursuing pleasure on all-fours, is a phe-
nomenon certainly worthy of attention, and probably
of admiration.

The unbending integrity of his nature, which made
him so very excellent a Judge, in all likelihood impeded his success as a counsel. He had it not in
him to deal in insincere smiles, artificial frankness,
laughter affecting to be hearty but hollow and greedy
as the grave, or to practise grinning politeness to

those who came to consult him as to how they could lie and cheat with impunity; and as there is frequently conscious dishonesty on one side of every dispute, and sometimes on both sides, his known want of charity to that kind of thing shut him out from listening to the tales of very many clients. His tendency to arrive at personal convictions, also, must have impeded his intellectual motions as a pleader; for while an earnest self-convinced pleader may sometimes succeed, and with an audience without foregone conclusions is most likely to succeed, yet as judges cannot help having foregone conclusions on points of law, the pleaders who succeed best are generally those who can argue all *pros* and *cons* without being self-convinced, and press, or pretend to press, most strongly upon those arguments that seem to fit into old grooves in the minds of their audience, and keep their own personal convictions in abeyance, carefully stifling every semblance of earnestness or of "zeal," as Lord Cockburn contemptuously calls it, as not likely to be of any use to their clients, while certain to be dangerous to themselves, and give the outer world, and especially the narrow circle of it that may happen to be present and listening, an idea that the counsel is a rash enthusiast who has got himself to believe in something which does not meet with ratification from the sublimely infallible occupants of the Bench. Hercules Robertson was not a man to conceal his own faith in a legal principle under jesuitical phrases, or to be careful to leave loopholes to enable him to escape from any opinion that he might put in writing; so it is pretty certain that, good and sound lawyer though he was, his views of what ought to be decided were not always confirmed by the Bench, and he was thus in the position of a general who has sustained a defeat and left no way of retreat open. Still, even in the field of consulting counsel, integrity is not without its reward, and he had it to no inconsiderable extent, for he was pretty frequently consulted in questions of feudal law and of teinds, to which latter obscure subject he devoted a great deal of his attention, and it is rumoured in early life collected materials for a book upon it. Some of his opinions on teind questions are very able and learned, and show that he could have written a better book upon them than any that exist in print as yet. So far as we are aware, he never came forward as an author, and, except in the field of law, we doubt if he had gifts that would have secured success as an author. Nevertheless, his judicial style is of great merit—always easy, clear, and keeping fast unrelaxing hold with very long arms of some central idea, establishing it against contradiction and developing it, and never introducing any foreign element, either amusing or fanciful, that can distract attention from the orderly working out and application of the principle or principles upon which, according to his judgment, the controverted question actually turned. He never joked, but though habitually serious he could understand joking well enough, and could smile at anything

funny—a beautiful half-angelic smile, as if gilded by
evening sunsets. We understand he was a loving
student of the fine arts, more especially of music.
The whole soul of him seemed given over to justice
and beauty, and to have purified itself from all taints
of earth as thoroughly as ever saint or devotee hoped
and prayed for in this world. The flight of years
had almost lifted him above the image of the earthly,
and carried him as close to the land of shadows as
those who wear the vesture of mortality can ever
reach. Beautiful with the rare beauty of old age,
weak in health for long, and wasted in body almost
beyond what could be credited, his mind was clear
to the last; and to him, far more than to most men,
death must have been a painless translation from
hard work, and weariness, and weakness of the flesh,
to such reward as the Highest has prepared for those
who serve Him faithfully to the end of this life's
pilgrimage.

LORD MACKENZIE.[1]

THIS eminent member of the Scottish Bench died at Upper Norwood, at the house of his brother-in-law, on 19th May 1875. He had been ailing for some months from what was reported to be violent rheumatism. When dressing to attend the funeral of his mother in November 1874, he was seized suddenly with violent pain, and was so prostrated as to be unable to follow her remains to their last resting-place. He returned to his official duties in the Court of Session so soon as —perhaps before—he was able, doing, for one thing, the work of the Judge in Bill Chamber during the Christmas holidays, though unable to get out of bed, and suffering the most intense rheumatic pain. Towards the close of last session he obtained leave of absence from the Lord President, and again for six months at the beginning of the present session. He went to England several weeks ago for the sake of the milder climate, and hopeful accounts of his health have been reaching Edinburgh; but these have been delusive. That he had heart disease, probably induced by severe professional work, has been long

[1] 'Scotsman,' May 21, 1875.

known to his medical advisers, and also, though perhaps not so clearly, to himself. It was thought to be latent, but a few days ago it manifested itself with deadly activity, being awakened from its latency either by the long-continued severe rheumatic torture, or being itself merely the same nervous malady affecting the nerves of the heart, and at last wearying them into death.

Lord Mackenzie was the son and namesake of Captain Donald Mackenzie, a fine, hearty, Highland veteran, who was maimed by a shot at Bergen-op-Zoom, we presume when serving under Sir Thomas Graham in that brave, but unsupported, and therefore unfortunate, attack made by a part of the British force in March 1814. His mother was Robina Jameson, one of the seventeen children of the sturdy, industrious, erudite, and notable Antiburgher minister, John Jameson, D.D., who wrote the well-known dictionary of the Scottish language, and several other less known works. Donald was born 22d June 1818, and was the eldest of a family of four children, all of whom he survived, though dying now at the premature age—premature at least for a judge—of fifty-seven. He originally devoted himself to study medicine, and finished his college studies with distinction, taking the degree of Doctor of Medicine at the University of Edinburgh in 1838, and becoming, in 1839, a Fellow of the Royal College of Surgeons. But he did not seek medical practice. He betook himself to the legal profession, being induced thereto probably by the circumstance that Robert Jameson, an eminent pleader, one of the very best of forty years ago, was his mother's brother. He was called to the Bar in 1842, and soon obtained a fair practice, having a strong and steady support from Glasgow, which of itself is sufficient to keep any young advocate's head above the waves. He had a vast amount of multifarious knowledge, not always exact, and so encyclopedic in its range as to form the subject of various Parliament House jests, but really much easier to joke about than to rival or surpass. He was appointed Advocate-Depute by the Whigs in 1854, and continued to act till 1858, and part of his work during the year 1857 was to sign Madeline Smith's indictment, and direct the preparation of the case against her, which he did with more hopefulness than was apparent among her other prosecutors. After a year of Tory administration, he again held the office of Advocate-Depute from 1859 to 1861, when he was appointed Sheriff of Fife. He discharged the duties of this important and not uncritical county greatly to the satisfaction of the inhabitants, both high and low. On 14th March 1870 he was appointed to the Bench of the Court of Session as successor to Lord Barcaple, and, except during his tedious mortal illness, he was unremitting and untiring in his judicial work.

Few men known to the Parliament House have been more universally liked than he, or better deserved to be in favour with all. He was free from most of the infirmities which are peculiar to the legal profession.

His truth and honour were beyond doubt. He had
no guile, and though he could throw out a fiery jaunty
taunt, like most men of hot Celtic blood, upon sufficient
provocation, he cherished no malice, and renounced
the luxury of having enemies. His word could be
relied on implicitly, and all sorts of paltry meanness
and selfishness were far from him. Indeed, like his
lamented predecessor on the Bench, he was too forget-
ful of self, and, like him, he erred in neglecting and
in stifling the instincts of self-preservation. Had he
been a little less self-forgetful, his place would not in
all probability have been vacant for many years to
come. His mother had attained the mature age of
eighty-four, and he seemed to inherit her constitution.
He was a tall, fine, and, though somewhat narrow-
chested, a strong man, who, until some two years ago,
when he caught cold from fishing in wet clothes,
seemed incapable of either bodily or mental fatigue, or
of realising in his own person what illness could be.
He plunged into all sorts of physical exercise, taking
enormous walks for the mere love of walking, or for
purposes of fishing and shooting; and instead of taking
such sleep as nature requires, and most men cannot
resist giving, sat up reading and writing half the
night. He had a medical education, and probably
had felt hints intelligible to him of some uneasy
grating of the springs of vitality within, but he gave
little heed to the warnings. He went on, rejoicing in
his strength, we fear squandering it; at least, not
saving it in any way. If he failed in any duty, it

was his duty to himself. His old soldier-father and his Highland ancestors, of whom he was not unnaturally proud, could not in any battle-field have shown more regardlessness of life than he did in his daily and nightly toil, though that toil was far from such as could involve in it the sympathetic enthusiasm of the battle-field. We believe it was a maxim of conduct with some of the agents that were wont to employ him, that it was quite superfluous to write abstracts or memorials for him; that the plan was just to send him a pile of papers with some short hint of what was wanted as a practical result, and leave him to find out all details for himself, which he did by reading carefully through every paper. And after his elevation to the Bench might have relieved him from this drudgery, we believe it did not, but that he continued, as was his habit, to examine and sift everything for himself. We could wish it had been otherwise, and that he could have taken a little more ease; but then, perhaps, if that had been, he might not have been the kind-hearted, self-regardless Donald Mackenzie that all his friends knew and loved so well, and will mourn with that reciprocal affection which even this selfish world cannot withhold from "the loving and true-hearted."

His reputation as a Judge was high, and deservedly high. He was strong in two essential judicial qualities —the one being untiring industry, the other a sensitive conscience. He always strove after the right, and he never wearied in that strife. It is said that his judgments stood the test of appeal better than the average; and that in some cases—two entail cases in particular —the House of Lords reversed the Inner House and returned to his interlocutors. This may or may not be good evidence of his judicial wisdom and success— it is what the world accepts as sufficient; but whatever became of his judgments elsewhere, we feel sure that no one who watched the man narrowly and intelligently, and noted his ready eager pursuit of new arguments, his wavering and fluctuations of opinion, his irrepressible indignation at falsehood in all its forms, could hesitate to believe that his judicial intellect worked under the highest sanctions, urging him irresistibly, though it might be unconsciously, to do the right, and that only. He was, we believe, in Church polity an Episcopalian, though the grandson of so distinguished a Dissenter as Dr Jameson. He did not profess religion much in public: he practised it a good deal, and lived by rules that ought to be common to all the Churches, and was really an unexceptionable man and citizen, and an upright, indefatigable Judge. The death of him is the going out of a light among all who were familiar with his presence; for he was a happy, cheery, human spirit, and walked abroad joyously, with step light and elastic as if he were begirt with perpetual sunshine. And yet, alas! the black shadow was there, and it has eclipsed him too soon.

He was married in 1843 to Alice, second daughter of Andrew Mitchell of Maulside, writer in Glasgow. He is survived by his wife and by six sons and four daughters. His eldest daughter, a beautiful and accomplished young lady, wife of a distinguished member of the Bar,[1] much loved by her father, died three or four years ago, and that greatly wrung his affectionate heart. His mother and she were two of the strongest of his ties to life, and the loss of them certainly told unfavourably upon his health, perhaps even to the extent of turning the wavering balance of his own fate.

[1] Now the Right Hon. John Blair Balfour, M.P., Lord Advocate of Scotland.

GEORGE GRAHAM BELL.[1]

THIS venerable and once well-known member of the Bar died at his residence at Castle O'er, in Dumfriesshire, on Friday last [18th June 1875], aged upwards of eighty. He did not die of any disease, or of anything that can be described as other than sheer old age. He was out attending to affairs on his sheepfarms three weeks ago, and since then the worn-out vesture of the body has wholly given way.

He was the son of Thomas Bell of Crurie, an estate which has been in the family since 1683. In early youth he had—or his parents had—thoughts of the Church as the proper arena for his talents, and we believe that he attended the theological classes in Edinburgh early in this century, in order to qualify himself for being a minister of the Church of Scotland. But somehow he began to have doubts of various kinds, and they resulted in sending him to the College of Justice to aid in the practical dissemination of one of the virtues instead of the dogmatic asseveration from the pulpit of all the multifarious propositions of the Confession of Faith.

[1] 'Scotsman,' June 21, 1875.

Mr Graham Bell passed to the Bar in 1819, the same year which saw the advent of Douglas Cheape, civil law professor and comic poet, a man of much wit and many merry friends; of John Tait,[1] late Sheriff of Perthshire, commonly and affectionately known among advocates as Father Tait, a man of uncommon natural sagacity and human kindness, and a wealth of old Scotch stories which Dean Ramsay might well have envied, if he did not go the length of actual appropriation; of Arthur Burnett, late Sheriff-Substitute of Peebles; of David Syme, present Sheriff-Substitute at Kinross, a brother of the late distinguished surgeon, Professor Syme; of Patrick Shaw, founder of the present system of law-reporting, a man of untiring industry and veracity, and of a geniality not to be guessed from the books that bear his name; and of two or three others that have been less known to the public. Mr Bell was at the Bar the most successful of any of them, as indeed he was of all his near compeers except John Marshall, who was known to all Scotland as Lord Curriehill, and believed to be the most profound of modern feudal lawyers. In 1858, on the elevation of Lord President Inglis to the chair of the Lord Justice-Clerk, Mr Bell was very generally proposed as a fit and proper successor to the then vacant honour of the Dean of Faculty's baton, and would have had a large support among the members of the Bar; but he gracefully waived his claims in favour of Lord Moncreiff, and actually proposed that he should be appointed Dean,

[1] Brother of the late Archbishop of Canterbury.

in a speech in which, among other memories, he recalled one to the effect that his earliest start in the profession had been due to some words of praise which his rival's father had given, in his place as Judge, to his first written legal argument—which praise had been of such incalculable service to him as to induce him to cherish gratitude through life to that great lawyer, and to refrain at that crisis from doing otherwise than helping forward the promotion of his son to this new and much-deserved honour. How much of this was the language of compliment, and how much of it strict history, no man could know, not even Mr Bell himself; for the currents in the legal flood that lead on to fortune—lead so far, and then fall short—are as inscrutable as the forces that shape and propel the clouds. But certain it is that, under whatever influences, Mr Bell did at one time command a great success at the bar, and for long possessed a large share especially of chamber practice, and that, in the judgment of all capable of judging on intellectual grounds, he deserved all his success; but that somehow or other he never reached the Bench, the true goal of an advocate's ambition, though it is very indubitable that far inferior men have reached it since his turn ought to have come.

He was possessed of an excellent legal intellect, clear, logical, ingenious, subtle rather than strong, and speculative rather than practical, but always keeping within close sight of reality, though tempted to pursue ideas fully further than most dull practitioners could quite see any necessity for or utility in. The days of written arguments were golden days for him. His written style of pleading could, and can still, quite well bear comparison with that of Jeffrey, or of Jameson, or of Rutherfurd, who were the demigods of their time. It looks like an easy, clear, graceful style; but we believe it was written and re-written, corrected and re-corrected, backwards and forwards and upside-down, as hardly any human composition, except an occasional sonnet, or Cambridge prize poem, or Brougham peroration, has been. His spoken style wanted fire and energy; but it was deliberate, unhesitating, in the main elegant, and carried distinct mature thought in it. He was an admirable lawyer, and would have made a Judge as good or better than most that this generation has had the pleasure to look up to. But his party—the so-called stupid Tory party—passed him by, for reasons unknown and probably unknowable, their plethora of men of genius being most probably not one of them. We believe that he was never offered any public appointment except that of a clerk in the Inner House, which he was by Lord Advocate M'Neill; but though £1000 a-year, without oppressive work, was a temptation of its kind, he rejected it, knowing that he had in him faculties that were worthy of a higher field for their exercise, feeling all the while grateful to that chief of his party who had sufficient justice and discrimination to remember him in his day of power and patronage. We do not suppose, however, that he ever felt unhappy at not having reached the Bench. He was too much of a philosopher to grumble over the inevitable. He had left the Bar shortly after he became advocate, in bad health, and gone to the country, it was thought to die of consumption; but he took to sheep-farming and fishing and wading to the neck in water, and generally following the instincts of nature in the teeth of medical advice, until he got better and returned to the Bar, it is said, with one lung, which has served him adequately for these fifty years, though this he did not himself admit. The country and its green fields and heathery hills and sunshine were very dear to him. He retired to it, to await his own appointed time, on the death of his wife in 1869; and he has just passed away in the extreme fulness of years, such as no discontented mortal could have reached, from among troops of friends and descendants, having enjoyed life more gaily and heartily than the vast majority of mankind, even of those who have robust health and every blessing of fortune.

Mr Bell married early in life Janet Martin, a daughter of a gentleman holding an appointment in the Chancery Office. Of the beauty of his wife tradition still makes mention, and his married life was long and happy. His family was large. His eldest daughter married the eldest son of Professor Wilson, who was an old and warmly attached friend, the Professor and he having been brought together not merely by their mutual love of fishing, but by their intellectual affinities. His third daughter is the wife of Lord Young. Altogether, Mr Graham Bell leaves behind him about forty grandchildren and several great-grandchildren. One thing, however, unfortunately, that he is not likely to have left behind him is, his collection of old Edinburgh and Parliament House stories. He had a splendid memory, and had been an accurate observer of men and manners. No man who has been seen on the floor of the Parliament House for the last twenty years could give such graphic and credible accounts of the famous men who have promenaded there, and vanished from it like ghosts within the third, fourth, and fifth decenniums of this current century.

LORD ARDMILLAN.[1]

LORD ARDMILLAN appeared last in his place in the First Division in or about the second week of July 1876, and since then has been confined to the house, with life slowly ebbing away from him, and but little hope of the tide turning. He retained all his faculties, and was able to see his friends and to talk with them till near the very last. He had still enough of vigour and of curiosity left to look out upon the monster crowd that had gathered before his windows from far and near to witness the Queen's inauguration of the Albert Memorial on the 17th August—the last of the big shows of time that it was to be his lot to see. His disease, an obscure affection of the stomach, involved starvation and considerable pain, the final relief from which came on the afternoon of 7th September 1876.

The deceased Judge was the son of A. C. B. Craufurd, the proprietor of the estate in Ayrshire from which, on his appointment to the Bench, he took the courtesy title by which he has since been known to the public and in official papers, other than those

---

[1] 'Scotsman,' September 8, 1876.

signed by him, which were, according to the custom of Scotch Judges who wear courtesy titles, always signed with his own name of James Craufurd. Though in feeling a "son of the land of Burns," second to few, and a Scotchman of rarely exampled patriotism, he was by some freak of destiny, of which no explanation is forthcoming, born in England. His birth took place at Havant, Hants, in 1805, so that he has barely exceeded the ancient limit of threescore and ten—a life rather too short in these days of enlightened physiology for an abstemious man like him. He was educated at the Academy of Ayr, the College of Glasgow, and the University of Edinburgh. What each of these taught him we do not exactly know, but believe that law formed, nominally at least, the chief of his Edinburgh studies. By way of living commentary and elucidation of the class of lectures to which he was privileged or doomed to listen, he occasionally haunted the law courts and listened to the voices of the great pleaders of fifty years ago. One of his lessons for the life before him was the trial of Burke and M'Dougal for the notorious West Port murders. He used to tell sometimes how, in his eagerness to see that great trial, he sat up all the previous night and stood from early morning about the door of the Court-room waiting until it was opened; how he sat all day and the greater part of next night among the uncomfortable, sweltering, anxious crowd, until the verdict was returned which sent Burke to the scaffold and his wife free; and he used to assert that Cockburn's much-admired, much-bepraised speech for Helen M'Dougal was superficial and only half-sincere, and not to be compared for earnest, argumentative power with Moncreiff's speech for Burke, who was condemned mainly upon the doubtful testimony of a scoundrel if possible more thoroughly infernal than himself. Burke was hanged on 28th January 1829, and some time in the course of that year James Craufurd passed his examination in Roman and Scotch law, and became an advocate. Five years later, urged by love, we fancy, rather than the desire to obtain the help of some one in spending his professional fees, he married a young lady named Balfour, who in those days was noted for her personal attractions, and she became the mother of five daughters, who grew to womanhood. Of these the eldest and the youngest but one predeceased their father—the eldest having died in Edinburgh of scarlet fever, caught from one of her children, two or three years ago, greatly to her father's grief and that of all who knew her to be one of the most ethereal and amiable of the human race. Those who knew Lord Ardmillan fancied that after her death the old sunshine never exactly seemed to come back to him, and noticed that his face, though calm and serene, wore the look of one whose happiness had become permanently divided between reality and hope.

At the Bar the progress of the young advocate from Ayrshire was not at all rapid or decided. The truth is, he never had much civil business, though for one thing he could address juries very effectively. But he did have a very considerable criminal business both in the Court of Justiciary and in the Church courts. He was rather a favourite in the General Assembly as a speaker, and to be so requires talents and culture of a sort more strictly literary than those which secure success as a pleader in civil suits. Some of his clerical clients did not pay him very munificently. There is a story of one of them, who was deposed for drunkenness, having fee'd him by handing across to him at the bar of the General Assembly (he had previously apologised for having no agent, &c.) a roll of something that looked in bulk like a fee of between fifteen and twenty sovereigns, but which on being looked at after his eloquent counsel had got home, and he himself got prayed over and deposed, turned out to be six round peppermint lozenges of the kind that is most effective for stifling the smell of whisky. In the Court of Justiciary, where he was chiefly employed, and where he was willing and ready to work without money if the cause was sufficiently interesting, he made many speeches, which were always as effective as the evidence would permit (for he had ample time to prepare), and were often really eloquent, they being the outcome of an honest, earnest soul who could see pretty clearly into the truth of facts, and who had a natural eloquence of expression which he had cultivated by a rather discursive study of English and Scottish literature, especially poetical literature. His eminence as a criminal counsel justified, if it did not secure, his appointment as Sheriff of Perth in February 1849, and also his selection for Whig Solicitor-General in November 1853. During his tenure of this latter office he conducted many criminal prosecutions, and among them that of Dr Smith of St Fergus for the alleged shooting of a patient whose life he had insured. The prosecution speech of Solicitor-General Craufurd against him ranks among the best prosecution speeches of this generation of lawyers. His appointment as Court of Session Judge took place in January 1855, and that as Judge of Justiciary dates from June of the same year.

If Lord Ardmillan ever exhibited any hardness of heart it was as a Judge of Justiciary. His sentences were frequently somewhat severe—that of poor visionary Hardie of Leith to twenty-five years' penal servitude for forgery being unexampled since the era of penal servitude began. But there can be no doubt the punishments he inflicted were intended solely as a terror to evil-doers. He would never inflict pain for the mere sake of it; and many a poor wretched woman who with the wild words of despair appealed to him to give her "only another chance," did not do so in vain. Except on the Justiciary Bench, Lord Ardmillan was one of the most genial and kindly of men. No man could rise to a higher pitch of happy enthusiasm at a Burns dinner or the annual festival of an Ayrshire club; and few could provoke more cheery

laughter around a private dinner-table than he. He
had a great fund of odd humorous stories, some of
them English, many of them Irish, but most of them
Scotch, which he could tell very well, he being gifted, in
addition to the proper supply of sympathetic humour,
with a fine faculty of mimicry, which does not often
survive elevation to the Bench, if it should happen to
survive even to come within sight of it.

Lord Ardmillan's popularity did not in any wide
sense begin until he had been for some time a Judge,
and then it rose and rose until he was the most
popular of Outer House Judges, and had his rolls
crowded with the causes of those who wished justice
declared, not by a learned hair-splitter or a jesuitical
jurist, whose version of the law and the prophets
varies every half-hour, but by a man whose conscience
was to him the guide of guides, and whose belief in
the absolute supremacy of justice was invariable—
crowded also to no inconsiderable extent, it must be
admitted, by those who were particularly indifferent
about justice but anxious for delay, and who saw in
his glutted court chances of delay not to be descried
elsewhere. When at the Bar, his professional income,
it was often said, never rose above £800 a-year until
he was appointed Solicitor-General, when, of course,
his position attracted to him, to some extent, the
attentions of those too numerous agents who have
no ideas of their own, except that it is safe to follow
the multitude and that their clients are bound to be
content if they have secured to them the services,

actual or nominal, of a counsel with a big blazing
name. But after he arrived at the Bench, in spite
of the neglect of the common herd of blind leaders
of the blind, and had acquired the reputation of
"doing well as a judge," they all rushed to him *more
suo*, following, as the common herd always ultimately
must, the lead of intellects better and truer than their
own. After his elevation to the serener judicial air,
those moral elements of his character which had been
little other than impediments at the Bar, heavier
than lead, became wings to carry him forward, in
the course of administering justice, high above the
entanglements of half - understood precedents, half-
expressed notions of institutional writers, and half-
concealed confusions in logic, and, in fact, of accomplished counsel and partisan witnesses. He was
possessed by an ardent desire to reach the right, and
he reached it by a sort of instinct, more in the manner
of a true woman than of a trained lawyer, often by
paths which he knew not of. His opinions, though
substantially just at the core, and dictated by the
purest judicial spirit—the spirit of doing and declaring
the right as you shall answer to the Judge of all the
earth—have never obtained, and probably never will
obtain, a high reputation among the busy tradesmen
of the law. The honesty of purpose disclosed in them
is plain—most lawyers who are fit for much, or indeed
almost anything at all, have intelligence enough to see
that; as also that they are seldom wrong, or, let us
say, inequitable in the result; but they have, from the

special pleader's point of view, too little critical examination and analysis, and setting forth of legal principle, too little material fit for use in argumentative
discussion; and they are undoubtedly thought by the
pettifogger tribe to have in them too much of ethics
and too little of expediency, or whatever else may
compose that system of morals which believes little
else than that man has a purse and a stomach, and
is, when not sufficiently cunning and discreet, capable
of being hanged. And it may be conceded that they
are too rhetorical and too little logical. They partake
largely of the character of speeches or of sermons.
They glow with emotion, they abound in declamation,
they sometimes burst out in poetry, and they hardly
ever argue, except by way of indicating the prominent
steps of a process by which convictions so earnestly
held and so ardently expressed have been arrived at.
They indicate the mind not of a calm logician, not of
a cold-blooded argumentative lawyer, but of an orator
or preacher who has not leisure or patience to reason
from link to link—of a preacher who has got into a
rather narrow pulpit, who cannot repress the burning
word, but who becomes occasionally half - conscious
that the word with him counts for a great deal less
than the deed which the word has leaped forth to
justify. Probably 300 or more years ago—perhaps
even in these days—the pulpit would have been the
right place for him; but even from the Bench, notwithstanding its many restraints and the chilling
audience that surrounds it, he did preach a faith in

righteousness not unworthy of the consideration of all
human creatures who have not finally made up their
minds, or other functional manifestations of the grey
matter of the brain, to anticipate no future state other
than to

" Be blown about the desert dust,
Or sealed within the iron hills."

As a man, an orator, and a judge, Lord Ardmillan
deserves to be long held in remembrance and in
honour. He was a man of warm sympathies and an
affectionate nature ; dear to all his friends, and to
whoever came into close relations with him ; not at
all a man to be either distrusted or dreaded. He was
of so catholic a spirit that, though an ardent Free
Churchman, and a leading member, if not actually
an elder, of the late Dr Candlish's congregation, his
admiration for Burns hardly stopped short of idolatry,
and filled his memory with the variegated poetry of
that strong son of Scotland, and with much kindred,
and, it may be, occasionally reprobated literature.
No one who was present at the great Music Hall
Banquet, in celebration of the Burns Centenary in
1859, can have forgotten the noble speech, as glowing in language as it was enthusiastic in delivery,
in which his lordship, somewhat suddenly called
on to take the place of Lord Brougham, proposed
" The Immortal Memory of the Ayrshire Bard." Dr
Candlish, on his deathbed, gave Lord Ardmillan his
father's copy of Burns, much read, long treasured,
and not without reason dear to both his father and

2 G

his mother—a gift in its character, in its date, and its recipient, suggesting strange comparisons between the narrow dogmas among which we live and the infinities that wait for us when we die, and reflections as to how thin the dogmas grow, especially the uncharitable part of them, in presence of eternity and those who have entered it.

Lord Ardmillan's speeches and other literary utterances, all of which are tinged with the qualities of the oratorical mind, are not what can be called great performances, and perhaps some of his lectures upon religious or rather ecclesiastical dogmas to Christian young men and the like were most of all open to hostile criticism.   But they all have the cardinal merit of sincerity; they mean what they say, and they carry with them that conviction which proceeds like contagion from an orator who is self-convinced; they are not deficient in literary grace and polish, though they are inclined to exhibit a tendency to turgidity such as occurs in the writings of young enthusiasts.   And indeed Lord Ardmillan was always young: though a Senator of the College of Justice, he was a boy at heart, especially in love of fun and in friendship.   He was not harassed by the cares that afflict the mean and the self-seeking.   He did his duty according to the lights of the hour, and he did not require to be vexed with the failure of well-devised schemes which involved the doing of evil that good may come, or of projects of positive immorality.   His life was as blameless as human life can be.   The

Divine Eye was above him evermore. He lived as
if he felt its presence: not the reckless life of those
who never think, and who would willingly claim
kindred with the beasts that perish, nor the hopeless
despairing, dreary life of those who have looked up
for the Divine Eye and have seen only "the bottom-
less eye-socket of Death." He aimed at living a
true Christian life; and if he fell short of the beautiful and grand ideal, it must be because nothing else
is possible for flesh and blood.

LORD NEAVES.[1]

ON Saturday morning, 23d December 1876, Lord Neaves departed this life. Though he had reached the somewhat advanced age of seventy-six, his friends and admirers were not without hopes during his last short illness that he had several years still to live. He was come of a long-lived race. His father, the late venerable Clerk of Justiciary, discharged his official duties until ·he was over ninety, and died in 1868, from the consequences of a fall. Lord Neaves had never lost his interest in life, or in accumulating knowledge, which was to him one of the chief interests of life. If it were true, as some have believed, or at least said, that no man dies until he is fairly tired of existence, he ought to have lived at least as long as any of his race ; for no man ever enjoyed the passing hours more than he did, or more industriously turned them to some sort of intellectual use.

By extraction Lord Neaves was strictly a Forfarshire man. The late Mr Charles Neaves had come from that county—so fertile in able men and other valuable commodities—to seek and find his fortune in Edin-

[1] 'Scotsman,' December 25, 1876.

burgh in the end of last century; and his distinguished
son, named after himself, was born in Edinburgh on
the 14th October 1800. The boy was educated at
the High School of Edinburgh, and there had copiously
implanted in him the seeds of those classical tastes
which kept green and flourished luxuriantly all through
his life. Tradition says that he was dux of the High
School—and one could not well conjecture what other
kind of a boy could have been dux if he was there;
but his love for classics and his classical culture
struck root far more deeply than falls to the lot of
the majority of duxes, who, too often, in after-life
retain little or no evidence of their school learning
except the poor prize for which they strove, as if it
had been the really valuable possession. After passing through the University of Edinburgh with distinction, young Neaves joined the Faculty of Advocates, almost as soon as his age would permit, in
1822. In a few years he glided into practice; and the
reports show that, in his early years at the Bar, he
was counsel in many difficult and important cases.
Those were the days of written pleadings, and his
literary faculty must have stood him in good stead, as
did also, doubtless, the friendship of Duncan M'Neill,
who could understand both law and wit, and approve
of both even in occasional combination; so that Mr
Neaves's barely repressible love of a joke did not
materially affect his progress in his profession, or
lead to his being sacrificed to the prejudices of those
ever - abounding and superabounding noodles who

doubt the validity of every argument which is not both spoken and listened to with a sepulchral solemnity of countenance. Indeed, many of the young Tory advocates, his contemporaries, had a pretty strong inclination to jocularity. Lockhart, "the scorpion who delighteth to sting the faces of men," was pacing the old oak floor of the Parliament House until 1825, when he left for London to edit the 'Quarterly Review.' Douglas Cheape, a kindred spirit, afterwards Professor of Civil Law, was there also—a man of true genius, now almost forgotten, or remembered only for a few jests and a few verses, most of them, like 'The King of the Breechesless Islands,' preserved only in tenacious memories or in tattered MSS. There, too, was George Moir, a man of great elegance of mind, and great delicacy of literary touch (witness, *e.g.*, his article on poetry in the 'Encyclopædia Britannica'), and of enormous culture, but of too little courage; and there was Patrick Robertson, ultimately a judge, the Falstaff of his time, though without the concentration of Falstaff—a kind of flabby self-indulgent genius, who, however, in mimicry and good-natured mockery reached to heights never before attained, or likely to be attained, by any member of the College of Justice. None of these wits succeeded in law as Neaves did, except Moir, who was, however, not sufficiently self-reliant to be a ready debater. In 1841, when Sir W. Rae was Lord Advocate and Duncan M'Neill Solicitor-General, Mr Neaves was appointed an Advocate-Depute, and held the appointment till

1845. He was Sheriff of Orkney and Shetland from 1845 to 1852. His professional success before 1835 had been such that in that year he adventured upon marriage. His wife, now his widow, was a daughter of Colonel Macdonald of Dalness, in Argyleshire. In May 1852, when Lord President Boyle resigned, Duncan M'Neill, Lord Colonsay, was promoted from the Outer House to the vacant presidential chair, Lord Advocate Anderson was raised to the Bench, Solicitor-General Inglis became Lord Advocate, and Charles Neaves was appointed Solicitor-General, which office he held until January 1853. In or about April of that year, on the death of Lord Cockburn, he was appointed a Judge in the Court of Session, and in 1858 he was made a Lord of Justiciary.

Such is an outline of the facts of Lord Neaves's career as a lawyer. He was a great lawyer—in the opinion of many, the greatest "case lawyer" of his day; that is to say, he knew whatever had been decided or half decided, and could out of a most tenacious and capacious memory refer by name to nearly every case in which anything important in the way of principle had been either agitated or settled. Probably there is not such another, or more than one such other, memory left in the whole College of Justice. We believe that no man living knew so much about the criminal law of Scotland as he did; and that no coming man is ever likely to know it, not merely in its broad principles, but in its minute details, especially of practice and technical form, so intimately as he did.

Few men can ever have the opportunity, and fewer
still the faculty, to learn what he knew, and which
is now sunk to the unfathomable. But Lord Neaves
was not a mere lawyer. He was honoured as a lawyer
by all who were capable of appreciating an almost unprecedentedly, or quite unprecedentedly, wide range of
accurate knowledge, an almost inexhaustible fertility
of apt argumentative illustration, a rare facility in
puncturing sophistry and all manner of wind-bags,
and a mastery of clear coherent logic; but he was
likewise honoured as a man of letters by thousands
who knew nothing, or next to nothing, about him as a
man of law; and his public life and reputation have
been fully more those of a man of literary culture and
faculty, even of genius, than those of a great lawyer or
a great judge. Hardly any literary celebration of any
importance has taken place in Edinburgh within the
last half-century in which he was not an important
performer. He was present at the famous theatrical
dinner in 1827, at which, in answer to the toast of his
health proposed by Lord Meadowbank, Sir Walter
Scott, for the first time in public, admitted that he
was the author of the Waverley Novels; and he sat on
into the night, no doubt aiding the fun, after Scott had
ceded the chair to Peter Robertson, and heard Peter
burlesque Scott's confession by confessing, as Scott
had privately suggested to him, that he was the mur-
derer of Begbie, a porter of the British Linen Company
Bank, who in 1806 was stabbed to the heart and
robbed in broad daylight; not to speak of a long series

of comic toasts, provocative of much laughter, of which
the memories, like the echoes, have all but utterly
passed into oblivion. He was present, supporting
Professor Wilson, at the Edinburgh banquet in honour of Dickens, given on 25th June 1841, and proposed one of the toasts—in honour of Wordsworth,
Campbell, and Moore—in a happy speech, which
Dickens, as is recorded in his recent bulky biography,
thought a "little too lawyer-like for my taste," though
its author was "a great gun in the Courts,"—the truth
probably being that Dickens had discovered by a sort
of instinct that that particular speaker was by nature
a born foe to much of the half-sincere, overstrained
sentimentalism and flashy philanthropy that abounds
in his books. We have some reason to believe that
Thackeray formed a higher and juster estimate of this
accomplished lawyer, who, having by that time risen
to be Judge, and conspicuous among the literary circles
of Edinburgh and of Scotland, was by universal assent
thought worthy and most suitable to preside at the
banquet given in his honour on 2d April 1857, and
who on that occasion paid one of the most hearty and
discriminating tributes that has ever been paid in
Edinburgh or anywhere else to the genius and labours
of the distinguished novelist — a tribute of which
there is, unfortunately, no very adequate record, any
more than there is of Thackeray's own inimitable
speeches, among the best he ever found the nerve to
deliver. Last year, again, as it were by the voice of
all Scotland, Lord Neaves was selected to preside at

the Leyden Centenary celebration, held at that notable
man's native village of Denholm on 4th September;
and he there proposed the memory of John Leyden,
poet, philologist, antiquary, universal *helluo librorum*,
in an eloquent, genial, and judicial speech, doing full
justice and no more to the gifted, enthusiastic, but ill-
starred son of the Borders. His lordship's position in
the world of letters also met with fitting recognition
when, on 20th April 1860, he received, in company
with Mr Gladstone, Dean Ramsay, and other eminent
men, the degree of LL.D. at the hands of his Alma
Mater; and once more when, in March 1872, the
students of St Andrews University did themselves
and him the honour to elect him their Lord Rector.
His installation address at St Andrews, delivered in
February 1873, was full of the wisdom of a man whose
studies had been directed to mankind and the ways
of the world as well as to books.

From 1830 until recently Lord Neaves was a contributor, both of prose and verse, to 'Blackwood's
Magazine.' He was the author of a celebrated series
of articles on Grimm's 'Teutonic Grammar' and
Grimm's 'Philological Magazine.' Philology had been
from boyhood one of his favourite studies, and he
could, and sometimes did, discourse on it with a
fulness of information equalled by few, and probably
excelled by none out of Germany, where men devote
their life to that sort of pursuit. One singular
merit his philological disquisitions had—they were
always intelligible, which is something very remark-

able, considering the rivers of muddy nonsense that
have been poured out upon such subjects; while they
were marked by a felicity of illustration, and not
unfrequently by a genial humour, all his own. From
one of his contributions to 'Blackwood' in 1871, entitled "The late George Moir," a good deal of information may be derived regarding his early contemporaries
at the Bar, and some information, also, regarding the
author of it, who is there seen looking back in a sort
of serene, not cheerless, sadness upon the laughter and
the light of other days, that had faded from every
memory but his. It is much to be desired that his
contributions to 'Blackwood,' and many scattered
papers in the Transactions of the Royal Society and
elsewhere, should be collected and published. They
are valuable in themselves, for they are all full of
real knowledge and thought; and even of themselves
they would form no unworthy memorial of their
author's versatility, industry, acuteness, and all but
universal knowledge of books. Several of his productions have already been published. Among these
are a lecture on "The Uses of Leisure," originally
delivered to the students in the School of Arts, and
well worth the perusal of all who can enjoy wisdom
walking arm in arm with wit; another on "Fiction
as a means of popular Teaching," and a third on "The
Character and Writings of Paley." There is also a
small volume, forming one of the Blackwood series
of "Ancient Classics for English Readers," on "The
Greek Anthology," full of curious lore and noteworthy

criticism, enough of itself to set up a man with a stock of out-of-the-way erudition, and *apropos* of which it may be mentioned that, recently, his lordship was engaged on a series of translations from the Greek epigrammatists, not now, we believe, likely to be published; and last, but by no means least, there is the volume entitled "Songs and Verses, Social and Scientific, by an Old Contributor to 'Maga.'" This volume of verses was published in the beginning of 1868, and several editions have since been called for. We turn to it now, not without a touch of sadness, which all its mirth cannot banish, oppressed by the reflection that so small a book should contain the best evidence left upon earth of the varied learning, the subtlety of intellect, the far-seeing sagacity, the love of truth and right, and the intense animosity to falsehood and pretence that covertly burned in the mind of its author. Upon the surface, Lord Neaves was a man not very visibly in earnest about anything; on the contrary, he wore a sort of semi-transparent mask of *nonchalance* and indifference. But it is impossible to read this book, and, indeed, it was impossible to watch him long otherwise, without seeing that somewhere about the deepest and strongest current of his nature was a hatred of every species of falsehood and humbug. He was manifestly born with a barely repressible tendency to lay violent hands upon, or at least to thrust some kind of edged instrument into, everything that bore the semblance of a sham. The next strongest force in his nature seemed to be an insatiable thirst for knowledge. Perhaps this may have been a modified manifestation of the love of truth; but it is not impossible that it was not, for it is pretty plain that he greatly, if not chiefly, wished to know all that could be known on every side of every question, and that then he could take the question to *avizandum*, and consider it with very great patience and without any overwhelming impulse to rush to a decision, as is too common, at least with half-enlightened seekers after truth. A talent for suspense of judgment, rare among song - writers, is distinctly visible in these songs. Few books of the same size contain so many exposures of error, or delusion, or imposition, as this book. Even those who may not agree with him must enjoy the fun he pokes at the evolution theory, with its "deer, and a neck that was longer by half, by stretching and stretching became a giraffe; which nobody can deny." With absolute impartiality the sharp instrument pierces the irrationality of Sabbatarianism, with its "zealots made up of stiff clay," that, in order to begin the week well, resolve to be "unhappy on Sunday;" and the quackery of the Permissive Bill, "a little simple bill that means to pass *incog.*—to *permit* me to *prevent* you from having a glass of grog." With equal impartiality he stabs the incredibilities of Plato and of John Stuart Mill, giving, indeed, in one of his most melodious and suggestive songs, a neater refutation of the latter's negation both of mind and matter than will readily be found in the deliverances of heavy - footed metaphysicians.

Irony is his favourite weapon in attacking absurdity. He fully accepts propositions in their most startling breadth, and with much calm unrelenting ingenuity follows them out to their ultimate ramifications, destroying them by the process of *reductio ad absurdum*. Almost every page is sprinkled with genuine wit, generally of a quiet, grave-faced, subtle order, very different indeed from the riotous half-seas-over joking in verse that has sometimes been produced by lawyers and been popular among them. On the score of delicacy no critic can object to Lord Neaves's publications, their delicacy being unexceptionable, both from a moral and an artistic point of view. For the most part, the touches that pierce the deepest are put in, as it were, with the point of a needle.

Lord Neaves was a man of so many talents and so many sides that we find it hard, if not impossible, to convey any adequate and complete conception of his character. His chief mental gifts were that power of wit or of humour that sees, as by a flash of lightning, the incongruity of things—a strong, surefooted, reasoning faculty, logical rather than metaphysical in its biases, and a memory that seemed to retain everything, great and small, that had ever fairly attracted his by no means languid attention. These gifts were kept in constant exercise, either by a constitutional restlessness or by moral impulses to industry of an exceptionally strong kind. Few men have practically known so little of idleness as he. And then in the moral region of his nature his ear was never deaf to the call of duty. He did the right merely as a matter of course, without making any fuss about it. In all relations of life he was faithful to the uttermost, true to his friends while they were living, and zealous to guard and perpetuate their memories after they were dead. And he was really kind—not obtrusively, but genuinely so—to many that only a considerate, benevolent nature would have thought of aiding or befriending. Of this many a junior counsel was well aware when he was in the Outer House, to whom, in the most casual and incidental, but still suggestive, way his lordship would drop hints of the greatest value to the inexperienced. On the Justiciary bench, while he held a singularly instructive attitude to the Bar, to the prisoners his attitude was always that of the merciful rather than the stern judge. He knew' enough of human ignorance and of human dishonesty to make him shrink from inflicting punishment with the confidence of one who had been temporarily endowed with the light of Omniscience. He was a successful pleader, inclined rather to be discursive than to be severely logical or pretentiously metaphysical. His literary knowledge and copious variety of expression gave him a great advantage over the ordinary tradesmen of the law, as did also his knowledge of physical science. One of his physical science illustrations in the first Torbanehill case was probably the best ever adduced in the Parliament House. The question then was whether the mineral let as coal was actually coal; and geologists, chemists, botanists, and other men of science, came forward to testify that this mineral was not coal, according to their view of the characteristics of coal. Neaves scouted the introduction of this scientific evidence when the true question was what had been the actual subject-matter of a bargain, and supposed the case of a Greenland sailor engaging himself to serve for a share of the proceeds of the fish, and the bargain being sought to be evaded by scientific gentlemen, with or without spectacles, stepping into the witness-box and deponing, "Fish; a whale is not a fish; it is a mammal-quadruped, with its hind legs turned up into its tail,"—an illustration by itself sufficient to sweep away several days of the scientific evidence in that protracted jury trial. A species of oratory, somewhat different from forensic oratory, in which his lordship had scarcely a rival, was that of after-dinner oratory. Speeches more amusing in their substance or more variegated in their complexion than those he made after dinner have seldom if ever been heard, and certainly never heard at circuit dinners at, say, Jedburgh and Dundee, under the presidency of any other judge. Nor did he scorn, on occasion, to entertain a company with one of his own inimitable songs.

We have already said that his lordship was a great Judge. His merits lay in his own extensive knowledge of law and in his readiness and eagerness to hear everything that could be said for or against

every important proposition. His infirmity, if he had
one, lay in an inability to make up his mind, and in
a tendency to give undue weight to considerations
that a less delicately constructed intellectual balance
would have found to be of little or no weight. But
his judicial attitude as a sifter into the truth of propositions, and all the nooks and crannies of a case,
was worthy of all praise. No counsel who appeared
at the bar of the Second Division, and had a sound
or seemingly sound argument to submit, could fail to
feel that in Lord Neaves he had an invaluable ally.
If the counsel could not exactly set his argument
on its feet, his lordship would certainly help him,
though he should help to knock it down again at
some later stage of the discussion. And then the
sallies of wit with which he enlivened the Inner
House debates—when will the like of them be heard
again in the Inner House, or in any other house in
Scotland? Wistfully we look back in fancy upon the
place of honour that shall now know that familiar
form no more, and sadly we shut out the vision of
the vivacious keen face of the most cultivated scholar
and the most real genius that has for many a year
found a chair among the Senators of the Scottish
College of Justice.

MRS STIRLING.[1]

SUSAN HUNTER or Stirling was born in St Andrews on 3d October 1799, and died in Edinburgh on 1st October 1877. She was the daughter of James Hunter, minister of the College Church, St Andrews, and Professor of Logic, Rhetoric, and Metaphysics in the United College of St Salvator and St Leonard, a man of conspicuous figure and not inconsiderable intellectual powers—and of his wife, Jane Wilson, long a prominent character in St Andrews, who for mental gifts, especially in the matter of wit, fell nothing short of genius. Dr John Hunter the great philologist, once secretary (whatever that may imply) to Lord Monboddo, had settled there as Professor of Latin in the United College, and became in course of time her father's father and head of a patriarchal family that still flourishes both in England and in Scotland, and can furnish instances more curious and numerous than most families of the hereditary transmissions and singular transmutations of intellect, marked with biases chiefly to criticism and literature. When little Susan saw the light St Andrews was a queer old

---

[1] 'Scotsman,' October 2, 1877.

isolated place, with grass on its streets, and lichens and wallflowers on its ecclesiastical ruins, except at places where it was most convenient for the non-venerating citizens to pillage them as a substitute for a quarry; having in it no industry, or next to none, saving the manufacture of golf - balls out of leather and feathers, and the manufacture of clergy-men out of raw lads gathered from the homes of the middle classes all over Scotland. In her early days in the nursery there were, for example, at the same time studying divinity at St Mary's College, John Leyden, from a Roxburghshire shepherd's shieling; Thomas Chalmers, from a small merchant's house in Anstru-ther; John Campbell, subsequently Lord Chancellor, from the manse of Cupar-Fife; and Thomas Duncan, afterwards Professor of Mathematics, and the author of several books on that not very popular branch of knowledge — through life the friend of all three, more particularly of Chalmers, and probably, though scarcely known to fame, the most clear, strong, sober intellect of them all—from a farmhouse somewhere in the Anstruther district; and all, except Duncan, breaking windows, dismantling sign - boards, learning to recognise the taste of toddy, and doing general mischief after nightfall, just as young students in small university towns have been wont to do from generation to generation. And in her later nursery days Lord Colonsay and his brothers, from their island-home in the west, were attending the United College; Duncan M'Neill specially distinguishing himself under

Dr Haldane as a mathematician, and all boarding in her father's house for the sake of their comfort and progress on the lines of Saxon or southern civilisation. During her youth St Andrews was full of "characters" —that is to say, human beings with interesting and obvious idiosyncrasies, it might be oddities, and not all circumscribed, polished, and outwardly identical as if they had been stamped under royal authority in some mint with dies and moulds accurately cut in steel.   The tide of respectable primness had not begun to rise over St Andrews until she left it; so that before the deluge of uniformity and dulness she was able to observe and lay up in memory traits of human nature and of human life which have unfortunately grown obsolete.   In her conversation it was sometimes the good fortune of her friends to hear of the ancient oddities of St Andrews; and in her last novel, 'Sedgely Court,' there are photographs of some genuine old Scotch ladies and their talk, all once vital in St Andrews, the like of which are not to be found in the world now.   For clear glimpses of the realities of fifty or sixty years ago in this ancient university city, we do not know where to look with such hope of arriving at the vivid truth as in this too little known novel of her writing, which, though in form a fiction, is truer than most histories, especially of prim men and women in solemn old cities, whose greatness is in the past.

She left St Andrews for Dundee in 1836, on her marriage with James Stirling, C.E., the joint inventor, along with his brother, the Rev. Dr Stirling of Galston, Ayrshire, of that ingenious piece of mechanism known and described in natural philosophy books as "Stirling's Air-engine." After her marriage, she amused herself and occupied her leisure by writing her first novel, entitled 'Fanny Harvey,' which had packed into it too much shrewdness and common-sense to be very popular, but which was all purchased, though a little slowly, by a not undiscerning public, and which still continues to be read by those who prefer the sensible to the sensational.

After a few years' residence in Dundee, she and her husband removed to Edinburgh, to which she had been a frequent visitor before her marriage. Her sister had married John Jeffrey, brother of Lord Jeffrey, and Lord Jeffrey's first wife was a sister of her mother. This double marriage connection with the Jeffreys led to her being frequently at Craigcrook, and was the means of her meeting there most if not all the celebrated contributors to the 'Edinburgh Review,' regarding many of whom her reminiscences would have been worth reading had she had the disposition, and latterly the health, to put them upon paper. Thomas Carlyle was one of her acquaintances, made there about 1828.[1] She saw him on the occasion of his first visit to Craigcrook; and she remembered and used to tell, what some people who talk of his

---

[1] See Mrs Carlyle's Letters, particularly the introduction to Letter 4. Carlyle there makes a mistake, as also in the Reminiscences, about Jeffrey's first wife. She was Mrs Stirling's aunt, not her sister.

later literary style as artificial and unnatural may
be surprised to learn, that he then, in his comparative
youth, just about the time that he was writing his
article upon Burns, the style of which gives offence
to no fastidious person, talked the disrupted, amorphous, emphatic style of the 'Latter-day Pamphlets.'

Her Edinburgh home was, so to speak, broken up
by the death of her husband in the beginning of 1876.
She continued in the old house, 11 Hill Street, where
they had lived together so long; but the shock of
parting with her life-long companion seemed to have
told upon her vital powers more fatally than could
have been expected, and since his death she has
been slowly, though intermittently, breaking down.
So long as Mrs Stirling was well, in few houses in
Edinburgh could such pleasant and interesting company be met as at her evening conversaziones, or
such pleasant untrammelled talk be listened to.   There
could be heard George Combe pertinaciously defending
his phrenological and kindred notions against the half-
mischievous doubts and suggestions of Alexander
Russel, or it might be the serious arguments of Dr
Crawfurd; Dr Chambers discussing the 'Vestiges of
Creation' as if he had been a stranger to their composition; Robert Cox dropping a pregnant hint or
strange fact out of his enormous store of theological
knowledge, gathered chiefly in his laborious explora-
tions into the Sabbath question; Sydney Dobell talking copiously and eloquently, but obscurely, on poetry
or on politics; Alexander Smith, of the 'Life Drama,'

shrugging his right shoulder, looking up with a shy, faint smile, and telling to a knot of two or three how much less than £20 he had obtained for the first edition of his last volume of poetry, at which he had worked for years, or how he liked the malignant accusations of plagiarism with which the 'Athenæum' assailed all his volumes as they appeared; and another modest Smith—William, author of 'Thorndale' and 'Gravenhurst'—sitting in a corner gently asserting that there may be a true idea at the bottom of Positivism, or maintaining that evil is only good in the course of growth, and that conscience as well as knowledge is "widened by the process of the suns;" and tens of talkers or of listeners besides, who are alive, and who must therefore be nameless, but who, while they live, will never cease to look back with pleasure and admiration to the kindness, the sagacious speech and not less sagacious reticence of their hostess, and the ample toleration which she, an authoress and friend of authors, accorded to the criticism of every printed or spoken utterance, and which she, a minister's daughter, and steady though not blind adherent to the creed of her father's Church, accorded to the expression of all speculative opinions, though scarcely compatible with orthodoxy, but rather suggestive of quarrel with or emancipation from all sorts of dogmatic creeds. In short, in that house neither Church, nor creed, nor coterie was safe from free criticism; but all, through the operation of some unexpressed law, which seemed to float in the air or to be promulgated by some kind

of mesmeric radiation, were free from coarse or unbridled abuse. The talk that prevailed there was not
talk picked out of newspapers and diluted or para-
phrased, but was natural and candid, and very often
brilliant and original.

It is not easy to portray Mrs Stirling's character
for the apprehension of those to whom she was not
personally known. But from her novels it is possible
with considerable accuracy to infer the leading features
of her intellect and disposition. The most striking
feature in her mind was a great strength of common-
sense, rather hard and masculine in all its character,
and quite free from all alloy of the nature of spasmodic or hysterical weakness. Had she been a man,
and educated in the ordinary branches of a man's education, probably her strength would have lain in un-
folding some branch of mental philosophy. She was
logical rather than poetical, though her taste for poetry
was pretty catholic and widely cultivated. It drew
her, we should say, much more strongly to Shakespeare
and Burns and Scott than to Keats, Shelley, and
Tennyson; and we rather suspect that reading her
friend Dobell's ' Balder' was gone about by her rather
as a duty than a pleasure. The most prominent
feature of her moral nature was a strong practical
benevolence. She would do an act of kindness wherever she could, and to those from whom she could
expect no return. Her shrewd venerable face never
looked so beautiful as when a slight blush came over
it when she, so to speak, girded herself up to do battle

for the absent, who, in her opinion, had been unjustly assailed, or too harshly if not quite unjustly. She hated humbug in a quiet way herself, but she did not care to see it exposed without mercy in others, and she was full of all sorts of charitable constructions for conduct that to rhadamantine eyes seemed only the more condemnable that it had within its reach a good many cloaks of pretence or hypocrisy. Altogether, a more kindly, friendly, true-hearted, clear-headed, noble sort of woman has seldom gone without reluctance or trepidation from amidst the living whom she loved, to join the solemn, silent company of those who have gone beyond the veiled portals that finally close on all the sons and daughters of men.

THE END.

PRINTED BY WILLIAM BLACKWOOD AND SONS.

32101 064203787

Lightning Source UK Ltd.
Milton Keynes UK
UKHW022127060519
342211UK00008B/658/P